Barry Davies MBE was introduced t... Radio's *Sports Report* before spending t... on *The Times*. He was selected to join the ITV commentary team for the 1966 World Cup and remained with ITV until 1969, when he left Granada for BBC Television. He became established as one of the corporation's leading commentators on football, as well as many other sports including tennis, ice skating, gymnastics and the Boat Race.

'. . . beautifully written memoir' *Independent*

'[Barry Davies] has an amazing wealth of anecdotes to draw upon, because he has been commentating on televised sport for more than 40 years . . . There is an awful lot to reminisce about, and a vast cast of characters to remember' *Daily Telegraph*

'This excellent book looks back on his distinguished career' *Blackpool Gazette*

'*Match of the Day*'s longest-serving commentator serves up a huge helping of nostalgia in this magnificent autobiography' *Good Book Guide*

'. . . hugely enjoyable read' *Yorkshire Evening Post*

'Barry Davies writes as he commentates: with geniality, fluency and an easy air of authority. These qualities make him as pleasant to read as to listen to' *Time Out*

BARRY DAVIES

Interesting, very interesting

THE AUTOBIOGRAPHY

headline

First published in 2007
by HEADLINE PUBLISHING GROUP

First published in paperback in 2008
by HEADLINE PUBLISHING GROUP

1

Cataloguing in Publication Data is available from the British Library

ISBN 978 0 7553 1423 2

Typeset in Goudy Old Style BT by Palimpsest Book Production Limited,
Grangemouth, Stirlingshire

Printed and bound in Great Britain by
Clays Ltd, St Ives plc

Headline's policy is to use papers that are natural, renewable and recyclable
products and made from wood grown in sustainable forests. The logging and
manufacturing processes are expected to conform to the environmental regulations
of the country of origin.

HEADLINE PUBLISHING GROUP
An Hachette Livre UK Company
338 Euston Road
London NW1 3BH

www.headline.co.uk
www.hachettelivre.co.uk

For Penny, Giselle and Mark

Contents

The 1980s

The 1990s

Acknowledgements

Many people have helped in the production of this book and, inevitably, not all have found a place on the page. I am enormously grateful to those who gave their time and should like to include here Paul Armstrong, Simon Betts, Andrew Clement, Michael Cole, Jimmy Dumighan, Chris Lewis, Terry Long, Ken Osbourn, Johnnie Watherston, Alec Weeks and Mark Wilkin, who all confirmed, added to or corrected my various wanderings down memory lane.

Jim Reside, Julie Griffiths and Alastair Scott kept me from falling on the ice. Alan Hubbard and John Goodbody filled gaps in my knowledge. Mike Penson painstakingly researched the BBC sports archive. Albert Sewell and Martyn Smith found answers when my grey cells let me down. And having Jack Rollin as sweeper – reading the supposed completed work – was a considerable comfort. However, as with commentary, if mistakes have been made the fault is mine.

I should further like to thank Nick Townsend who kept telling me I should write a book; Jonathan Harris for making me believe I could do it; Helen Simpson for helping me see the wood from the trees; and the team at Headline, Lorraine Jerram and David Wilson, for their guidance and patience.

And finally the trio to whom this book is dedicated, who advised and then advised again, read and then read again: they know how much they contributed and how much it was appreciated. My typing improved but without my wife the publishers would still be waiting.

Preface

It is said that you should never judge a book by its cover. In this case I would request that the cover be examined lest the wrong conclusion should be drawn about the book's title. 'Interesting, very interesting' were words I chose thirty-three years ago at a moment of anticipation while commentating on a football match. It seemed to me that one of my favourite players, the ebullient Francis Lee, was setting himself to mark his return to his old stamping ground, Maine Road, Manchester, in style. He had left there in some discord six months earlier after seven eventful seasons in the blue of Manchester City. Now, cutting in from the left, he saw the chance to score against them for Derby County. A right-foot shot of some ferocity was truly aimed.

He turned in triumph and his face filled the television screen; his expression mixing a schoolboy's cheeky grin with adult appreciation that this was a special moment in his career. That my words were thought by my peers and members of the public to have captured the moment, with a further repeated phrase, 'Look at his face, just . . .' suggests that for a commentator it isn't so much what you say as how you say it. In searching for a title for this book it struck me as a good choice because through much good fortune it is a pretty fair definition of my life. Whether it is also true of the book is not for me to say.

Writing it has certainly been an 'interesting' journey, arduous at times, a happy wander down memory lane at others; and then there were the stiles to cross. Doubts were frequent companions on the route, most notably when meeting others' encouragement. 'You must have a good tale to tell,' many people said. But have I? As simply an observer, how much has remained in the memory? Would what some regard as a laid-back style of commentary be an inhibiting factor in bringing moments to life on a page? Would those who wrote so generously, in print and privately – particularly when I left *Match of the Day* – be disappointed by my written word?

My hobby, for that is what my job has been, has taken me to ten World Cups, ten Summer and seven Winter Olympic Games, seven Commonwealth Games, twenty-three Wimbledon Championships and countless other sporting events. I've had a privileged seat to watch the world's sporting heroes and have met, and interviewed, many of them. I have also worked, and at times been in competition, with the best of Britain's commentators in five decades of enormous change in the television coverage of sport.

Like the Saturday evening programme that gave me my big chance, my story can only be presented as 'edited highlights'; some moments have inevitably finished on the cutting-room floor (now the electronic dustbin) and some names aren't given the credit they deserve. My guides along the way all have my gratitude. Without them, and the support and love of my family to boy and man, there would be no tale to tell.

1

Dusseldorf '77

The men's 100 metres line-up was awesome – better than at the previous year's Olympic Games in Montreal. The commentator was an athletics novice, who had learned only that morning that he'd be doing the race.

True, he'd stood in as a substitute for half a season four years earlier, but his only previous attempt at the 100 metres had been in a fairly low-key inter-counties championship. On that occasion, to his left the low roof of the main stand had slightly obscured the start. To his right was the only monitor. Naming the competitors as they took their places on the blocks had been simple enough, but the gun signalled total confusion.

Peering under the roof edge at the start, he said something of little consequence and then turned to his monitor, which showed a head-on picture – from racing left-to-right they were now seemingly running from right-to-left. What few words were said were barely discernible before they finished: in line abreast.

'Well,' said the producer, with a sympathy and amusement which deflated the would-be commentator all the more sharply, 'it's safe to say things can only get better.'

For the record, seven of the eight runners were split by only two-tenths of a second. And that was in the days of hand-timing.

The eight runners on the track at the Rheinstadion in Dusseldorf in September 1977 were taking part in the inaugural World Cup, a team competition involving the five continents; though the United States and the two Germanys, one from either side of the Berlin Wall, had their own, non-continental teams.

The three main contenders had all missed the Montreal showdown. Steve Williams of the United States, a pre-Olympics favourite, had pulled up hurt in the American trials. Eugen Ray, the East German, had also been injured. Silvio Leonard, from Cuba, in Dusseldorf representing the Americas, went to Canada nursing a cut foot and was eliminated in the heats. Now he boasted the season's fastest time of 9.98 seconds, with Ray next best at 10.12 and Williams 10.16. All such facts were said by the commentator reading from the race card prepared by the BBC's highly regarded statistician, Stan Greenberg, a supreme Nut (a member of the National Union of Track Statisticians). But the opportunity to impart more knowledge – such as the fact that Leonard's time was achieved at altitude and that Williams had been running into a headwind – was denied me by the producer, John Shrewsbury, sitting at the other end of a commentary box which, along with Stan, also housed Ron Pickering and Stuart Storey. The former was a guru of the sport and the coach of the 1964 Olympic long jump champion, Lynn Davies; the latter was an Olympic high hurdler of recent vintage. Both were long-standing members of the Beeb's athletics commentary team which, in those days, had only three paid-up members. The team captain, David Coleman, the finest athletics commentator television had known, was out of contract: I was his deputy.

'There was a problem with the sound,' said John. 'Start again.' The broadcast was what the Americans call 'live to tape' – not, in their language, a contradiction in terms. Put simply, the commentary would be done live and a recording would be shown to the British public shortly afterwards. There would be precious little time to correct any error.

Take Two: I had barely finished saying, 'Williams in lane one' before the message came once more: 'Start again.' And again. The tracksuits were off, the leg muscles flexing in search of the blocks, the perspiration on the commentator's brow increasing by the second. Never mind the race; my concern was whether I'd be able to finish the starting line-up before they reached the tape. I tried not to rush it, but the adrenaline was flowing fast.

Chatting with Shrewsbury the previous evening I had been daft enough (maybe arrogant enough) to suggest that I'd try to resist the common trick (I thought) of focusing on one runner who was either 'well' or 'poorly' away, and instead wait to pick from the field. Ray was the fastest starter; there was no doubt about that. Williams struggled a bit. Leonard was well enough away from the blocks to be in with a chance. It was quickly brute force against rhythm – between the German and the American – but very close. And the smoothness of Williams' acceleration in the closing stages won the day, or so I thought – and said. But Ray thought he had won and so did the close-up cameraman. The crowd were fulsome in their appreciation of a cracking race (and in the moment a facetious thought occurred to me – something I've been prone to over the years, sometimes to my cost): 'That was kind of them . . . How did they know it was my first try?'

Suddenly I became aware that Shrews was beckoning me from the other end of the box. I started to speak, but he clearly wanted me at his side. 'I think I was right,' I said.

'So do I,' he replied, 'though as we aren't on the line you were taking a chance. But there was a problem.'

'What?'

'They lost sound.'

'Huh! They'll never believe I got it right,' I said, as I walked away feeling pretty dejected.

'Where are you going?' he asked.

'Well, there's nothing to be done,' I said. 'They're not going to run the bloody race again, are they?'

'No,' he said, 'but you are. I'll start the watch: make damn sure you're well out before ten seconds.'

And so, staring at the stopwatch hand ticking round, I

commentated again: Williams just, Ray second, Leonard third, Pietro Mennea of Italy fourth, and the time . . .

Barely fifteen minutes later, viewers at home watched the race 'live'. The sound now matched the pictures.

'It worked brilliantly,' said the London editor, Paul Lang. 'I think we'll get Barry to do it like that every time.'

Looking back, it was probably the best example of a feeling that has grown throughout the years: live outside broadcasts, particularly abroad, are at least as much *in spite of* as *because of*. But they've been my working life for forty years, in the ever-evolving, crazy world of television: it's been a love-and-occasionally-hate relationship.

As we left the stadium a couple of hours later, Shrews said, 'Do you fancy doing the women's hundred tomorrow?'

The 1960s

'And you are Barry who?'

2

A Change of Career

A captain from the Royal Electrical and Mechanical Engineers was the only other officer in the mess when I went in.

'I hear you're on BFN [British Forces Network] on Sunday,' he said.

'Not exactly,' I replied. 'I'm only going down to Cologne with some details of the local services matches. I volunteered to help them.'

'Well, that's not what they said on the radio just now. I was listening in my room and the announcer mentioned *Sportsman's Diary*, and said something about hearing from Second Lieutenant Davies.'

I suppose the next line, to fulfil the requirement of commentators and clichés, should be: 'And so a broadcasting career was launched.' I could add, 'And it went down the slipway with grace,' because the presenter and producer of the programme was Alan Grace, who later became the official historian of British Forces Broadcasting. That organisation – so precious to the troops – was a starting-point not just for me but for many of radio and television's most famous broadcasters. But I was hardly picked for talent. Alan's later observation that 'We were desperate for forces personnel who knew something about sport' tells a truer tale. I'd been mad on sport since my schooldays, so I did at least know 'something'.

The conversation in the mess of 113 Company, Royal Army Service Corps (RASC), in Mülheim Ruhr, West Germany, is indelibly written in my memory. Of the broadcast itself I remember nothing, though I imagine 'ropey' would be a generous description. However, I became a regular contributor and even managed a little commentary and reporting – enough to be able to suggest, some years later (when ITV were seeking commentators for the 1966 World Cup), that I had some experience to offer. That, however, was a long way ahead.

From time to time, when World Cups and Olympic Games have led newspapers to print potted biographies of the television teams set to bring the event to the living room, among the sometimes cryptic observations there has been the statement: 'Barry Davies is a qualified dental surgeon.'

That should have been true, but it isn't. Through lack of application, too much time involved in sport, mainly football then, and a deal of boredom – break-time conversation always seemed to centre around the molars of Mr Smith or Mrs Jones – I flunked out (an Americanism, I know, but very expressive). Even so, I'm almost certainly the only sports commentator to have made a full upper and lower denture. The recipient, at the Royal Dental Hospital in London, was a 6ft 4in Guardsman with a mouth like a horse's. With the amount of mixture needed to take the impression, I nearly choked him.

Quite why I wanted to be a dentist is a mystery. Well, I didn't really: I wanted to be a doctor, and had done since the age of ten. Later I felt sure I'd be a surgeon – a feeling confirmed when, as a medical student, I watched my first operation, craning behind the glass of the theatre at Charing Cross Hospital, and found myself pushing for a better view. But I failed to achieve the exam marks I'd hoped for, and was persuaded that to be a dental surgeon was my best hope. Lack of maturity or just madness? Either way, it didn't take me long to realise my mistake. Actually, looking back on it, the whole thing is laughable – as anyone who has seen my ten thumbs struggling with DIY will confirm.

After I failed to fill teeth, my life quickly turned to an obsession with the opposite end of the body, the feet – or more accurately what covered them: boots. I was in the army, and the early life of a national serviceman revolved around the shine on the toecap and the fear that someone or something would harm it. Then there were the hut inspections, with every piece of kit – never mind if it was still wet – folded to precise dimensions on the bed. Shining floors, sparkling windows, everything in its place: all to no avail – a speck of dust on the very top of the door. Another inspection tomorrow. Corporal Skelton was his name. I wonder if he later found a job as a security heavy at a football ground: 'It's more than my job's worth . . .' He did have a softer side, but it wasn't until he'd knocked us into shape that he gave us a glimpse of it. Home, because I had arrived from studying the subject, was with the Royal Army Dental Corps in Aldershot. Did that horse-mouthed Guardsman know?

Fairly soon, though, I was off to Mons Officer Cadet School, where the boots were required to be several shines higher and the drill was in a different league. I kept quiet about the fact that I'd passed out top in drill during the army's inspection of the Combined Cadet Force at my school, Cranbrook: sensible, really, because it was only through a lucky decision. There I was, marching on my own, the rest of the group having gone in the opposite direction. There was a shriek of ''Alt!'' and the approach of pounding feet which concluded with a stamp to tremble the parade ground.

'What's your *name*?' The question cut the air.

'Cadet Davies,' I stammered.

'Daaaviiiiies, I *like* you.'

Faced with an unintelligible command, I'd been the only cadet who guessed right. Hence pole position and a salutation which lasted the term at school and remains in my ear to this day.

The square at Mons was rather larger and the assembled company stood in awe of Regimental Sergeant-Major Lynch, who could spot a misaligned foot, or a badly timed rifle movement, through the back of his head from a mile away. The important thing was not to find oneself too close to what Lynch referred to as 'an *overseas cadet*'. They were his signposts. 'That man there, third rank, four along from the *overseas cadet*. Take his name.' Extra drill was the punishment. It was, I suppose, a form of racism, but it was left on the parade ground.

Mons was a pretty intense six weeks of written and practical challenges, where being a team player was an integral part of searching for personal success and showing leadership. (Among sports coaches it has become a cliché to talk of character, but getting the best from different talents and people who don't necessarily like each other is their aim, and it's a quality which deserves praise. Integrating the supposedly wayward character is the hardest part, and the failure to do so reflects as badly on the coach as it does on the player.) The assault course, the army games – leading a group through supposed hostile territory, making the best use of the little and sometimes obscure equipment provided – and all the other exams were both character-building and character-questioning. I have no idea what percentage of cadets failed, but if my group was in any way typical there was no lack of determination or fear of failure.

So there I was, crouching in a bush and counting army vehicles leaving the Essen–Cologne autobahn at a Mülheim Ruhr *Ausfarht*, feeling lost, cold and hungry. After a couple of hours, I was collected and taken back to the officers' mess of 113 Company, RASC, and given the chance to start unpacking, which I hadn't been allowed on arrival. Tea was served in the lounge by two very bolshy mess waiters, who kept interrupting and adding their own comments as two other subalterns vied with each other in running down both other officers and just about everything about the unit. To cap it all, one of the waiters dropped most of the contents of his tray in my lap. It was a very confused Second Lieutenant Davies who retired to his room to change. Half an hour or so later I returned with some trepidation, to be warmly greeted by the same foursome. But the officers were now the waiters. My first afternoon as an officer in Her Majesty's Army had been a total wind-up.

Many good days followed as I took over the platoon of one of my tormentors; suitably B platoon, which became known as Barry's Bandits – draw your own conclusions. I still have the engraved glass boot – the vessel for a yard of ale to be drunk in one continuous gulp – thus inscribed. (These days, it stands in the corner of my study, jammed full of accreditation passes from sports events around the world.) They were a good bunch, and I have often been accosted at matches by 'Remember me?' – some even adding 'sir.' At the last Royal Tournament, the seniority was rather different. I came down from the commentary position to find my erstwhile company commander, Major Gavin Jenks, waiting to greet me. He it had been who told me, when, after some technical error on an exercise, I came clean rather than trying to brazen my way out of it, 'Mr Davies, you will find that in the army honesty is not always the best policy.'

The 1962 Cuba crisis, when Kennedy and Khrushchev eyeballed each other after the USA discovered Soviet missile sites on the island, meant I served two and a half years in uniform, and to my surprise collected a second pip on my shoulders. I spent six months in Berlin, where we played a sort of cops and robbers – driving through Checkpoint Charlie with my driver, Jeff Bentley, to nose around trying to pick up an East German or Russian tail. The enemy guns trained on our barracks from over the wall concentrated the mind a bit, but I didn't believe the British Army of the Rhine would have been able to do much about it if Khrushchev's lot had decided to advance.

I often wondered what it would be like to come under fire and how I'd react, but the nearest I got to confronting the enemy came on the return journey to our Mülheim base – and it might have become an international incident. I was responsible for some eighty men and thirty trucks, and on arrival at the border checkpoint at Helmstedt I found that my collection of identity cards was one short. What made it worse was that the missing one was mine.

I asked my sergeant how he fancied Siberia, but this was no joking matter. There had recently been a number of problems in the 'corridor' between the two Germanys, and some British and US convoys had been made to wait several hours or been sent back.

I presented the cards.

The East German guard looked at them and, unfortunately, could count. 'There is one missing,' he said.

'I know,' I replied. 'It's mine.'

His glare would have got him the film part. 'Where is it?'

'I don't know. Perhaps your chap at the other end kept it.'

He proved he was capable of looking even grimmer.

Just behind him was a very large, fat Russian, who asked what I had said. On being told, he looked a darker thundercloud than the German. Then suddenly his belly began to wobble like a saucepan of milk coming to the boil. The wobble rose up and up until it emerged from his mouth as a roar of laughter. On a dull, boring day in a dull, boring job, he'd been amused. The perplexed German was instructed to wave us through. The missing ID was found at the Berlin checkpoint and arrived back in Mülheim a week later.

A month afterwards, it was time for my farewell interview. I'd wavered for a long time between the army and broadcasting as a career; broadcasting won. 'We'd like you to stay, but unless you go out and give it a go, every time you look at that fellow David Coleman you're going to think, "That could have been me"': the words of Lieutenant-Colonel John Wright, Commanding Officer, HQ Company, RASC, to Lieutenant Barry Davies. 'But if it doesn't work out, provided you don't take too long we'd welcome you back.'

I was still torn, the more so on the day of departure when most of 113 Company and some from 5 Company (who were sharing the barracks) turned out to say goodbye. My departing autograph book included the observation: 'This officer went through his entire career pushing all doors marked Pull.' National service was good to me, and it changed my life.

3

From Towser to *The Times*

Victoria Station in the evening rush hour, circa 1962, en route to the family home in Herne Bay. Had I left the army to join this? Too many people in too small a place rushing head down to catch the train home, most of them looking as though their job, indeed their life, brought them little joy. I joined them in not feeling particularly happy, because I'd been to see Gerald Sinstadt – number two to Angus McKay at BBC Radio's *Sports Report* – and my hopes of entering the world of sports broadcasting had taken a severe jolt. Alan Grace's kind recommendation had cut little ice with the man who had previously been his boss in Cologne. No openings, lots of competition; Gerald painted a very bleak picture. I still had the uniform and the Sam Browne . . .

A walk across the clifftops to Reculver the next day, talking over the problem with Towser, our Border collie, failed to disperse the clouds. There was no local radio in those days; nowhere except BFBS (British Forces Broadcasting Services) to gain experience. But a phone call from Gerald brought a ray of sunshine: he was one person short for the next Saturday programme, and would I like to help out? I would, and I did so for the next six months, for the princely sum of six guineas a week.

My father supported the growing overdraft. Mother was a constant source of optimism that it would all work out. Initially I took a job in a bookshop but I gave that up to work full time with the Beeb. I was still only being paid for Saturdays, but Uncle Syd, who had first taken me to watch football as a kid, offered me lodging in north London.

Brian Moore, the BBC's newly appointed football correspondent, often invited me to accompany him to interviews, and, as I wasn't supposed to be working there, no one could say I couldn't go. (Security and identity cards were some way in the future.) I became happily involved in programme discussion, and every Saturday, in *Sports Report*, could be found at the elbow of Eamonn Andrews, checking the facts of the script he was about to deliver. (That was the only time in my life I smoked – with a cigarette holder, because Eamonn used one.) I even did a little broadcasting for the overseas service. But when a vacancy occurred in the sports room Angus turned to Vincent Duggleby, then working in the newsroom and later to be the voice of *Money Box*, and told Gerald to get rid of me.

I ignored the sacking. They still wanted me on Saturdays, so how could I be sacked from a position I didn't have? Years later, Gerald recalled that it was only when he saw me *in situ* on the Monday morning that he began to take me seriously. And I stayed until Brian fixed me up with a job as a sub-editor on *The Times* sports desk, where he had worked before turning to radio.

Looking back, I have to concede that, for all my disappointment at the time, Angus was right. I wasn't up to the high broadcasting standard required in those days. (I was happy, though, not to remind him of his decision when he later claimed me as one of his boys.) In fact, he did me a favour. If he had appointed me, I might have been trapped in a staff job as a producer and only occasional broadcaster. I'm grateful, too, for the discipline instilled in me by the department – the 'who, what, why, when, where' demanded of a good report; for the encouragement I received from Gerald and Brian and all the behind-the-scenes people in the sports room; and later for the particular help given me by one of them, Pat Chambers, whose friendship with Frank Keating – then of Rediffusion Television, afterwards a gifted, amusing columnist in the *Guardian* – led me to 1966 and all that followed.

But the most important thing *Sports Report* did for me was to introduce me to the love of my life, who worked there as a secretary until she was old enough to become a stewardess with BOAC. It took six years and many takings to, and collections from, Heathrow airport before Penny and I decided we were right for each other. But what started with complaints about the scribbled writing of scripts to be typed is now nearly forty years of marriage.

Three years at Printing House Square, just round the corner from Fleet Street, was an education. *The Times* was a great newspaper in those days. It was, though, going through a period of change, with first the front page of advertisements reluctantly giving way to news; and later the purchase of the title by the Canadian Roy Thomson. What might now be perceived as a Dickensian decorum pervaded the large sub-editors' room. The foreign, home news and sports desks – that being the order of seniority – stayed remote from each other, which on the evening of 22 November 1963 led me to resolve that this would not be my life for too long. The sports editor's wife telephoned him to say she'd heard that President John F. Kennedy had been assassinated. When I enquired of the foreign desk if it was true, I received the reply, 'Oh, yes, old boy, we knew about it twenty minutes ago.' My protestation that this was a piece of news which might be of interest to all in the room was greeted with a mixture of surprise and indifference.

Penny was that night working for *Radio Newsreel*, which broke the news having received the wire barely a minute before going on air. She met me after work at eleven and we strolled by the Thames from Blackfriars to Big Ben, she trying to persuade me that the world hadn't come to an end.

The sub-editor's role on the sports desk certainly had its boring parts. Things like the racing results, the Worplesdon Foursomes and the Bumps charts from Oxbridge were things to avoid, but set against that was the privilege of reading some of the finest sports writers of their or any other generation – John Woodcock on cricket; Geoffrey Green on football and tennis; Peter Ryde, golf; Neil Allen, athletics; and Rex Bellamy, rugby and many racket games. Rex gave me a piece of advice I've never forgotten: it was in a way a gentle put-down of one whose head was crammed with sporting facts probably too often delivered. 'Young man,' he told me, 'the time will come when you'll realise that the important thing is to know where to *look up* the information you're seeking.'

Rex, in my opinion, was a far better writer on rugby than the then correspondent, who rejoiced in the name of U. A. Titley. The pomposity suggested was not without foundation, particularly on the evening I phoned him with news of the Scottish team selection for the Calcutta Cup, asking for comment. 'How dashed inconvenient,' he responded. 'I'm just sitting down to dinner.' I also argued with him about using Shakespeare's *Henry V* – 'And gentlemen in England now a-bed / Shall think themselves accurs'd they were not here' – as an intro to a London XV's victory over the All Blacks: I thought it quite inappropriate. John Hennessy, the sports editor, adjudicated. I lost.

Hennessy was later of great help to me in understanding the technicalities of figure skating, but while on *The Times* caused me some irritation in the manner in which he allocated football reports for Saturday matches. (Later television sports heads caused me similar problems!) My competitor, in the shadow of Geoffrey Green, was Jacob Ecclestone, later a senior figure in the National Union of Journalists, and who did which match was determined by whether or not he was travelling home to Sheffield for the weekend. As both of us paled into insignificance alongside Geoffrey, it had little relevance for the paper; but it was very important to ambitious me. I wanted the decision to be made on merit.

The great Green had an amazing ability to deliver wonderful prose over the telephone from a few scribbled notes. To sub him was a joy, unless he'd been denied the odd warming Scotch. Too many wasn't a problem, necessitating only the removal of a few adjectives to facilitate the flow: a tot too few was much more difficult. 'There's no secret to it,' he once told me. 'Just imagine you've come into the room and are asked what happened. Tell them, old love.' I remembered it well when deputising for him in Switzerland when Lausanne Sports played West Ham en route to Bobby Moore's team winning the European Cup Winners' Cup. The phone rang just as the players were leaving the field. The news that Geoffrey was sick hadn't reached the copy-taker. I decided I couldn't ask him to phone back, so I 'told them'.

The Times then still had anonymous correspondents and staff reporters, and it's as one of the latter that my report on the third-place match appears in the official book of the 1966 World Cup.

During my university days, when he felt I was spending too much time playing and watching games, my father had said, 'You'll never make a living out of sport.' Now, he scrupulously collected all my attempts at reporting, in scrapbooks which I still have. In terms of my playing talent which, sadly, has never matched my enthusiasm, he was certainly right. In time, Hennessy gave me – and therefore my father – greater employment, and I enjoyed many an afternoon and social evening covering schools and university football in the

company of David Miller, whose considerable career has yo-
yoed between *Times* and *Telegraph* (he was then with the
latter); and Henry Blofeld of the *Guardian*, long before 'my
dear old thing' became such a distinctive and distinguished
member of the *Test Match Special* team. At the time he was
covering football while trying to break into television with
ITV's very occasional coverage of cricket, but, as with two
other great and very different cricket commentators, John
Arlott and Brian Johnston, radio proved to be Henry's scene.

Arlott, if memory serves, was also an excellent football
commentator, and I recall one very pertinent comment from
my schooldays. 'The best centre half in England is currently
playing at outside left; the best outside left is playing for
Finchley' (then amateurs in the Athenian league). Jack
Froggatt, of Portsmouth, played for his country in both positions but George Robb, by then of Spurs, was given only one
chance, against Hungary in the 6–3 defeat at Wembley in
November 1953. I once had the great pleasure of interviewing
Arlott for a programme called *On Reflection* produced by
British Forces Broadcasting. Ian Wooldridge, then the *Daily
Mail*'s cricket man, and I were joint interviewers at Arlott's
home in Arlesford, Hampshire. The conversation ranged from
aquatints to wine, from his first editions of Thomas Hardy to
his time standing as Liberal candidate for Epping. There were
so many facets to the man that the interview comfortably
made not the usual one but two forty-five minute programmes.

I well remember asking him the obvious but probably
required question: 'If you could have been present at an occasion before you became a broadcaster, what would it have

been?' I expected W. G. Grace or Jack Hobbs or something of the sort, but he replied, 'Gladstone's Midlothian campaign.' My lack of preparation or knowledge of the subject was perhaps disguised by the simple follow-up: 'Why?' Arlott then waxed lyrical about Gladstone's quality of oratory before the use of microphones.

I later met George Robb when he became a schoolmaster at Ardingly College, Sussex, where for a while he passed on his knowledge to the First XI. There were a number of characters serving that role on the independent schools circuit, none more fascinating than Ken Shearwood at Lancing, the only man in football who was a match for Bill Shankly – as quick with the comment, as clipped with the humour or acerbic line, as in love with his team, and held in awe by the boys. He was an authoritarian, demanding of play and standards of sportsmanship; but a bit of a football Mr Chips.

At Bradfield was Peter Jones, assisted from time to time by Maurice Edelston, a former amateur international who had played for Reading and who, with Brian Moore and Alan Clark, was in the BBC radio commentary box for the '66 World Cup final. Maurice was also instrumental in helping Peter build a second career which made him the best-known sports broadcaster on radio for two decades. In 1971 it seemed he was about to move to television, but Sam Leitch, BBC television's head of football, had other ideas. He turned to radio to strengthen his team, but instead of Jones chose John Motson.

I doubt that Peter, who went on to cover state occasions as well as all the top sports events, much regretted Leitch's decision. His style was once amusingly, but certainly not mendaciously, summarised by Maurice en route to a match in Sheffield. I enquired where Peter was. 'He's introducing *Sport on Two*,' he replied, adding after a brief pause, 'Under an Oxford Circus sky, no doubt.' Peter's painting of word pictures was often vivid in colour, and he certainly brought things to life. His own was full in many ways, but too short. His last words were with microphone in hand covering the Boat Race in 1990. He collapsed, and two days later, aged only sixty, he died.

In time, I was given more opportunities to report instead of sub-editing, with a range which came to include cricket, tennis and rugby (and even a couple of pieces for the *Literary Supplement*), but no task was more enjoyable or testing than covering schools football. Accuracy and constructive criticism were at a premium. The reports were scrutinised far more thoroughly than any involving professionals.

I was delighted, therefore, when within a couple of weeks of standing down from *Match of the Day* in September 2004, I received an invitation to be the guest of honour at the Walkers Stadium in Leicester to present the Boodles Independent Schools' Football Association Cup the following spring. The Schools' Association chairman, David Elleray, would definitely make my top five list of best referees; the president, Chris Saunders, succeeded Jones at Bradfield before becoming headmaster of Eastbourne College. At the time of writing, his son Jonny is one of the reporters emerging from the pack at Radio Five Live.

4

From North to South

Most people will probably remember the 2002 World Cup mainly for Ronaldinho's free kick, which knocked England out of the championship. But my own most lasting memory is of an undulating sea of red-clad fans smiling and yelling approval. The winning penalty of the shootout had been struck. Spain, like Italy and Portugal before them, had fallen by the wayside and the streets of South Korea's major cities mirrored the scene and the noise of the stadium at Gwangju. The hosts were through to the semi-final.

Later that evening, Philip Bernie, the BBC's senior figure in the Korean half of the competition, congratulated me on my reaction to the decisive moment. 'You didn't say anything for about forty-five seconds. It was wonderful.'

'Ah,' I replied, 'I'm the world's best commentator when I keep my mouth shut.'

The Koreans had presented me with some sort of symmetry: the South had today provided the chance to emphasise that the commentator's best weapon is often silence; the North, back in 1966, had offered a key to the identification of players which served me well over the next five decades.

So much of life is about being in the right place at the right time, and for me the World Cup finals coming to England in 1966 couldn't have been better for they provided the lucky break which gave me the chance to become a football commentator. TV coverage of the tournament was by a consortium of the BBC and Independent Television, who pooled their resources to provide the facilities and the pictures for the world's broadcasters. The result of that decision was that for the first time ITV could compete directly with the BBC in the domestic coverage. *Match of the Day*, introduced and commentated by Kenneth Wolstenholme, was two seasons old, and the Beeb had a number of established names to cover the matches in the four areas of the country: David Coleman, the presenter of *Grandstand* since 1958, Alan Weeks, Frank Bough and former Wales and Arsenal full back Walley Barnes. In contrast, ITV had only one football commentator, Gerry Loftus, and such was the Beeb's dominance of sports coverage that he, like the network, had few chances to prove his worth.

One of his commentaries did make headlines, but for the wrong reasons. I watched it happen in a studio in central London. A remark by Gerry, after England had lost 3–2 to Austria at Wembley in October 1965, was partly responsible.

Speaking to camera after the match, he began, 'Well, Alf Ramsey will have to get out his chopper tonight.' The resulting mirth, not least his own, cut by a good ten minutes the time the videotape editor had to present the tape for transmission, and in the days when scissors and sticky tape were the tools of the trade he, poor chap, cut between two corner kicks and left the winning Austrian goal on the floor. The result on ITV was a 2–2 draw.

Loftus seemed certain to be one of ITV's four commentators for the championship, but the search was on for three more and thanks to my days with *Sports Report* my hat was in the ring. My trial for one of the coveted positions began at Rediffusion House in London's Kingsway. I was asked to commentate on a recording of England versus the Rest of the World from October 1963. Fortunately, I'd seen the match, in which Denis Law scored and Lev Yashin, the great Russian goalkeeper, signalled his departure at half-time by holding his arm horizontal so that a shot hit his fist and with one bounce reached the halfway line. The sound of the original commentary was turned down, so atmosphere there was none. But I did well enough to be invited, along with several others, to commentate for some ten minutes each on the Youth Clubs' Cup final at the Crystal Palace National Recreation Centre. I wrote to both clubs asking for short biographies of their players and six-by-four photographs which, for a week before the match covered the living room floor of the flat in Hampstead, north London, I shared with two others. Extra contributions to the beer kitty were required.

I'm not sure that my commentary was any better than the others', but, being in the second half, it – as Frank Keating later put it – 'awakened the dozing'. I knew the players and had something to add. It established a reputation, which stayed with me, as a commentator who did his homework. Further tests at Football League level followed, including one at Fulham where the sound mix was such that another contender, Hugh Johns, and I found it hard to avoid borrowing each other's thoughts and finishing each other's sentences. Then, in February of World Cup year, Graeme Turner, head of sport at Rediffusion Television, put his neck on the line by contracting me to commentate on Chelsea against AC Milan in the Inter Cities Fairs Cup, followed two weeks later by England versus Germany. The programme of the first remains a valued possession. It's signed: *'Here's to the first of many – Jimmy Greaves.'* He had, of course, played for both clubs. He could not have been more helpful as what was then called a 'summariser', and it was a fine match in which Peter Osgood, pulling the ball out of the air with one foot then lashing it home with the other, scored one of the best goals of his career – and as a watcher mine.

In contrast, what turned out to be a rehearsal for the World Cup final was pretty turgid, decided by an untidy goal finally credited to Nobby Stiles, though claimed at the time by Roger Hunt. The praise received after the Chelsea match was somewhat tempered by the Wembley affair. (I would learn that 'good commentary', though well intentioned, usually meant 'good match'. Few appreciate that praise is often much more deserved for a bad match.) But I made it to the final four, along with John Camkin, a journalist on the *News Chronicle* and a director of Coventry City, who would cover the Midlands; Gerry Loftus on his home patch in the north-west; and Hugh Johns, who, in company with former Welsh captain Dave Bowen, won the prize of Wembley and England's matches. My beat was the north-east and the Parks of Roker and Ayresome.

I suppose I was a little disappointed, but I had no right to be and certainly didn't express it. And looking back, not being heard too often as I learned some of the tricks of the trade was far more beneficial in the long term. I was also lucky that I had one of the stories of the championship, although nothing that I said in commentary matched the beautifully simple phrase of the BBC's Frank Bough, who began his end-of-match report with his voice rising in disbelief: 'What's happening here? Korea have beaten Italy.'

By the time Pak Do Ik wrote his name into World Cup history I'd become an expert on North Korean football. Rather cheekily I'd insisted on being sent north a week earlier than ITV had planned, persuading John Bromley, the executive editor, that the unknowns from the Far East presented a bigger problem than any other of the sixteen teams. Even with that extra time, the 'expert' had one blind spot, called Yang Sung Kuk – number 21 in the squad – who in fact didn't play until the third match. Somehow, matching his photograph with his style and movement failed, until it was pointed out to me that the full head of hair had, just before leaving home, been given a crewcut.

The World Cup grounding given to me that year by the

Koreans – as well as the Russians, Chileans, Italians and, in the quarter-final, the Hungarians – has meant I've seldom needed to rely on numbers for identification. It made me something of a rarity. The BBC's Walley Barnes once commented on air, 'I can't tell you who it is, he's facing me'; and Billy Wright, deceived when a forward called Paolo Barison wore the number 3 shirt, told viewers, 'We don't have full backs who can shoot like that,' a remark which also betrayed how insular English football was before the 'home' World Cup. These days, of course, players wear all sorts of ridiculous numbers, and commentators and the public alike have had to get used to it.

In 1966, at least I had no problems watching teams in training. Now, the media are made to leave the stadium after ten minutes of jogging and stretching exercises. Television executives whose companies pay the money that has enabled sport to flourish have done nothing to help their men at the end of a microphone who are expected to know the scorer of the first-minute goal. True, there's now masses of video footage to study, but nothing's as good as doing the homework 'live'.

In theory, ITV's four commentators in 1966 all had an equal chance of covering the World Cup final. We were required to phone in after the quarter-final to hear the decision. The 'young man in the north-east' – I was very much the baby of the team – told John Bromley, before John had the chance to say anything, that he'd be mad not to keep his Wembley team in their seats. I doubt that he ever thought otherwise.

On the day of the final I stood quietly at the back of Hugh's box, barely opening my mouth; although I did tell the German commentator in the adjoining box, sick though I was at the late equaliser, that his country deserved to be level at ninety minutes. Peter Lorenzo, ITV's reporter in the England camp, later accused me of being un-patriotic. But I have always felt that it was in extra time that England played like true World Champions. Alf Ramsey's simple motivational comment – 'You won it once; now go and win it again' – deserves its place alongside his very early forecast that 'England will win the World Cup' in football's folklore.

Equally lasting for me, in a very different context, was a comment made by Bill Shankly. At the pre-competition conference, John Bromley had explained that our experts – all members of the current great and good – would be asked to report their views to the pitch-side camera after the match. Bill, who was ITV's man in the north-west, looked thoughtful for a moment and then said, 'You mean you want me to talk to you from Goodison?' He did so after much persuasion and with great reluctance, looking down at his microphone as though it were the camera: the pride of Anfield apparently not wanting it to be known that he was standing on enemy territory.

Being at the England hotel that evening – the Royal Garden in Kensington – and later on the streets with the crowd, was to be part of a very special atmosphere; something, I imagine, like VE day. It was total celebration; joy and pride in full measure. Many must have had trouble remembering the details the following morning, but I recall no sign of aggression; an age of innocence which has slowly been destroyed. It was still alive among the Liverpool supporters who thronged the team hotel in Rome when the European Cup was won eleven years later. But in another eight came the Heysel tragedy. And for all the improvement in stadium safety which, much too late, came from that and the disasters at Bradford and Hillsborough, aggression still seems endemic in the national character at football matches. When did the need to jeer come before the wish to cheer?

Returning to the *Times* sports desk was quite hard after a month in the world of television, which I knew I wanted to join. I'd now commentated on seven matches (nine if the pre-World Cup games were included) and had drawn favourable comment from the two directors in the north-east for the ITV/BBC consortium, Chris Palmer and John McGonagle. But the World Cup was now history, and there were no openings at any of the independent companies. With Hugh Johns rightly considered the Number One, there would be little chance of even the occasional mid-week match for Thames.

Then, unexpectedly, came a phone call from John Bromley with an offer to cover six matches for ABC Television's *World of Soccer* programme, one-match recordings to be broadcast on Sunday afternoons in the north and the Midlands. Their commentator – who had not, incidentally, made the ITV World Cup squad – had asked to be relieved of his contract.

Martin Locke, a Rhodesian from Salisbury (now Harare in Zimbabwe), had been offered a position with the South African Broadcasting Company. With a six-week guarantee in my pocket, I handed my notice to John Hennessy.

5

Mexico '68

D-Day, 6 June, for Penny and me in 1968 meant our wedding day. We'd got engaged on the first day of spring of that year, so no danger of forgetting the most important dates; I don't think I ever have. But I hadn't realised how often June would be the month of a major football championship.

We were married in St James's Church, in Fulmer, Buckinghamshire, by a delightful vicar called William Taylor – he'd have been ideal for the role of Dr Chasuble in Oscar Wilde's *The Importance of Being Earnest*. It was the most perfect summer's day, and the reception in the garden of a friend's house in Farnham Common could not have been bettered. My suntanned bride, who had just returned from a trip to the Far East with BOAC, looked stunningly beautiful.

The *World of Sport* team, led by John Bromley and Dickie Davies, turned out in style, other friends having to put up with the fact that our wedding day was a Thursday in order to accommodate the sports fixtures. Among the relatives were Penny's antiques-dealer French uncle and his family from Paris, who had somehow found a way out of their city which had been brought to a standstill by the student riots. His brief speech, though probably not understood by many, took the prize for its expressiveness, worthy of his country's actor Fernandel. Penny and I left for Rome that evening and the next day hired a Fiat Cinquecento to journey on down to Positano, returning a week later to fly to the city of Penny's birth, Alexandria. There would be the chance of a second honeymoon in October, because I'd been included in the ITV team for the Mexico Olympics.

In the run-up to the Games, I was briefly tried as an athletics commentator. I remember it fondly for two things: for the chance to commentate on the fine American middle-distance runner Jim Ryun (Kip Keino was too much for him in Mexico and then he fell in his heat in Munich); and for the small amount of jogging I did with my fellow commentator, who strode with the bounce of a wallaby – he'd played a big part in Britain taking silver in the 4 x 400 metres relay four years earlier in Tokyo – disconcerting for a hack jogger. Adrian Metcalfe's knowledge was clearly way ahead of mine, but much though I enjoyed his company, in and out of the commentary box, I felt he didn't have the voice for the commentator's role he clearly preferred to that of the expert.

In his sport and at that time, I didn't, either, though there were moments, listening to the man chosen for the role – the Canadian Lionel Pugh, a former coach of note – when I felt both disappointed and a little hard-done-by. Competition against Coleman and company was very different, and, as in the World Cup, it was a good thing that I was used on the side roads rather than Main Street.

The coup ITV felt they had made was to land Christopher Chataway as the main presenter, and at the launch of our Games team, he understandably took the main headlines. His participation in the first four-minute mile and in the Helsinki Olympics, and especially his 1954 5000 metres world record at White City, defeating Vladimir Kuts in one of the enduring classics of the track, had secured his place in sports history. In contrast, I was tail-end Charlie and, until Brommers's intervention, anonymous.

Bill Ward, ATV's executive producer of the Games, gave Chataway a big build-up, but came eventually to the end of his introductions: 'And last, but by no means least, we come to two men who have to be ready at a moment's notice to turn their hands to anything, to cover all the other sports which make up the Olympics – and for this role we have Neil Durden-Smith [applause, applause] and . . . and . . .'

John Bromley jumped in to reveal my identity.

'And you are Barry who?' said our grinning boxing commentator, Reg Gutteridge, afterwards.

It was Reg who, an hour out of Mexico City, among a group of us sitting together in first class, broke a silence which had lasted some five minutes from the moment we hit an electric storm. 'I wouldn't mind,' he said, 'but he'd get all the head-lines. I'd just be "Also on board were . . ."' The 'he' was David Coleman travelling alone in row one. He and Harry Carpenter were the only members of the BBC team permitted first-class travel – a fact I discovered only after I'd signed the contract that took me to the BBC eighteen months later.

ITV were intent on having a happy team (they even built in a five-day holiday in Acapulco after the Games). In many respects, they also had a successful one; but it was not helped by the politics of 'us' and 'them' between the London and Mexico production teams, and a failure to trust their commentators at a moment which would have brought positive headlines to offset the predictably low viewing figures.

For a considerable time in the long jump, the BBC had Britain's Sheila Sherwood in the gold medal position; they'd somehow missed the first jump of Viorica Viscopoleanu of Romania. Now with computer updates that would be virtu-ally impossible; but in 1968 physically tracking every jump of each round of the competition was a necessity. Predictably, Mary Rand, the champion in Tokyo four years earlier, got the blame; star names as commentators – more of that later.

The ITV team had it right, but in London the BBC output was being monitored; and London thought they knew better. Metcalfe and company were instructed to correct an error they had not made, and eventually, on the threat of dismissal, they succumbed. Of course, they then had to apologise a second time, and the ITV wires between Mexico and London were red hot. The Beeb, incidentally, also missed the giant leap of Bob Beamon, though you'd never have guessed it from the excitement in the words of Ron Pickering which were delivered moments later and speedily dubbed onto a recording: 'Oh, it's an enooooormous one!'

My Games had their downside, not least being well away from the main stadium at big moments such as when David Hemery won the 400 hurdles in classic style, breaking Olympic and World records in the process. Coleman was criticised for his comment, 'Who cares who's third?' because it happened to be John Sherwood of Britain. Such was Hemery's mastery and the margin of his victory that I felt the criticism was unfair. Coleman was just unlucky, and when, years later, Hemery was a subject in the *Maestro* series of interviews I conducted, I made sure that the commentary – for which, incidentally, Coleman later publicly apologised – was clipped.

Thirty-seven years on in Singapore, leading London's successful bid for the 2012 Games, Sebastian Coe made it very clear in his speech in the prize-winning presentation that he had cared very much who came third: John and Sheila Sherwood, husband and wife – who, like Seb, hail from Sheffield – had been, he said, the inspiration for his career in athletics. As the only man to defend the Olympic 1500 metres title successfully, in 1984, it could be said that he struck gold for a third time when the IOC awarded the Games to London.

For me, the greatest disappointment of Mexico '68 was missing a scoop. On the evening of the men's 200 metres final and the demonstration of Black Power on the rostrum by Tommie Smith, the winner, and the bronze medallist, John Carlos, I happened on the latter at a downtown hotel in

Mexico City and persuaded him to be interviewed by our crew, who were due to arrive in the next few minutes. Not only were they late, but their equipment then failed. The departing Carlos was later secreted away in a different hotel before a 'live and exclusive' interview by the BBC at prime time back home.

My crew missed another moment which would have made picture headlines. Just before I met Carlos, Avery Brundage, the much- criticised, autocratic president of the IOC, fell into the hotel fountain in the foyer while looking back at his attractive secretary standing by his car. His two attempts to extricate himself, and his dash back to the car, dripping wet, were comical in the extreme, but sadly, unrecorded – Chaplinesque, but never making the limelight.

Bill Ward's comments about Durders and me needing to be ready to turn our hands to anything certainly rang true, though how much if any of it made the reel – was actually broadcast – I had no idea. Obviously it is not possible to send a specialist in every field, so the all-rounder requires a certain ingenuity. It is useful to have, or to acquire, knowledgeable friends. The form was to go to watch an event and then commentate on the summary provided by the host broadcaster later that evening.

At the weightlifting I found myself in conversation with an authority on the sport, and on many others, John Goodbody, of *The Times*, who expressed some doubt about the legitimacy of a lift by one of the favourites. When the lift came up in the summary I did the same, and thereby suggested knowledge somewhat greater than I possessed. Whether it fooled any of those who watched from their living rooms I know not, but my producer was suitably impressed.

But the biggest test definitely caused me to be economical with the truth. I'd been to watch the cycling road race, and was struggling to make some sense of the fifteen-minute edit which concentrated more on setting the spokes of wheels against a background of rhododendrons than on giving such useful information as who the leaders were. At that point the door of the cubicle opened and a note was thrust to my attention. 'You do know you're doing the start of the marathon, which follows this, don't you?' it read. I scribbled, 'No.' A second note said, 'Well, you are and here's a list of the runners and a map.' Fortunately I'd been to the Zocalo where the event would start, but what comfort that gave me was quickly dismissed by a third note which said, 'You'll be live into *News at Ten*.'

As the runners turned out of the square, the producer's countdown echoed in my ear. I correctly identified the first three runners, and thought I'd survived. But my luck deserted me: over-confident, perhaps, I said, 'And in fourth place . . .' Horror! His number was one more than on the list I'd been given. With a quick check that his skin colour wasn't going to betray my mistake, I gave him the name of the athlete carrying the last number on the list.

6

Back Home

Back in our little house in Windsor there was much to look forward to. With Penny still travelling the world with BOAC, and then the Mexico Games, we hadn't spent much time there together since our wedding in June. Now there was, among other things, a nursery to prepare. Come April there would be three of us.

On the work front, the granting of new Independent Television franchises also required some adjustment. I retained my contact with *World of Sport*, but I was now the commentator for Granada, whose franchise in Lancashire, previously for five days, now included the weekends. ABC Television was no more, its area being split into three – Granada, Yorkshire Television and, in the Midlands, ATV who had also expanded into a seven-day company on being moved from their weekend role in London.

I greatly missed the Sunday lunchtimes at the local of one of my producer/directors, Geoff Hall, in Cheadle Hulme, a hotbed of football chat where straight-from-the-shoulder criticism taught me many lessons. Though being recognised in public out of context – in a restaurant or at the theatre for example – was for some time a clear embarrassment emblazoned on rosy cheeks, I've always found 'the man in the street' a generous and useful critic. The embarrassment in later years – though not now so obvious – has been the way people have been able to quote verbatim what I said at various matches and on various occasions. It has also, I confess, given me a warm feeling of satisfaction, though not, I hope, smugness. It was nice to know 'they cared'.

The rivalry between the new and established companies was very keen, and at times co-operation was minimal. London Weekend, with Jimmy Hill joining as head of sport from Coventry City, soon after taking them into the First Division, was the new kid on the block. Outside the capital, there was a determination that LWT should not be allowed to take over; inside, there was wariness from the company they followed in the Friday evening schedule, Thames (the successor to Rediffusion), though while the name changed many of the personnel stayed in their roles.

The arrival of Brian Moore at LWT was a blow on two counts: first because I would have liked the job, and second because it was clearly going to move me down the pecking order. But, given that Jimmy Hill always did things his own way, I wasn't altogether surprised. Brian brought with him considerable experience as the BBC's football correspondent (a curious title, because it applies only to radio). I had made no attempt to seek the position, and it was not until much later that I learned from Brian's autobiography, *The Final Score,* that my case had been strongly fought by John Bromley. 'You were family, old love. Of course I supported you' was Brommers's comment when I tackled him on the point. Brian wrote that we might have been in opposition in the television commentary box in reverse order, he with the BBC and me with ITV. I don't know if Brian knew it, but Jimmy later told me that listening to Brian's radio commentaries while travelling to mid-week matches made up his mind because 'He said nothing that upset me'. I've never asked him what it was I said that did.

Jimmy and Brian went on to form a strong partnership on *The Big Match,* as presenter/commentator and expert, and backed by John Bromley created a new and different style of studio panel for the 1970 World Cup. John always believed that ITV had to be different to compete, and the informality of Jimmy, Malcolm Allison, Paddy Crerand, Derek Dougan and Bob McNab, with Brian, in the chair, trying to keep some semblance of order, was certainly that. For all his reputation in commentary, it can certainly be argued that presentation was Brian's greater strength, and his expertise in that area enabled Hugh Johns – unceremoniously ousted from the network commentator position he'd rightly held since the '66 World Cup – to be reinstated for the next three World Cup finals.

So competitive and so insistent on using their own commentator were the separate companies – or more accurately their sports departments – that I often found myself sitting a few feet away from Brian when the best match involving a north-west club was in London, or from Hugh when the same applied in his new realm, the Midlands. Yorkshire used Danny Blanchflower, who, for all his wonderful playing career, found television, like management, too restrictive. In conversation he could be enthralling as well as Irishly charming, although his advice, seriously given, that a football commentator's working life should be no longer than a playing career, I somehow failed to take on board.

Danny provided a moment which encapsulated the fact that the fans often know best. Before a match at Elland Road, the director called him into the scanner to point out that he was over-using the word 'chance', as in 'chance for Smith; chance for Brown'. The Irishman was not best pleased, claiming that he would have himself become aware of the habit. As he passed a group of supporters on their way to the ground, they chanted, 'Chance, chance, chance.' He said nothing, but the point was surely made.

Distance may lend enchantment, but I have the impression that life at London Weekend was champagne days. Although I wasn't their commentator, I was fully involved with the beginning of *On the Ball*, introduced by Brian, which we all felt was much more lively and original in thought than the Beeb's *Football Preview*. A special occasion was not needed for someone to crack a bottle of bubbly.

The only disappointment was the cowardice of the programme controllers, who failed to give a decent chance to a serious sports programme introduced by Michael Parkinson. Poor early figures saw it moved from Friday evening to Sunday afternoon, where it predictably died a premature death. The chance to have a sporting equivalent of the old *Panorama* or *This Week* was lost. *Pace* recent programmes by Messrs Hansen and Lineker, the sporting press are right in their criticism that serious investigative journalism is a rarity in TV sports departments.

In the old days at the BBC, the concern was about losing contracts. Perhaps that's still the case for some, but as every football manager from Alex Ferguson down seems ready to take umbrage at any comment made by programmes, either local or national, over which *Match of the Day* has absolutely no control, the sports department would do well to set up a proper documentary branch. (At least *MotD* is now more prepared to follow the style of news programmes and say, 'So and so was invited but declined . . .', something I advocated for years.) And then, turning from poacher to gamekeeper, it could exert some influence over the timing of programmes such as the edition of *Panorama* that came close, by showing the IOC in a less than flattering light and thus upsetting the IOC members who would be voting, to undermining the London 2012 bid, which BBC Sport was supporting. The original transmission caused problems enough, but the repeat on BBC World was broadcast even closer to the Singapore Congress of the IOC.

To return to the 'old days' with ITV, live interviews from

grounds – which were a regular part of *On the Ball* – were not entirely welcome around the regions, in part because of the lunch break, and in part because it was an LWT programme. It was a rare Saturday when there was not a critical barb or two. To talk of eggshells would perhaps exaggerate my position, but with most of the mortgage being paid by Granada there was a need to tread carefully. On the other hand, doing pieces to camera was a new experience and one such perhaps played a part in fashioning my career.

That may be a romantic notion, but as the story involves Manchester City it's entirely in keeping with the club's history down the years. City were an exhilarating side, full of characters gelled together by two more of disparate variety. Summerbee, Bell, Lee, Young and Coleman is a forward line which trips easily off the tongue. Joe Mercer, the manager, was a joy; the provocative Malcolm Allison a wonderful coach of good players (he'd have been excellent in that role – though not, I think, as manager – for England).

Towards the end of 1968, the year in which they won the championship, beating Newcastle 4–3 to clinch the pennant, I offered the forecast in a match report from Maine Road that, come next May, they would win the FA Cup. Considering their talent it could not be said to be an extravagant forecast, but it turned out to be right and some City supporters remembered it. Up on the Wembley balcony on Cup final day, waiting to do a small interview, and watching David Coleman strut his stuff, I was spotted by Blues fans who, just as the BBC cameras panned on to them in Wembley Way, broke into a chant of 'There's only one Barry Davies'. (I suppose Bryan

Cowgill, the BBC's head of sport, might just have been aware of my existence. On the other hand . . .)Two months later I became a close-season transfer.

For the next few hours, though, I was very much a member of the ITV team in what became known as the television punch-up final. Manchester City had signed an exclusive deal with the BBC which, in theory, left ITV with only the players of Leicester City to interview. But at Wembley Summerbee and co were quite happy to talk to us, and he came close to thumping someone who tried to pull him away while he was talking to me. It was all rather handbags stuff, but the row simmered on for quite a while. The following season an arranged football match between the two sports departments was hastily cancelled when the BBC manager was told by Bryan Cowgill to withdraw his team.

There was no real doubt that I would accept the BBC offer, but I asked David Warwick, the boss at Granada, about the chance of a Friday-night preview programme and a studio introduction to the Sunday afternoon match. The response was, 'Not next season, but possibly the one after'. It duly arrived then, to the delight of the man who followed me in the Manchester chair, Gerald Sinstadt. Indirectly, it was a favour returned: he had given me my first chance with the BBC. Now Bryan Cowgill and the *Match of the Day* editor, Sam Leitch, were offering me my second. The stay was to be rather longer this time round.

One curiosity of the timing of my arrival at Television Centre in July 1969 was that the previous May had seen the conclusion of the season-long commentators' competition run by *Sportsnight with Coleman*. It was said he thought up the idea while on holiday, to give the public a chance to see that commentating wasn't as easy as they might imagine. There was a big response and some people believed I was the eventual winner. Among them was a man who for years ran the press box at Lord's. If he's reading this, I apologise for never having had the courage to correct him when he so warmly and admiringly welcomed me, each time I visited the home of cricket, as the man who made it all the way to the top after winning 'that' competition.

For the record, I didn't actually enter. The victor was a Welshman called Idwal Robling, ahead of Ian St John of Liverpool and Scotland fame. Sir Alf Ramsey had the casting vote and, so it was said, would never entertain the possibility of voting for a Scotsman. Sadly for Idwal – cruelly christened Awol Ribling by some at ITV – there were only occasional opportunities in Wales and the West Country after his prize-winning appearance in the BBC team in Mexico. In contrast, Ian St John forged a successful career in television, particularly in company with Jimmy Greaves in *Saint and Greavsie*. Among others who made the top six, Ed Stewart – 'Stewpot' of 'Hallo, darling' fame – returned to disc jockeying, acting and the undying support of Everton; and Tony Adamson took his fine delivery and usage of English to tennis and golf as a distinguished broadcaster with BBC Radio 2 and then Five Live.

7

Early Days Back at the Beeb

The BBC gave me a gentle introduction with a minor in-vision role at Ninian Park, Cardiff, in a pre-season match celebrating the Football Association of Wales's seventy-fifth anniversary. With Ken Wolstenholme I already had a passing acquaintance – quite literally: along the gantry boxes at Wembley – but it was my first meeting with the senior outside broadcast (OB) football director, Alec Weeks. In those days, the OB was pre-eminent in the sports department, providing the basis of the BBC's world-wide reputation for coverage of sport and events. The studio's role was to support them. Times would change!

Alec's was a classic office-boy-made-good story. He'd risen from the ranks through engineering and studio-managing on radio before moving, as one of the pioneers, to television in 1959. Seven years later his choice of pictures was seen around the world when England won the World Cup. It's easy to forget that the 1966 championship was, as a whole, the first to be covered by electronic cameras and videotape. The only part of Alec's working life away from the BBC was spent as a PE instructor in the RAF. He'd been a more than useful boxer, twice going into the ring in inter-services contests with a man who went on to become middleweight champion of the world, Randolph Turpin.

His physique and a certain pugnacity not far below the surface suggested Alec wasn't a man to be crossed. There was a problem at Ninian Park about some advertising hoardings for which agreement had not been reached. Shortly before kick-off Alec gave orders to a man whom I took for a fixer-cum-bodyguard. 'Boy,' he said (I took a little time to appreciate that this was an often-used salutation), 'go out there and kick them over.' The 'bodyguard' was in fact the caption artist, Ron Suckling – in those days captions were figures and letters on a felt blackboard. The debate about advertising not allowed by the BBC Charter was then a regular occurrence, for which the director was made responsible and often hung out to dry by the bosses back at base. Today, as they say, it's a whole new ball game: flicking ads everywhere you look.

On Charity Shield day, David Coleman introduced the new format of *Match of the Day* with a map of the country split into five regions. He and Kenneth Wolstenholme were to share the commentating in the south-east; Idwal Robling, the winner of the competition, the west; Walley Barnes, Wales; Alan Weeks, the Midlands; leaving me, in company with Stuart Hall, back where I'd been with Granada, in the north – as I put it when David Coleman welcomed me to the team during the programme, 'from Merseyside to Leeds, from Manchester to Newcastle'. I watched the recorded match in company with Don Revie in the Leeds studio and afterwards interviewed him and later the new manager of Sheffield Wednesday, Danny Williams, and his big signing from Celtic, Tommy Craig. The cost of the transfer was £100,000, £65,000 less than the new British record Revie had paid to take Allan Clarke from Leicester City.

Between my live interviews David presented what amounted to a trail, with action of Clarke, George Best, Roger Hunt, Bobby Charlton, Martin Peters, Ron and Wyn Davies, and Bobby Moncur used to justify his claim that, 'The Football League in this country possibly produces the best value for money of any form of entertainment anywhere in the world. Where else, for as little as five bob, can you see players and moves like this?'

My first commentary, a week later, was to be from Elland Road, a venue where I would witness many significant moments in the coming decade. Now it was Leeds United *v* Tottenham Hotspur. At the Queen's hotel in Leeds on the Friday night I met John McGonagle, the BBC OB director who, in the consortium put together with ITV in the '66 World Cup, had covered the matches at Ayresome Park. The last time we'd worked together was the night three years earlier when North Korea beat Italy, though then he'd have listened to Frank Bough. Now it would be different, and I was anxious to make a good start.

John liked to do things in his own way and in his own time, and he liked to ease himself into the day. He had a penchant for good whisky, although it was not the effects of that which meant that he preferred breakfast to be taken quietly, but simply habit. He would look with disdain at anyone who awoke 'full of beans'. But our first breakfast together was brief and calculated to put not only him off his stroke.

Kenneth Wolstenholme, suffering from flu, wasn't rostered to work on the opening day, 9 August. David Coleman was to commentate on the main match and then introduce the evening programme. But when he awoke that morning he'd lost his voice. McGonagle was instructed to organise transport – a role given to his ever- efficient and helpful assistant, Sybil Jenazian – and with barely time to down the cornflakes I was on my way to Selhurst Park. On the M1 there was a lot of thinking time but of a very general nature, for I had no specific notes on the teams. Manchester United was no problem: I'd been commentating on them regularly for the last three years, and in those days United were still the country's favourite team. But Crystal Palace had only just won their place in the big time. Their manager, Bert Head, became my first interviewee for 'Football Preview' on *Grandstand*.

It was a good opening match for the programme and not a bad one for the new commentator. Alec Weeks seemed pleased enough and encouraging, and the four goalscorers were rightly identified. But if there were any laurel leaves to be found there was little time to rest on them: car and chauffeur were waiting to take me back to Lime Grove studios in Shepherds Bush. There I joined Frank Bough, who was deputising for David Coleman, and interviewed two Scottish recruits to the Palace side, Roger Hynd and Gerry Queen; Roger admitting that it had taken him the first half to adjust to the pace of the First Division, and that he was at fault on the first United goal.

Six weeks later I stood in for David as *Match of the Day* presenter. My commentary match was just round the corner at Loftus Road so I had plenty of time to think about the task – probably too much time. Sam Leitch, the editor, soon had the frame of the programme worked out and together we scripted the opening. Looking back, I can't believe that nobody suggested recording my opening lines: it would have meant much less pressure, plus the chance to re-record in case of glitches. When Jimmy Hill moved from ITV four years later this was a regular occurrence, and by then he'd had far more experience of working in a studio. But now I was just sitting in for David and the understudy was expected to read the lines in the same way. It was, I suppose, a compliment – but as the signature tune faded away and the producer, Brian Venner, said, 'Cue Barry,' it was a very nervous presenter who opened the programme.

The first item of news on 20 September was that Dave Mackay's new team, Derby County, had beaten his old one, Tottenham Hotspur 5–0, with the beaten manager, Bill Nicholson, telling Brian Clough his newly promoted team had played exceptionally well. There was no coverage of the match. Instead the action was provided by Chelsea against Leeds and, in the south-east, QPR *v* Swindon, after which I probed Rodney Marsh, strongly – but without the slight grin ever leaving his mouth – about the fact that the day had seen the fourth penalty given for a tackle on him at Loftus Road and the season wasn't yet two months old.

Over the next four seasons I was occasionally used as the

programme's presenter, but never had the run that I believe every presenter needs to feel comfortable in the role. It therefore irked me when some years later, as I discussed my progress and prospects with the new head of sport, Jonathan Martin, he claimed that I'd been given my chance in the presenter's chair. My view is that I was only ever driving a vehicle designed for David, whose introductions were clipped, staccato phrases, earnestly delivered around brief highlights of the games to follow. Usually his rehearsal was no more than ten minutes before the scheduled start, his late arrival keeping everyone on their toes and creating a tension which he seemed to relish.

I wouldn't presume to compare myself with David or his successors, but for choice I was nearer the Des Lynam laid-back school of presenting. However, while I could compete with the one-liners – as I hope some commentary would attest – I'd certainly have had difficulty with the quiver of the moustache, the raise of the eyebrow and the presumed style with the ladies; to say nothing of the mop of grey hair. When he wanted to be, he was by some distance the best (as he often proved when he arrived as *Match of the Day*'s presenter nineteen years later).

Jonathan concluded that I was a better presenter in the field – at the OB – and I was to enjoy that role in tennis, skating, hockey, badminton and gymnastics, though in all those sports I eventually finished up as a commentator; so it would now be hard to argue with his comment then that my greater value to the Beeb was in the commentary box. Even so, although I know the decision owed something to unavailability, I was delighted when Jonathan's successor as editor, Brian Barwick, invited me to present *MotD*'s twenty-fifth-anniversary programme in 1989.

The regional second-match format lasted for only one season (1969–70). In the north, the opt-out earned the nickname 'The Mad Movies', such was the often outdated equipment we had to work with. More than once the scanner – the hub of the broadcast for sound, vision and picture quality – was a make-do van fitted with monitors and so forth, with the producer's assistant balancing stopwatches and notebooks on her knees. Sometimes the matches were covered on film and many a time the commentary had to be either synched-up or added after-wards – occasionally live on air. It was light years away from the multi-camera coverage of today – if we had two cameras working that was a luxury – but it had its amusing as well as testing moments.

I had more than my expected share of the big matches and stories; among them Liverpool being thrashed 4–1 by Manchester United at Anfield on 13 December, with a 1–2 and a clap of thunder by Bobby Charlton completing the rout: and Barry Endean providing the season's cup shock, scoring the goal that beat Liverpool at Vicarage Road. But along with that opening Saturday the two things I recall most fondly from my first season with *MotD* are Jimmy Greaves, my sidekick four years earlier on my commentary debut, completing his perfect record of scoring debuts for every new club – and, of course, for England – playing for West Ham at Maine Road; and finding words, too, for the team who may have helped me reach the Beeb, as in the pouring rain at the totally uncovered Prater stadium in Vienna, Manchester City beat Gornik Zabrze of Poland to win the European Cup Winners' Cup. The celebrations, though, were somewhat marred for the players' wives and sweethearts whose hairdos lost by many curls to the weather.

The 1970s

'And Leeds will go mad, and they've every right to'

'Hunter has to win this ball'

'The smile of the season, the performance of the season, the trophy of the season'

8

Chatting with Alf

In seven World Cup finals since England's victory in 1966, the media's preview of the coming tournament has varied only in the degree of hype of England's hopes. The supposed God-given right to be among the favourites, which was severely undermined when England failed to qualify in '74 and '78, and took a further blow in '94, resurfaces every time the flag of St George, in various forms, is carried to the party (actually it used to be the Union Jack, which I frequently complained about). Only twice have England come close.

The most recent was in 1990. Luck played a big part on the rollercoaster to the semi-final, but there deserted Bobby Robson's men when they were, in my opinion, the better side and would surely have beaten a desperate Argentina in the final. The other occasion was in 1970, when England were the cup-holders, and the hype was less and the hope of success more realistic than at any time since. I'm one of those who felt that the squad and the team that fell in the quarter-final were a few notches higher in quality than the boys of '66.

Shortly before Mexico '70, I spent a couple of hours in the company of Brian Moore for another programme in the *On Reflection* series produced by British Forces Broadcasting Services featuring a leading sporting celebrity of the moment. Our subject was Alf Ramsey. I can only assume, looking back, that Alan Grace, the producer, played the 'speaking to the troops' card in persuading the man whose life as a professional footballer, which began at Southampton, owed something to having played against them for the Duke of Cornwall's Light Infantry. Alf was perfectly affable before and after the programme, but much of the interview itself reminded me of the profession I'd decided to forgo. It was not too far from pulling teeth.

His answers, sprinkled with his favourite expression, 'most certainly', were painstakingly delivered, and little was given away. But there were moments which threw some illumination on the character of an essentially shy man. When asked to pick from the thirty-two internationals he'd played for his country, he replied without a moment's hesitation, 'England's defeat in the 1950 World Cup finals by the United States.' Sixteen years later his 'fury' at the last-minute German equaliser in the 1966 final was because he believed a German player had handled and his comment 'We should have had a free kick' had all the strength of an immediate post-match interview. And yet when talking about the moments immediately following that goal, when he had to go out to talk to his dispirited team, he described himself as very controlled. Ordering his players to stand up instead of sitting on the Wembley turf was because, 'We had to convey to the Germans that we were looking forward to the next half-hour.' He said he was embarrassed to admit that, 'We weren't concerned with entertainment,' but he purred like a proud father when talking of the goals scored by Bobby Charlton and Geoff Hurst: 'They were beautifully taken. There was such poetry in those seven goals.'

At that time Ramsey provided the yardstick by which other sports measured the requirements of their national coach, even more than when Clive Woodward led England to the rugby World Cup in 2003. But that began to change one hot afternoon in León, and reached its nadir a little under three years later on an October evening back at the scene of his triumph. Substitutions too soon; a substitution too late: how finely the line is drawn.

Back in 1963, when he was appointed England manager, he said very early that 'England will win the World Cup' and for most of the next three years inwardly cursed falling into the trap. But what else could he have said? And he was proved right. Before 1970 he was far more guarded – 'Most certainly England will try their best to retain the World Cup' – but proved equally prophetic when, back in the studios of BFBS, he responded to a query about the problems he faced with 'altitude, heat, boredom', and then, after a pause, 'food and drink'. Had it not been for Gordon Banks suffering Montezuma's Revenge, no one would have queried the decision to substitute

Bobby Charlton with Colin Bell, keeping England's senior citizen fresh for the semi-final. Using the squad, especially in such conditions, is a key to success. And no one knew then that Bobby Charlton's international career had come to an end with his 106th cap. In León it was Peter Bonetti who shared the blame with Ramsey, which was tough on Gordon Banks' understudy forced with little practice on to centre stage. The goal that began the turnaround was, so Franz Beckenbauer told me years later, no more than a hit-and-hope which he didn't hit well. But from being comfortably in control, two goals up, England lost 3–2, with the introduction of a pacey German winger, Jurgen Grabowski, a telling factor in extra time.

All this I watched later on a recording. On the day, I was in the highest stadium in the championship in Toluca, covering the hosts, Mexico, in their quarter-final against Italy, whom I had followed through their usual highs and lows and clashes of personality; not to mention the urgent need to banish the memory of four years earlier when tomatoes rained on them on their return home from defeat in Middlesbrough by North Korea. In the first half, the Mexicans – players and supporters – were on a high befitting a venue at 8,774 feet. It was 1–1 at half-time.

But this was the day when Luigi Riva came good, scoring twice in the second half under the prompting of one of my all-time favourite footballers, Gianni Rivera, who remained a substitute throughout the competition. In the semi-final Rivera scored the winning goal at 4–3 against Germany, in an extraordinary match which had seen him amazingly clear off his own line a minute earlier. But the coach, Ferruccio

Valcareggi, opted for the defensive needs, Rivera playing only the last six minutes of a final which had already been decided. It isn't only England coaches who view the most naturally gifted with suspicion. Players have to be sweating or they aren't trying. Though in those conditions everybody sweated.

The other venue of Group Two, Cuatemoc, in Puebla, was a deal more attractive than La Bombera, 'the chocolate box', as the Toluca stadium was known. And it was in Puebla that I covered my first live match for the BBC, a very testing goalless draw between Italy and Uruguay. The start was hardly propitious as there was little time to identify the first anthem – Uruguay's – before the band struck up. In my ear, Bryan Cowgill, from the studios in Mexico City, shouted, 'It's the Italian national anthem.' He repeated it three times. I kept silent. 'And now,' I said as the music changed, 'the Italian anthem.' 'Oooh, sorry!' said the voice in my ear.

The next day, Ginger, as Cowgill was known, announced that yesterday's had been the greatest football commentary he'd heard. Unfortunately, he was talking about David Coleman in Guadalajara, as England fell to Pele's invitation to Jairzinho to score the only goal of a match which contained the best save, by Gordon Banks, of any century. That was probably a fair comment, but it was a great match, and one which should have been repeated in the final.

Alf Ramsey alone made it to Mexico City as a pundit for the BBC. I met him by chance, looking very lost, in the foyer of the Aristos Hotel. I don't recall now for whom or what he was waiting, but when I invited him for a drink of something he responded with a smile, 'Yes, I think I'd like a cup of tea.'

We spent the next forty minutes or so idly chatting about foot-ball, present and past. There was no guard, no suspicion, none of the usual scepticism of a journalist's view or the question 'What authority do you have to say that?' – an approach he often adopted with those who hadn't played professionally. He was a hard man to get to know, but for all his inflexibility and his distaste for what he described as 'the embroidery which surrounded the job', he was a very genuine person.

Like his successors – not one really appreciated the lone-liness of the role until the day when he had no commitment to club affairs – he was happiest when he was on the training pitch with his players, but even there he kept a certain distance. No player could be a hundred per cent certain of his place in Ramsey's choice. The identity of the player who after one match said goodbye with the comment 'See you next time, Alf' has changed so often as to make the story apocryphal. But, while he was certainly a players' man and always supported them, the response 'If selected' was entirely in keeping with his attitude.

In very different times – salaries through the roof, a larger media, fans more demanding – I believe Ramsey's successor at the World Cup forty years on should have remembered that dictum. Several others who have held the role have allowed – quite often with the encouragement of the media keen to build and sometimes to destroy – certain players to hold a place above the team. It never happened in Ramsey's day.

The Brazilians of 1970 who kept the Jules Rimet trophy after winning for the third time, by beating Italy 4–1, were 'most certainly' the best international side I have seen, in, admittedly, conditions which favoured them: the brilliant Pele and the almost-as-good Tostao, the chain-smoking Gerson and the crucially important ball-winning and ball-using Clodoaldo, offered so much invention. The conclusion was perfect, with an enhanced replay of the goal that had beaten England; Pele, again, with arrogance, poise and simplicity setting up the final scorer, though Carlos Alberto had to run a little further and hit the ball a deal harder than had Jairzinho. The most lasting memory, however, came not in the final but in the semi-final when Pele, running through on the Uruguayan goal to reach Tostao's pass, sold the most outrageous dummy to Mazurkiewicz before, behind the confused goalkeeper, tapping the ball just the wrong side of his left-hand post.

Kenneth Wolstenholme's commentary made clear the general amazement, and fully captured the moment, but the boss had other plans for the final. His agent, Teddy Summerfield, had to insist that the relevant clause in his contract be honoured, or Ken would have lost the seat for the final. Cowgill wanted Coleman to do it, and even tried the compromise of using Ken for the many countries taking the BBC output, with David exclusive to Britain. Ken's right to the first choice of all major football wasn't included in his next contract, and after one more FA Cup final, his twenty-third, he and the BBC parted company. Little did he know that by the time the next international championship finals came around, the European of 1972, Coleman, too, would be at odds with his employer. As a result I got the chance not just to watch but to commentate on the second-best international team I've seen.

9

Questions of Criticism

I'm not sure how deeply I thought about commentary in the first couple of seasons with *Match of the Day*. I was just wrapped up in the game and thrilled to be with the top football programme. After the match I had almost complete recall of every incident and what I had said about it. I spent hours studying tapes of matches and was pretty hard on myself, but the criticism was mainly about missing things or simply not getting it right. Penny, never a football fan, assumed I knew what I was talking about, but she had a sharp ear for pronunciation and grammar and a keen eye for mannerisms on camera (she actually appeared on the box before I did, during her days at the Arts Educational School). I was grateful for both.

There were strict commentary rules then about things like not talking over goal kicks, and making only brief comments over close-ups of managers, because, though editing matches was becoming more sophisticated, it was still early days. Standards were high, and commentators and match editors alike could expect to be carpeted on the Monday if a mistake got through on the Saturday (though the occasion when Brian Kidd of Manchester United apparently threw the ball to himself was a gross exception to the general standard). The imminent arrival of a doubtful edit often produced a phone call from the videotape area to the studio gallery in the hope of distracting the editor at the crucial moment.

My criticism now of the commentator I was then would include: 'Somewhat given to over-excitement and with a need to pitch his voice lower.' Although it struck a chord with the fans at the time, I'd love to re-voice my reaction to the 'Not offside' decision that probably cost Leeds the title in Arsenal's double year, 1971 – the most blatant example I can recall of not playing to the whistle. The words 'Leeds will go mad and they've every right to go mad' probably stand the test of time on paper, but the way my young voice said them doesn't (see criticism above).

The match was Leeds *v* West Bromwich Albion at Elland Road on 17 April 1971. As Leeds pushed forward, looking for a winner, Colin Suggett of West Brom was clearly offside. The flag was raised and play briefly came to a halt. The referee, Ray Tinkler, although shaken by the resulting furore, was prepared to talk to me about it in his dressing-room afterwards, though by making sure he knew what I'd said on the tape, which was already being edited in London, I gave him every reason to show me the door. He insisted that Suggett hadn't been interfering with play, which was why he'd allowed Tony Brown – who'd intercepted Norman Hunter's pass just inside the Albion half – to run on and present Jeff Astle with the winning goal. The decision was probably as costly to the referee as to Leeds, for Tinkler was in line to officiate at the Cup final that year. (Interestingly, today's interpretation of offside would put him in the clear.)

The 'sickened man', as I described Don Revie, came to be interviewed breathing fire, and against all journalistic judgement I sent him back to the dressing-room to cool down. He returned a little later looking as he had just after the goal, and paid no fine to the Football Association, while still speaking his mind.

A few years later, Ron Greenwood, who succeeded Don as England manager, accused me of being a Leeds supporter, which shows that a commentator can be labelled, even by the cognoscenti, simply by being in the commentary seat at a time of success. Most of us have, at some stage, been thought to wear the colours of Liverpool or Manchester United; more recently Arsenal or Chelsea.

Bias is the first criticism aimed at a commentator, and I made rather a fetish of keeping secret the team I supported as a boy. I believe I survived my thirty-five years on *MotD* without anyone being able to point a finger with any confidence. But naturally I was affected by style, and the ebb and flow and fortune in a game. Passion, while it should never be forced, is part of commentary, and being lifted by the play of one side can often be perceived by the committed as being against their opponents. A team which I felt wasn't getting the rub of the green certainly gained my sympathy. And then, of course, there are those moments which lift you from your seat.

On the question of criticism, two conversations come to mind. The first was with Don Revie, who, in the days of what would now be looked upon as a more formal style, was the best I worked with in the commentary box. He brought his managerial eye to the task, taking the moment to turn away from the immediate action to look at individual performance and devise tactical plans in his head, so as to be able to offer answers to basic questions like, 'Why are Team A beating Team B and what can Team B do to change the situation?'

On this occasion, though, in May 1972, his remarks were made on the journey back from Hampden Park, where Scotland had been playing England. I forget the specifics but I'd made a couple of points in commentary about the performance of Rodney Marsh, whose run in the team was giving rise to conflicting opinions. I asked Don, who'd watched the match from the studio at the ground as a pundit, to comment.

'The first thing you said needed saying, and I said to myself, "Well done, Barry." I also happen to agree with your second point but I was praying you wouldn't make a third. You'd be telling an international player how to play.'

That's a line David Pleat felt I crossed when Bobby Robson took two of David's Luton Town players to the international against France in Paris in 1984. Paul Walsh did quite well in an inexperienced losing team, but Brian Stein 'froze' and joined that unhappy breed of one-cap players. 'You were right,' said David at the Football Writers' dinner that season, 'but because you said it millions of people, the viewers, thought it, too.' There is no more fervent advocate of the game than David, and he delivered the line not so much as a criticism as like a distraught father whose son had been dropped from the school team. I think he gave too much status to the commentator, but I took his point to heart.

In subsequent years I worked alongside him in the box many times and I loved his enthusiasm and insight. At times, when it came to a quick delivery of words, too much of the former inhibited the latter, but he was a huge source of knowledge and great to work with.

Covering England brings different demands, because the audience is supporting only one of the teams. Getting the right balance between objectivity and looking at the contest through English eyes can be difficult. Obviously one must present England's hopes, enjoy their success and react to their disappointment, all of which should come naturally; and criticise if required. But it's easy to fall into the trap – we've all done it – of using 'us/them' and 'we/they', which should be avoided, especially at the British Broadcasting Corporation. In the days of the old Home International Championship, this was particularly important. Locally based commentators were often used alongside the network man, but there are plenty of Irish, Welsh and Scots living in England and the last of those groups led the way with accusations of bias. There are no such problems with foreign teams, and having been launched as a commentator by seven straight such internationals in the '66 World Cup, I've always enjoyed the freedom of comment they offer. In recent years even the identification has become easier, thanks to the multinational Premiership.

10

The Tragedy of Munich

It was to the Mexico World Cup and the West Germans' recent display at Wembley that Brian Moore and I referred, on a summer's day in 1972, as we stood watching them in training before the European Championship final at the old Heysel stadium in Brussels. (In passing, we noted our different methods – he, a former radio commentator, matching names with numbers; I just noting looks and movement.)

This was the summer of the talent of Gunter Netzer. In the late spring he'd stridden, blond and imperious, about the Wembley turf in a 3–1 victory on 29 April 1971 which led to England playing the second leg of the quarter-final as a scoreless, damage-limitation exercise. Now, in the four-team finals, a German side of the known – Beckenbauer and Muller – and the new – Breitner, Hoeness, Heynckes

– responded to the wave of his wand. Having just a moment's doubt when the Belgians made it 2–1 at the end of the semi-final, they strolled to victory over Russia in the final, scoring three goals without reply. There was an effervescence and freedom about their play which, for me, places them just behind the Brazilians of the previous World Cup. As hosts in the next, the Germans would find those qualities elusive.

One other memory of summer '72: in June, Alec Weeks and I were delayed for some three hours at Brussels airport. On its outward journey the British Airways Trident that should have brought us home crashed on the A30, a few miles west of Heathrow. There were no survivors.

It hardly seemed possible, but when I returned from Belgium there were only a few weeks before I would be involved in a second Olympics. So much had changed in the four years since Mexico City.

Then I'd been the new boy, albeit with three years with *World of Soccer* and *World of Sport* behind me. But the future with the change of the ITV franchises was only a season-by-season arrangement. Now I'd completed three seasons on a programme which emptied the pubs on a Saturday evening with regular audiences of 11 or 12 million viewers; and a new contract was on the table.

On the home front, always for me much the more important, Penny and I had twice sent out invitations to a christening lunch – 'Giselle, a production by Penny and Barry Davies', in the summer of '69 and then 'Davies Mark 2, a 1971 model'.

For Penny, Gigi and Mark were now a full-time occupation, and for parents and grandparents a pride and joy. Sadly, for my mother for all too short a time. She died very suddenly in January 1972, just before Mark's first birthday. A lovely lady of strong, determined character, and I adored her. In earlier days she bore a close resemblance to the Queen Mother and during a very happy childhood spent in north London and in Kent, my sister, Maureen, and I became quite accustomed to strangers doing a double take. And like Her Majesty, Mother was born on 4 August; but two years later.

In Mexico in '68 the Games themselves had been friendly, with comfortable security which allowed me to bring my new wife into the media area for a few events. But a show of dissent by students before the Games began, which had brought a savage reaction from the government, and Smith and Carlos's Black Power salute on the podium, had shown that the glare of the Olympic spotlight made the Games extremely vulnerable to political demonstrations.

The German authorities were keenly aware of this, and the security in Munich was such that at an early press conference one British journalist, J. L. Manning of the *Daily Mail*, asked why it was easier to get into the site of Dachau than into the Olympic Village. Though it was a tasteless remark, it made the point that the organising committee of the Games were well prepared to risk the ire of the world's media to ensure that their security measures succeeded. But they failed; and the attack on the Israeli athletes – which resulted in eleven deaths – by the Black September group of Palestinian origin changed the world of major sporting events for ever.

The fear is always there: so the security, as in many other areas of life, increases, while everyone knows it can never be enough.

I recall turning on the television in my hotel room after oversleeping a little, and at first struggling to understand the German commentary while wondering why there was no early coverage of the Games. The unmoving but so moving pictures of Block G where the Israeli team had been housed filled the television screen for hour after hour, as deadlines of the threat to kill a hostage came and went. The horror was in the mind, about what had already taken place and what might still. How other commentators coped with finding the right words I know not, but David Coleman was absolutely brilliant – a voice of authority and sensitivity in one.

Eighteen years later, in a programme to mark the centennial Games, the *chef de mission* of the 1972 Israeli team, Shmuel Larkin, told me he still believed the choice of lodging for his team had not been accidental. I should like to think his continued suspicion owed more to the ongoing failure to resolve the hatred between Israeli and Palestinian which most undermines world security.

I have no doubt that the International Olympic Committee made the right decision to carry on. I thought so at the time and still do so with the advantage of hindsight. But Avery Brundage was like a gravedigger handling porcelain. His speech lacked both sympathy and understanding, and he seemed in a rush to put a difficult – no, an impossible – situation behind him. In fact, the Olympic ideal was, and still is, a source of hope in an uncomprehending world, through all humanity's imperfections, including those of its own members and participants.

The Games offered me the chance to commentate on other sports for the BBC, though I wasn't as stretched as I had been for ITV in Mexico. This time it was other ball games: hockey, handball and volleyball joined football. In hockey I was supporting Peter West, whom I'd first met at Cranbrook School when he returned to play cricket for the Old Boys. It had been my task to whiten his pads.

Peter was a thorough gentleman and a fine, unflappable broadcaster, as was clearly seen in the classic recording of him being blasted by the public-address system as he started a live interview. 'I thought we might have problems with that,' he said nonchalantly, as the camera pulled back to reveal the offending large speaker a few feet away, and he continued with the interview. That his reputation as a cricket and rugby commentator suffered because he accepted a contract to present *Come Dancing* was totally unfair. Darren Gough, Mark Ramprakash, Colin Jackson, Matt Dawson and Peter Schmeichel all seem to have enhanced their reputations by taking part in the modern version, *Strictly Come Dancing* – how attitudes change! Peter West deserves a place among the great pioneers of sports broadcasting.

His autobiography, *Flannelled Fool and Muddied Oaf*, includes a passing remark that he believed I could equally well have chosen to commentate on the oval ball. I think he was a little too kind, but I do enjoy the game of rugby. It has, though, changed much since Peter's heyday – not least in the increasing use of substitutes which so interrupts the flow of the game. As for lifting in the lineout . . . !

In Munich, the flow of the volleyball final was my stiffest test. I covered it off-tube – that is to say, not at the venue but back in the broadcast centre gazing at the monitor – in the company of one of the best of a fraternity much under-valued, the OB stage manager. Harry Coventry never forgot who had served and so whether a point had been gained or not. The voice in my ear belonged to Bryan Cowgill, who had the reputation of getting rather excited – not to say annoyed – from time to time. But now his control was perfect, his words helpful and encouraging.

During the Games, I returned to commentate and intro-duce *Match of the Day*. I well recall Bryan ringing the studio gallery in London, wanting to hear how the Sunday news-paper critics had reviewed the BBC's coverage of the Games in the opening week. He was particularly interested in Clive James, whose spiky but clever, perceptively written column in the *Observer* was a regular must-read. Jonathan Martin, then studio producer, was instructed to read it to him while the second match was on the air. The boss was left feeling very happy with life. Flying back to Munich on Sunday morning I read the piece myself. It bore little relation to what I'd heard in my earpiece the previous evening. By judicious sub-editing and, from time to time, altering the emphasis, Jonathan had changed the balance completely and quite bril-liantly. I didn't wait around when I handed in the late editions.

11

'74 World Cup

The 1974 World Cup finals were among the most enjoyable of the ten I've watched. They were also among the most demanding. John Motson and I were used as reporters as well as commentators, and covered many a kilometre up and down the German autobahns.

John had joined the *MotD* team at the start of the 1971–72 season, and I remember well our first conversation, in which he said that he would welcome any advice I could give him. With tongue in cheek I responded by saying, 'Well, for a start, if you reach the age that Ken Wolstenholme is now, and the Beeb offer you a new contract like the one they offered him last April, sign it before they change their minds.' Little did I know then that he would put Ken's twenty-three FA Cup finals in the shade, after being given 'lift-off' by Ronnie

Radford's goal for Hereford against Newcastle in the third-round replay on 5 February 1972. (For the record, Ken was only fifty-one when he left the BBC in 1971.)

1974 saw the best Scottish side to play in the World Cup finals, the worst Brazilian, and the most gifted team, Holland – third in my all-time list – lose in the final. Emlyn Hughes's comment, 'I don't care who beats them [Scotland] as long as Zare ['Zaire', but pronounced like 'dare'] do,' didn't come true, but it was because they beat the little-known Africans only 2–0 that a side boasting the likes of Bremner, Law, Lorimer, Dalglish and Jordan failed to reach the last eight. They more than matched the defending champions in their second match, in which the great Rivelino seemed often to mistake Bremner for the ball, but drew 0–0; and then offered only a late equaliser when they had to beat Yugoslavia. So the Tartan Army, which was really mustered for the first time and seen in such colourful fashion in Dortmund and Frankfurt, made what has since become a regular early journey home.

Perhaps it was that which led the BBC's football boss, Sam Leitch, a Scot, to make Brazil, who had won Scotland's group, first choice for matches in the second phase. David Coleman argued long and rightly that the Dutch were the team to follow in live coverage. There was an edge between the two men from then on. Having already had live the match which more than any other before or since justified the word 'historic' – the only meeting ever between East and West Germany – as a result of David losing the argument I saw two of Holland's matches, albeit recorded. To watch the skills of Johan Cruyff, Johan Neeskens, Ruud Krol and company was a joy, a team uninhibited to the point of sometimes taking the breath away; a reflection, perhaps, of their nation. Only Pele and Maradona stand in front of Cruyff in my 'greatest' list.

I was also lucky enough to cover live probably the best match of the whole tournament, West Germany's 4–2 victory over Sweden on a rainy evening at the Rheinstadion, Dusseldorf. Their defeat by East Germany in the final match of their opening group had actually served West Germany well, because finishing second meant they were in the easier second-round group. The victorious East were left to face not only the Dutch but Brazil and Argentina.

But to lose on home soil to a regime which occupied half of it, and which erected a defensive wall on the football field as well, sent the West German media into paroxysms, questioning every aspect of a team they had expected to win. There was much talk of internal bickering, clashes of egos and all the usual dark rumours associated with failure. Although they had won their other two matches, the performances against Chile and Australia had been far from impressive. Gunter Netzer, after an injury-ridden season with Real Madrid, had played only the last twenty-one minutes in a losing team.

It's generally thought that Franz Beckenbauer took over the running of the side (there's nothing new about player power) but, having had the advantage of reporting and inter-viewing as well as commentating, I believe that the 'wily old fox' Helmut Schoen, the manager, lived up to his nickname and wasn't unhappy to allow Beckenbauer to knock a few heads together. Rainer Bonhof, introduced in the second phase, brought drive to the midfield, and the only change in the line-up for the last four matches was Wimmer against Yugoslavia. When he was substituted by Hoeness, the final team was established: Beckenbauer and Wolfgang Overath were the only survivors from Wembley eight years earlier. The right balance had been achieved, with Overath an elegant left-sided creator back in the role that Netzer craved.

They were rarely the slick machine of two years earlier but they were a team who never stopped running – a fact which Holland forgot. The early penalty in the final for Vogts's tackle ending Cruyff's run gave them the perfect platform, but it seemed that they wanted to prove themselves a 'superior race'. On the pitch and in the stands, the desire of the men in orange to enjoy the moment was palpable. But history drained them, and when it was most needed the team who were said to play total football – all defenders when necessary, all attackers when desired – failed to live up to the sum of their parts. The theory, of course, became an excuse which could be readily called upon, and it has been, by both those who played and those who watched. It's a trait of the Dutch character seen in other sports – hockey has provided a few examples – when the ability is clear but the vision out of focus.

During a report for radio on the 1972 Olympic final in Munich, I'd suggested that if Poland, the new champions, hadn't been unlucky enough to be drawn in England's group, they were good enough to make the top three in the World Cup finals two years thence. The Poles were a fine side, and some of the observations made on that miserable night in

October 1973, when what felt like a Silesian winter descended on Wembley, were well wide of the mark.

Tomaszewski was no 'clown', as Brian Clough called him, though the luck was certainly with him. (It took a long time for it to be appreciated that the different style of Continental goalkeepers often works, though the observation may seem strange today when they dominate the Premiership.) Lato and Gadocha had great dribbling skills at pace. Deyna was becoming world-class. Lubanski, who had picked Bobby Moore's pocket in the first match in Warsaw, was already there. ('Cool by Moore; too cool' was a brilliant recovery by David Coleman in the commentary box, which the England captain couldn't match.) Doing the recorded commentary for the BBC at Wembley, I could offer 'Hunter has to win this ball' as one of my better lines of the second match.

I'd spent much time with the Poles, particularly with their coach, Jacek Gmoch. They knew they'd be under pressure for most of the match but believed their pace on the counterattack might catch England out. The England defence looked stretched as Hunter, preferred to Moore in Ramsey's selection, came to claim the ball down in front of the royal box. But he dallied, trying to keep it in play with his right – that is to say, wrong – foot. Gadocha was away, and, with Hughes scrambling to get back, Domarski's shot gave Poland the lead. He didn't strike the ball particularly well but, hitting it close to Shilton, watched it go under the goalkeeper's body. Pat Jennings, the wonderful goalkeeper for Northern Ireland, Spurs and Arsenal, would probably have kicked the ball away, but Shilton was textbook, and he turned the page too slowly.

England had chance after chance to score more than the penalty calmly put away by Allan Clarke. The second substitution – the late, late arrival of Kevin Hector – simply added to the tears. It's easy to say it wasn't meant to be, but England in the World Cup finals *was* meant to be. The inventors of the game had always been there since a rather reluctant entry after the Second World War. The emptiness was like nothing before or since. Present and past international players were joined in disbelief. Seven years on from triumph, England was nowhere. John Shrewsbury – directing the recorded match for the BBC with his cameras alongside those of ITV, who were live – said afterwards that he thought I'd been sucked in by the emotion of the occasion. He was right.

The Poles did their best to soften the blow by their performance the following summer and might have done even better had torrential rain not hit Frankfurt on the day of the decisive match in the second round. Half the pitch at the Waldstadion was a swamp. Germany defended it in the first half and, try as they might, Lato and company couldn't find a way through, their pace almost totally nullified. At half-time drying machines were brought on and the Germans reaped the harvest with Gerd Muller's goal – and that after the 'clown' Tomaszewski had saved a penalty. The comment by Alan Wade from the FA Coaching Department that you have to adapt to the conditions only added to my belief that the Poles had been done. I was delighted when they won the play-off for third place, beating a Brazilian team which – under the same coach, Mario Zagallo, but lacking many of the big names of 1970 – played throughout the tournament in a style which insulted their country's football pedigree.

Back home my dad proudly showed me a newspaper cutting which claimed that the BBC's own research had established that I was the most acceptable commentator. Later on in my career he'd probably have descended on Television Centre brandishing the article, but in October my lifelong supporter suffered a fatal heart attack. He was the best.

12

Making Choices

The first chance to commentate on a sport other than football came when I'd been with the BBC only thirteen months but I declined the offer. Harry Carpenter was away and David Vine, then number two on boxing, was doing something else; so Bryan Cowgill asked me to cover Cassius Clay's return to the ring following the ban imposed on him for his refusal to accept the Vietnam draft. He was to fight Jerry Quarry in Atlanta, Georgia, on 26 October 1970. I didn't feel qualified to compare his form before and after his imposed absence. I hadn't realised that Henry Cooper would be alongside me; but I had no regrets that Alan Weeks filled the other seat. Although I was there that night at Wembley in June 1963 when the said Mr Cooper put Mr Clay on the floor, boxing is very low on my long list of favourite sports. I have, however, interviewed both Cooper and Muhammad Ali (Clay) for radio.

In the late '60s and the '70s I was a regular contributor in that medium for the international sports programme produced from Bush House by Alex Turnbull (his son Gordon became head of BBC radio sport) and for *London Sportsdesk*, produced by Alan Grace at British Forces Broadcasting. I shared the presenter's seat with Bryon Butler, successor to Brian Moore as BBC football correspondent, and Gerald Williams, whose love and knowledge of tennis surpassed even his lifelong support of Crystal Palace. A regular involvement in the news and personalities of the sporting week was very satisfying, and the best programmes were those which had the last five minutes still to be filled late in the day; they were as up-to-date as possible, keeping the team on its toes.

In June 1973 I was offered another chance by Cowgill, this time for a sport which was much more my cup of tea. 'I need you to hold the team together like he did': I was being asked to fill in for David Coleman in his strongest sport, athletics, at the British International Games in Edinburgh. Negotiations were said to be continuing for the renewal of David's contract between the BBC and his agent, Bagnall Harvey, who was, at the same time, discussing Jimmy Hill taking over from David as presenter of *Match of the Day*; Bagnall was the man who had strongly supported Jimmy when, as PFA chairman, he negotiated the abolition of the maximum wage. No easy task satisfying egos.

If Ron Pickering and Stuart Storey felt theirs a little bruised by my arrival, they disguised it well. They could not have been more helpful. Although I enjoyed watching athletics, and had from an observer's seat been lucky enough to fit Valeriy Borzov's sprint double and Lasse Viren's 5000 metres into my 'ball games' schedules in Munich the year before, my knowledge was as nothing compared with that of an Olympic coach and an Olympic competitor only five years before who was now coaching the British champion shot-putter, Geoff Capes. Ron was, I found, a father-figure to the British team. In Oslo for the semi-final of the European Cup I lost count of how many athletes came up to him to discuss their performance or seek his advice.

My role was mainly setting things up, dealing with the results and filling in as needed, with a few bits of commentary thrown in, but nothing less than 400 metres. For every race and field event a detailed card was produced by our statistician, Stan Greenberg. It sometimes arrived late in the day because of line-up changes, but was always a saving grace; though not to be seeking a fact just as a significant move was being made on the track was a hard knack to acquire.

What started in Edinburgh in June progressed to European team competition in Oslo, where for probably the only time in major competition there were three false starts in an 800 metres. (The Italian runner, Marcello Fiasconaro, well named for the situation, was eventually disqualified, producing long Italian protests.) I was on course to travel behind the Iron Curtain and back to Edinburgh for the European Cup final, but my athletics summer came to a sudden and surprising end in Minsk.

We were there for the USSR against the USA, an

international match notable for the entry of fourteen-year-old Mary Decker, who had the temerity in the 800 metres to beat Niele Sabaite, the silver medallist in Munich. It also produced a convincing victory for the Soviet Union in both the men's and the women's competitions, the latter including a one–two in the 400 metres for Kolesnikova and Kulichkova – two stunning, long-legged Baltic beauties whom Stan, always taking his preparation very seriously, had watched in training. When he became aware that he, too, was being closely watched by a Soviet coach, he self-consciously remarked what good form they were in, and was more than a little surprised to receive the reply in English, 'Yes, but they should be in the Folies Bergère, not here.'

Harry Carpenter had joined us on the trip as an observer but it was only after the event had ended that I discovered why. Over a drink back at the hotel he was musing over his time, some years before, covering athletics for the *Daily Mail* and wondering aloud whether he could pick it up again, when he said, 'But when Ginger said you didn't want to carry on . . . ' My expression stopped him in mid-sentence. 'Oh,' he said, 'I see that you know nothing about it.' I learned that Sam Leitch had demanded I be available for the start of the football season. Alan Mouncer, the athletics producer, and the BBC's most-gifted OB director, wanted me to complete the season with the high-profile European final, which he would direct. Ginger Cowgill came down on Sam's side, and the fact that it was clear I had wanted to go to Edinburgh might later be seen as an own-goal on the football front.

The somewhat hazardous journey to Minsk, though, came

to an end with a proclaimed victory. On the way out we'd had to change planes in Moscow and at the domestic airport had been ushered, in the dark, across the tarmac and runways, amid flashing lights in a scene to suggest we had suddenly been projected into a film probably starring Steve McQueen. The second flight was bumpy in the extreme and prompted us to wonder whether, if the worst happened, anyone would learn of our demise. Soviet internal airlines did not have a good reputation, and disasters were often hushed up.

The first leg of our return journey found our little propeller-driven twenty-seater aircraft containing several unwanted 'passengers'. We were accompanied by a journalist from the French sports newspaper *L'Equipe*, and before take-off he and I proceeded to swat the flies with rolled-up newspapers. As my final backhand, with a delicate touch of topspin, removed the last intruder, Harry Carpenter solemnly announced, 'Game, set and *mouche* to Great Britain.'

My next opportunity at a summer sport came two years later, in 1975, courtesy of Cowgill's number two, Slim Wilkinson who, as the editor responsible for Wimbledon, offered me a test as a tennis commentator. The venue was Bournemouth for the British hard-court championships.

It was what Ilie Nastase described in his autobiography, *Mr Nastase*, as a grey, grisly day, during which he tried to keep the crowd happy by clowning around a bit. I'd barely started my test commentary when his angled smash against Patrick Proisy, at 4–5 and 15–love, the Frenchman serving, was called out. After initial protest and several minutes of debate the Romanian was defaulted by the referee, Mike

Gibson (who was also the Wimbledon referee). To this day, I don't know if my efforts were even recorded. Suffice it to say that it was eight years before I commentated for the first time at the championships of London SW19.

The shuttlecock on racket came long before the ball as, following a feature for *Sportsnight* in spring 1977 with Gillian Gilks, the British number one, whom the Badminton Association felt to be too outspoken, I was asked to present the All England Championships at Wembley. A year later I commentated on badminton in the Commonwealth Games in Edmonton, Alberta, with the former men's number one, Derek Talbot. Tennis followed the same pattern: in 1979 I was back at Bournemouth, not to commentate but to present the hard-court championships.

August Bank Holiday that year saw the last highlight of my brief three-act play at being an athletics commentator. The second World Cup had taken place in Montreal over the weekend, and only Stuart Storey was required to travel overnight from Canada for duty at Crystal Palace for the Rotary Watches International Games. He was there for the field events. I was to cover the track in company with Chris Thorneycroft-Smith, an executive of DAF Trucks who was being given a trial as a possible addition to the athletics team. To my surprise, David Coleman turned up as well and stood behind me as I made a bit of a mess of the 400 metres.

The main event of the afternoon was to be the mile, featuring the highly promising Steve Ovett and the West German winner of the World Cup 1500 metres, Thomas Wessinghage. I offered David the microphone but he declined.

It was a cracking race: ten men went under the four-minute barrier, and Ovett beat the German in what was not only an all-comers' record but a time – 3 min 49.6 seconds – bettered only by Sebastian Coe the same year and the New Zealander John Walker four years earlier.

Years later, chatting about old times with John Shrewsbury, I recalled the occasion when David came back from Montreal to listen to 'that chap from some motor company'. John immediately came up with the name, and added with a knowing look, 'But he didn't come back to listen to him, he came back to listen to you.' I can honestly say that that thought had never crossed my mind. I was later offered the chance to continue with the sport on radio. It was very tempting but I would have had to forgo introducing the tennis; the position subsequently went to Alan Parry.

It's sometimes said that I turned to other sports when football selection began to go against me. It's truer to say that producers in other areas had already offered me opportunities. Whether accepting them led to my losing a football contest with someone who, at a crucial moment, made it clear to the boss that he was only interested in covering that one sport is a matter for conjecture.

13

Motty and Me

The saga of Motson and Davies isn't easy to write, for however I tell it some will perceive it as sour grapes. Be that as it may, I am resolved to present the facts and leave the reader to judge.

Let me say at the outset that there is no animosity between Motty and me and there never has been – despite the fact that a *Match of the Day* editor once wrote to my agent that having both of us feeling that we weren't being given a fair share of the fixtures was a small achievement, but his own. We agree that our contrasting styles have been good for the programme, and played a big part in our collective longevity; and I've always proffered the thought that one man's commentator is another man's irritation.

The last time I had a chat about the position with Niall

Sloane, the head of football, I suggested that perhaps 30 or 40 per cent of viewers preferred my style, and that that should be reflected in his commentator choice. He responded by telling me that he thought the figure was at least 50 per cent. 'Incredulity' does scant justice to my expression, and I left his office knowing that, whatever I offered to football commentary, it would never be enough.

The minor soap opera, which frequently took the attention of the television critics, lasted for a quarter of a century, ending with the European Championship in Portugal in 2004, when the fact that I was not invited to commentate on a single one of England's matches, not even recorded, made my position absolutely clear.

It began in April 1977 with newspaper headlines proclaiming that 'Davies does not get the Cup final'. The negative is significant. With David Coleman declining the new contract he'd been offered, it had been expected that I'd deputise. What the newspapers didn't know was that a month before the announcement Sam Leitch, editor of *Match of the Day*, had told me that the final was mine and that a statement would be made in due course. Nothing more was said between us. The announcement came as a bolt from the blue. I sent a letter of resignation, not because Motty had been given the final but because of the way I had been treated. I was sent for by Cliff Morgan, head of outside broadcasts and events, who did his best to placate me while making it clear that the BBC would hold me to my contract.

The following Sunday, David Hunn wrote an article in the *Observer* quoting Morgan berating commentators who came to him to whine, and how they should appreciate their privileged position, which was the envy of many. I was bracketed with Ron Pickering as being guilty. I protested that it was Morgan who'd asked to see me, but I achieved nothing; and Alan Hart, head of sport, put out the BBC spin that in giving John the Wembley final and me the European Cup final we'd been treated fairly and equally. Much as I enjoyed the evening in Rome on the Wednesday following, the Cup final then stood above everything else in the British game.

The die had been cast.

Coleman was back the following year and then quit football completely – and I have to say inexplicably – after commentating on the 1978 World Cup final in Buenos Aires. It was no surprise that Motty returned to the Wembley final the following season, and it was to be sixteen years before I was given a chance. The longer John's run continued, the more difficult it became to make a change. Every April, the choice was debated within the Beeb and without. Every major championship led to press speculation. Every time the answer was the same. Eventually the BBC stopped saying that we were equal number ones. It would, however, be wrong of me not to point out that the man ultimately responsible for confirming the decision – the head of sport – changed five times in those sixteen years.

In Italia '90, there was a groundswell of opinion among the BBC team in Italy, and in the press coverage at home, that this time it would be my turn, but our team leader in Rome, Jim Reside, cautioned me not to get my hopes up too high (there was no possibility of that). Even the local Italian drivers working for the BBC became aware of the argument – 'Deserves his chance . . . Unfair to drop him' – and commiserated with me at the usual outcome.

But then, after the 1992 European Championships in Sweden had followed the pattern of the past, the *MotD* editor, Brian Barwick, decided 'to break the mould', as he put it: after the quarter-finals of USA '94 I was told that the World Cup final was mine. John was given the news, by phone, while he was celebrating his birthday in a bar in New York. He surely could have been told more gently. His (presumed) understandable drowning of his sorrows, along with his celebrations, was followed by an announcement that he would be taking a sabbatical from *Match of the Day*.

In 1995, I at last occupied the seat at Wembley but soon afterwards Barwick was moved up to be head of Sport production. The new *MotD* editor, Niall Sloane, told me early in the New Year that he felt the decisions about the end of season matches were taken unnecessarily late, and I agreed. Nothing more was said on the subject until I received a message to phone Niall; I was in Tel Aviv doing some interviews for a programme celebrating the centenary of the modern Olympic Games. When I called he simply asked me to go and see him as soon as I returned. I pushed aside a nagging irritation and concern, and completed the far-from-easy task of talking to the *chef de mission* and one of the surviving athletes of the Israeli team who had suffered so monstrously at the 1972 Munich Olympics.

Back in London Niall told me he'd decided that I'd do the FA Cup final and John the final of Euro '96. It was clear that John already knew, so it was a waste of time arguing – though I did – that the best man on the second Saturday in May should, all things being equal, still be the best man six weeks later. Niall's argument, and it was hardly a vote of confidence, was that to drop me from the Cup final would lead to the press having a field day. The statistics of matches in John's favour was not, in Niall's opinion, a factor to be taken into consideration. It can be said he did me a favour because the best match of the championship, the England *v* Germany semi-final, came my way. But while we got on perfectly well, there would be no more 'favours'.

In the build-up to the '98 World Cup, the BBC let it be known that no decision about the final would be made until after the early rounds had been played. With the *Daily Mail*'s Charlie Sale in the lead, journalists and TV critics were looking for clues. I covered the opening match live – Scotland doing well before presenting Brazil with the victory – and England's first, the 2–0 success against Tunisia in Marseilles. The second match with Glenn Hoddle's team, against Romania, was live on ITV. I covered it, recorded, for the BBC. The third, against Colombia, was Motty's, live on the last day of the first round. The previous day I'd seen an interesting match in St Etienne and, because of my commentary, I believe, persuaded Niall – forecasting a Mexican comeback from two down against Holland (it ended 2–2) – to delay his intention to switch coverage to the other match in the group. En route to Lyons with a camera crew and two of our interpreter/fixers, there was a call on the phone of my producer, Simon Betts. It was Niall, for me: John was doing the final. He had yet to commentate on England. When we got back to our hotel the new head of sport, Bob Shennan, rang to say that he supported Niall's decision.

I regret now that I fired both barrels. I hadn't expected I'd get the final but I was incensed. I believed the decision had been taken long before. I broke the news to Simon who, bless him, was incandescent.

The mould had been well and truly repaired. John will know the statistics and the records, and good luck to him. For me they are more difficult to understand.

14

A Night in Rome

'Saw the Pope this morning and he's supporting us. He was wearing red': Scouse humour on the day Liverpool appeared in their first European Cup final in May 1977. That evening I began the commentary by adapting a line from Fräulein Maria, nanny to the von Trapp family: 'The hills [of Rome] are alive to the sound of Merseyside' (*The Sound of Music* was very much my children's favourite at the time).

It was a special day for Liverpool, only four days after they'd been denied the League and Cup double, losing to Manchester United in the FA Cup final at Wembley on the Saturday – a match they felt they should have won. It would be a day to test the avuncular man who, three years earlier, had been reluctantly promoted to succeed Bill Shankly: Bob

Paisley had already led Liverpool to two championships and twelve months earlier to victory in the UEFA Cup.

Shankly had achieved those titles and the FA Cup, but had fallen at the semi-final stage in Europe's major club competition. Now Paisley could stand with two other greats of the British game, Jock Stein and Matt Busby, and be the first Englishman to do so – not that such thoughts would have crossed his mind. But ending on a high must have been much in the mind of Kevin Keegan, who would be playing his last match in a Liverpool shirt having agreed to join Hamburg in the Bundesliga to further his football experience.

There was another in the party which travelled out from Speke (now John Lennon) airport who felt he had something to prove. On the Saturday, I'd played my usual interviewer's role at Wembley, examining the replays with Lou Macari and Jimmy Greenhoff to clear up who had actually scored United's winner, as the former's shot hit the latter to cause a change of direction too far for Ray Clemence. All the Liverpool players had looked drained. It seemed, though, to have been put behind them as team and media (no segregation needed in those days) checked into our Rome hotel. But I remember thinking they'd need a good start; and I hoped I'd have one, too.

How so many Liverpool fans made their way to Rome, let alone found a place at the match, is part of Liverpool folklore. The Tiber had flowed into the Olympic stadium and its colour was red. It was an amazing sight, and the players told afterwards of their shock at seeing so many of their supporters – at least five times the expected six thousand – and how they felt they had to win for them. A banner to left back Joey Jones showed the fans were in no doubt that they would. 'Joey ate the frogs' legs [St Etienne], made the Swiss roll [FC Zurich], now he's Munching Gladbach' – Borussia Mönchengladbach, their opponents in the final who had just been crowned German champions.

It was certainly a feast in football terms, though not all of it was to Liverpool's liking. Rainer Bonhof hit a post before Liverpool took the lead with a classic goal in speed of movement, appreciation of space and timing of pass involving Steve Heighway and the scorer, Terry McDermott. But they were pulled back six minutes into the second half, and then had to answer a number of searching questions which brought thoughts of the Wembley defeat to mind. A great goal by Allan Simonsen – a searing drive across Clemence after he'd seized on an errant pass by Jimmy Case which fell behind the advancing Phil Neal – set up what, until the extraordinary contest in Istanbul twenty-eight years later, was much the best of Liverpool's finals.

At home the next day my six-year-old son asked me the score. 'Borussia one [won],' I said. He looked and sounded distraught. 'Liverpool three,' I continued, enjoying the moment and recalling how I'd once been caught out by Uncle Syd in the same way. But Mark's beaming smile hid a secret, later revealed, that he had 'borrowed' my radio and, hiding it under his pillow, had listened to the whole match.

Among the TV critiques which compared the performance of Motson on the Saturday and Davies on the Wednesday I especially remember a comment in the *Daily Express* by

James Lawton. Tommy 'the Tank' Smith took a thoroughly untypical attacking position at Heighway's corner and headed the ball firmly into the German net past a giant of a goalkeeper called Kneib, turning the match back in Liverpool's favour. The Tank had announced that he'd retire at the season's end, and my reaction to his goal was: 'What a way to end a career.' Lawton argued that there were still twenty-eight minutes left and I shouldn't have committed myself so early. I doubt if anyone switched off.

When Neal rolled in the third goal from the penalty spot seven minutes from time, after a typical Keegan charge into the box had brought a challenge, too late, by Berti Vogts, I contented myself with, 'And with such simplicity the European Cup is surely won.' When it was all over and a smiling Emlyn Hughes held the trophy aloft, I saluted 'the smile of the season, the performance of the season, the trophy of the season'.

A few minutes after we went off the air I was hit by a wave of exhaustion intermingled with dejection. Alec Weeks and Lawrie McMenemy left me to my thoughts, but Sam Leitch wanted to know what was the matter. There was no simple answer; I just felt drained. Fortunately, my head cleared a lot more quickly then than it did the following morning after much of the red river had flowed on to our hotel. The sun rose with many a fan and some of the players still lounging in various postures around the pool. For many reasons that match has a place in my 'most memorable' top ten, not least because, though I may not have proved the point to others, I did so to myself.

Because of the Wembley decisions, I have seen almost as

many European finals as Motty has FA Cup finals. The first in the senior competitions – these days 'major' and 'minimus' would be better words – was watching Johan Cruyff toy with Internazionale in Rotterdam in 1972, and I was the commentator at three of Liverpool's seven finals.

In the early days, long before Sky, the BBC and ITV alternated the coverage of the European Cup and the European Cup Winners' Cup. So the following year, 1978, I went to Paris to watch Anderlecht put four goals past FK Austria, while Brian Moore commentated on Liverpool's retention of the European Cup, with Kenny Dalglish scoring the only goal against Bruges at Wembley – a rather more sedate occasion than twelve months earlier. The smooth transfer of Liverpool's number 7 shirt, at a cost of £400,000, from Keegan to Dalglish, was one of the features of that season, but it wasn't enough to prevent the return to the top of Brian Clough, who not only claimed the title with Nottingham Forest but won the League Cup as well.

At the start of the new season *Radio Times*, then the only magazine giving details of BBC programmes, marked the five-hundredth edition of *Match of the Day* with a front cover showing John Motson and me on either side of the new presenter, Jimmy Hill, with the Wembley scoreboard in the background recording the milestone (a laminated copy still has an honoured place in my study).

But, as one newspaper put it, the big news was that 'Old King Coleman is back' (though not until the third round of the FA Cup): David and the powers that be had ended the dispute that had allowed me to sit in his athletics seat, though not his football one. The turning-point had been the party for the five hundredth, which Bill Cotton, controller of BBC 1, persuaded David to attend. Over drinks rather than in court, as once threatened, a way of resolving their differences was found. Paul Fox, a former controller of BBC 1, was, I believe, the most influential voice in the debate. A friend of David since their days together at the start of *Grandstand*, he did not allow the fact that he was now managing director of Yorkshire Television to prevent him from offering advice to the benefit of his old employers.

In another article dealing with Coleman's return and the competition in the team, Shaun Usher of the *Daily Mail* claimed that *MotD* had never been more popular and that 'No major game has really taken place until dissected, talked through and instantly replayed on BBC One'. Among its twelve million viewers – 'from dons to dockers' – were, he claimed, Michael Caine, who was an addict, Omar Sharif when he was in town, and the Archbishop of Canterbury when he had time. I had rather lesser rank than the last-named, being described as 'looking rather like a tea-swigging curate in mufti'. I sent Mr Usher a telegram: 'Bless you, my son.'

15

Cup Final Day

The best thing about finally being in the Wembley commentary seat in 1995 was that sitting next to me was my son, Mark, now in his last year at university; he'd yearned for the day as much as I had. When I put down the microphone at the end of the match, he gave me a big hug. It was a very special moment. Unfortunately for both of us, it wasn't much of a match. Everton upset the odds by beating Manchester United, a solitary goal by Paul Rideout proving decisive.

To be honest I over-prepared for the occasion. I was aware I was doing so in the days leading up to the final, but even though I knew I was at my best if I felt I hadn't done quite enough, I seemed unable to stop myself. Things like the lead into 'Abide with Me' being absolutely right, and making sure that the kick-off had no accompanying words – just the referee's whistle and the crowd's hum – assumed far too much importance. It wasn't a bad commentary but I was too anxious that it should be my very best.

In the build-up I much enjoyed interviewing the two managers together, a rare occurrence for opponents in the Cup final. Joe Royle and Alex Ferguson enjoyed each other's company and both revealed the more relaxed side of their natures. This was not too difficult for big Joe, but I remember one simple remark from Fergie which suggested a rather different character from that usually seen. When talking about the role of the wife who waits wondering whether there will be the need to protect the cat or dog, he said, 'You go home thinking about the game, what went wrong and so on, and she greets you with "Do you know, that gardener didn't come again today – he said he'd be here and I waited in . . ." It's good for you; helps to keep things in perspective.'

Alex and *Match of the Day* have had a pretty rocky relationship, in which I think the BBC has often been too timid. After Jimmy Hill had made some criticism of Eric Cantona in a match at Norwich, Alex was quoted in a newspaper lumping us all together as being Liverpool supporters – a list including Bob Wilson! I wrote to him saying he could be as critical as he liked about my commentary but to accuse me of supporting a particular team was out of order. To my surprise, he rang me at home to say that he hadn't meant to involve me in the quote. On another occasion when he wouldn't talk to the BBC, he came over to me in the players' tunnel after a match to say it was nothing personal.

Alex would have been a good deal happier after my second Cup final commentary than he had been after the first: United beat Liverpool through a late volley following a corner by the said Cantona. The goal, though, was the only thing worth recalling from another poor match. The following day I was telephoned by the *Liverpool Echo* and asked for my considered view. It didn't differ from what I'd said in the commentary. Did I think it was a question of both sides cancelling each other out tactically? 'No,' I replied, 'I think neither played well on the day.' 'Funny,' came the response, 'that's just what Roy Evans [the Liverpool manager] has just told me.' My wait had been too long and the day was no longer one of the crown jewels of the English sporting calendar, but doing the commentary was now on my curriculum vitae adding to all the other television roles I'd played at the old stadium on Cup final day.

In the late '60s and the '70s it was a day out for the nation at Wembley via the television screen. We were on the air four hours before kick-off. Just about any programme with a sporting connection, from *It's a Knockout* on, had its Cup final version at some time. But the bulk of the build-up was with the two teams, from early-morning reports at the team hotels, to the 'team-all-together' interviews, to the coach-journey interviews, to the pitch pre-match interviews. It became quite an art for reporters to plan questions through the day to ensure a change of subject, or at least a different angle on the same subject. It's fashionable now to dismiss the 'team-all-together' interview as old hat and much too staged, but I enjoyed the challenge of acting as the ringmaster, always prepared to accept a certain amount of flak from the players. In fact, the more banter, the more relaxed they were and the better the interview.

The best such occasion was with the Sunderland team in 1973. I was with them for three days at the Selsdon Park Hotel in Croydon which long enjoyed a reputation for being the lucky Cup final hotel. They were a pretty easy bunch to get to know, and as rank outsiders quite enjoyed the presence of the electronic media. On the evening before the match, I watched ITV's preview with the manager, Bob Stokoe, and two of football's greats, then Sunday newspaper journalists, Jackie Milburn and Len Shackleton. The programme compared the parts of each team and gave marks for each category. The longer it went on the more annoyed Stokoe became as, predictably, Leeds United's points total soared and they won every category, including 'creativity', which especially seemed to annoy Bob: at the programme's end, the hotel's television was in severe danger.

'They've done your team talk for yer, man,' quipped Len. 'Just tell the lads that.'

With Jackie chiming in on the same lines, and with the assistance of the night porter, the anger was replaced by increasing confidence, and Bob departed for his bed with a 'we'll show 'em' look which was still there in the morning.

His players came to the set interview grinning and promising some fun, and what was already relaxed and apparently nerveless chatter came close to hysterics when Billy Hughes set off a laughing machine. The more banter, the more relaxed . . . The joke was certainly on me. We ploughed on to complete the allotted time, and then with the cameras off mostly fell about again.

Suddenly their attention was drawn to the monitors and what had replaced them in *Grandstand*. There for all the world was a set of tailors' dummies in ties and double-breasted suits. 'Cor, look at them!' was the chorus. Leeds United were being interviewed, and they looked almost scared about the contest to come. The contrast between the two sides could not have been more marked. The confidence of Stokoe's men soared.

The bus journey was a-buzz and when we turned into Wembley Way there was nothing to be seen but red and white. It can happen, for the other team's supporters are at the other end of the stadium. But the last time Sunderland had been there, the last two digits of the year were the other way round – 1937 – and I hadn't been born! The interviews on the pitch were mainly about the supporters and the atmosphere. So confident were Sunderland that they were going to cause an upset that on arriving in the television gantry I bet Bobby Charlton five pounds that they'd win.

It shouldn't have happened but it did. Jim Montgomery's magnificent double save – Peter Lorimer hit the ball too well and so hard that it flew up off Monty's parry as Coleman called 'One–all—no!' – ensured that Ian Porterfield's goal was decisive. It also caused me some embarrassment, because I leaped to my feet in the gallery to acclaim it, forgetting that right next to me was Leeds's injured full back, Terry Cooper. I admit that I became completely wrapped up in wanting

Sunderland to win. (It would never have happened if I'd been the commentator.)

That year was only the second time I conducted the post-match interviews, which, save for the closing moments in the studio, were the last round of the day-long competition between the BBC and ITV to offer the better coverage. Twelve months earlier, when Leeds had been the victors, marked my debut, succeeding David Coleman who, with the departure of Ken Wolstenholme, was commentating as well as presenting. I viewed the daunting task of filling the shoes of 'the master of the art' with some trepidation.

All the interviews for both channels were conducted in one room, divided by a curtain, adjacent to the first aid department above the Wembley tunnel. To reach it, the players were brought by helpers (producers and assistant producers, in the main) either through the dressing-rooms – which could be tricky as there was always the chance of losing one's man there – or up another staircase and across the public concourse. For television these interviews were serious stuff and, whereas there was a cordial draw before the match as to which company had first choice of whom, the poaching of the day's stars was common and the pat on the back on the Saturday came well before the heated phone call at editor level on the Monday. It was definitely a case of 'All's fair in love and Cup finals'.

Having little if any idea of the order of the players' arrival, the interviewer has to be flexible and to save questions until those most involved appeared. In 1972 this was further complicated by a late injury to Leeds's Mick Jones, whose cross had set up the winning goal for Allan Clarke. Jones was still feeling the effects of colliding with a post, and very nearly a television camera, just before the match ended. As the presentations began at the royal box, the noise in my ear made it clear that there was much argument between the editor and producers as to whether the pictures should be the traditional ones or those of the brave Mr Jones – the problem being accentuated by the availability of the choice being made by ITV. The debate continued during the lap of honour.

My expectation of guidance on my first attempt at the role was misplaced. Suddenly the players were there and it was 'Cue Barry'. The rest was down to me, with the producer playing recordings of the day's high points – complete, it was to be hoped, with the hero of the hour smilingly telling the audience how it had happened. Actually, the best moment that year, and maybe in all the years in which the role was mine, was of thirty-seven-year-old Jack Charlton looking down at his winner's medal. No narrative was needed.

After Sunderland's victory, Don Revie, very much a BBC man, was brought to the interview area far sooner than I would have wished. I resisted bringing him before the cameras for quite a long time while the victors in high spirits enjoyed their moment. I was sure that the atmosphere would change the moment he was introduced, but I had physically to prevent his accompanying producer from forcing him forward. It would have been very embarrassing had he left to appear first on ITV. But I felt I knew my man, and after a few words with Bob Stokoe I brought Don forward. His offered hand and magnanimous words provided a near-perfect ending, and I had no explaining to do on the Monday.

As for the structured pre-match interview, nothing quite matched Sunderland, but three years later, though without mechanical help, Southampton came close. I was delighted again to be with the underdogs, but I didn't know until I arrived at the same Selsdon Park Hotel that I'd been requested by Lawrie McMenemy. 'I want you to do what you did for Sunderland,' he said. 'I want them nice and relaxed on Cup final morning.' Interestingly, he'd brought with him a dossier from Don Revie about Manchester United, their opponents, and 'doing the right things on the day'. (That interview from Leeds's hotel three years earlier had actually been recorded on the day before the final.) Micky Channon, as usual, and Peter Osgood were good value, and another Second Division side won against the odds.

Then in 1981 there was Ossie Ardiles singing about 'Tottingham' as we tried a complicated hook-up with his and Ricky Villa's families in Buenos Aires.

After the long delay and the staggering cost of building the new stadium, how long, I wonder, will it take for the word 'Wembley' to regain its former status in the world of sport? 'The Venue of Legends', it was called – the title of a video I was asked to present – and while for me it was also a venue of contention, I'm glad I was around in the days when television took half the country to Wembley on Cup final day. It was a day which had a special place in the nation's psyche.

But times changed, dating, I believe, from when ITV won

the right to cover the final exclusively. I mean no criticism of Bob Wilson, who by then was the network's senior football presenter, or of another mate, Brian Moore, who was the commentator. But to leave Wembley after 'Abide with Me' for a commercial break before the teams came out destroyed the feeling of being there. For a long time now it's been just another live match, often undervalued by the managers involved. The days of the outsiders seem past as well, and the major clubs are reluctant to allow interviews at their hotels, let alone co-operate with a television producer's request for something different. On the other side of the coin, the demand for instant comment after the match denies the players the time to enjoy the moment – or recover from it – to which they are surely entitled.

The new Wembley, without the twin towers of which people around the world became so fond, is impressive, and, for all the fact that the match was disappointing, it was fitting after the long wait that the 2007 Cup final was between the country's two top sides – Chelsea and Manchester United – its first full-scale event. But attitudes will need to change if it is to remain the most important date on the stadium's calendar. And the FA have hardly helped their cause by denying the television viewers uninterrupted coverage. The decision which has left my former colleagues with only Premiership highlights and no England or FA Cup matches after the 2007–08 season is, in my opinion, spiteful, stupid and stinks of greed.

16

A Life with Brian

Who'd be a football manager? Les Cocker, Don Revie's right-hand man at Leeds and later a member of his England training staff, once asked me if I'd considered it. I assumed he was taking the piss, but a discussion about man management which followed, and his observation that 'You could find yourself a good coach', almost convinced me he was serious.

The question of man management came up when I applied in 1978 for the vacant editor's position on *Grandstand*. Alan Hart, the head of sport, had appointed a New Zealander, Harold Anderson, who had previously had an attachment with us, but was told that the job had to be advertised. In true BBC democratic style there would need to be a 'board' to pick from the best candidates. It seemed pretty clear that this would simply delay Anderson's confirmation, but I'd once told the programme's producer, Martin Hopkins, that I'd always fancied the job, and he called my bluff.

Hart arrived in Buenos Aires in the early stages of the '78 World Cup and buttonholed me to tell me that I'd been 'boarded' in my absence.

'How did I do?' I asked.

'Well, you didn't get the job,' he replied with a smile, 'but it was a very serious application and you did very well. There was one concern, however. We weren't sure you'd be all right with man management.'

Somewhat rudely, I just about stifled a laugh.

'Why do you find that funny?' he asked.

'Well,' I said, 'for a start I've yet to come across any leader in the department who seems to have much idea about man management; and secondly I'd have thought that two years in the army, being responsible for the blokes in my platoon, not to mention often having to answer questions or solve problems posed by their wives and families, would have given me some qualifications in the matter.'

'Oh,' he responded, 'I suppose that would have become clear if you'd had a personal hearing.'

'How does the air fare from Buenos Aires compare with that from Auckland?' I asked.

It was, though, all very casual and tinged with humour; and I think we both knew that, had they appointed me, it would probably have ended my front-of-camera/microphone career (one way of getting shot of me) and made the mortgage payments a little more difficult.

At the start of the 2006–07 season fifty of the managers in senior football had been in their positions for two seasons or less, and those fifty included ten plying their trade in the Premiership. There is no role in life which truly compares. Where else does a man spend all week preparing for something, and then when it matters most, hand his fate over to others? And when one of his fourteen players loses his concentration, or forgets what was planned, or simply doesn't feel it's his day because of a side issue like a row with his wife, it's the manager's fault. How it happened has then to be explained to the waiting media and, more importantly, to the chairman and the club board, who will make it clear that results are the only true judgement.

Most do it, of course, because it's their drug of life; the continuation of a playing career, though never quite the same. For some, it's a second chance after not being the player they wanted to be. For others, it's a search for consolation because injury cut them down in their prime, and in that category there's no better example than Brian Clough. Only Kevin Keegan, in his first spell as manager of Newcastle, came near to producing the atmosphere to be found during Clough's days at Derby. It was electric, even on non-match days – provided, of course, he was in residence.

In one of the many interviews I conducted with him over the years he admitted that everything at Derby 'was done in a blaze' and that he 'wanted the best out of the second time round'. He had scored 250 league goals more quickly than anyone else since the Second World War – a fact in which he rejoiced, while regretting that few were in the top division and none in the two games he had played for England. 'The thrill it gives you at that particular second is indescribable.' Seeking that, confined in his place in the dugout, was the key to his managerial approach. 'If you're entertaining, you know you're playing well; and the more relaxed you are, the better you can portray everything you have to offer.' But the idealist could also be the pragmatist; just as the confirmed old Labour socialist knew how to enjoy the trappings of success.

During his first attempt at winning the European Cup he used to hold court after the mid-week evening match at Derby's Midland Hotel. Just after midnight on one occasion, I thanked him for his hospitality and made to leave. He reproached me for my early departure, and I explained that I had to be in Coventry by ten the next day, that the train journey was both complicated and long, and that I needed an early start.

'Sit down and have another drink', he said, 'I'll fix it. Have your breakfast at eight and I'll be down at half past.'

Without further sensible consideration I did as instructed, and in the morning, bang on time, there he was in the hotel foyer bright and breezy. He threw the keys of his Mercedes to the third-team coach and said, 'Drive Mr Davies to Coventry.'

On the day he was sacked at Leeds, I sat with him in the referee's dressing-room at Elland Road. He had agreed to be interviewed before things blew up and we – producer Bob Abrahams and I – fell on the story. Well, up to a point, because he'd granted an exclusive to ITV and to the writer of his Sunday newspaper column. He'd hardly endeared himself to the players by telling them to put away their medals because they'd won them by cheating; and a group of them, with the recently departed Don Revie giving tacit support, had ousted him. Manny Cussins, the chairman, could only reply to my question, 'How is Brian Clough not the right man now when he was forty-four days ago?' with the comment, 'We've been spoiled by Don Revie.'

Later, Bob and I were among a group of journalists and television reporters sitting round a large table chatting informally with Brian over a few drinks he'd supplied when he suddenly said to me, 'You don't look too happy.'

I replied that I couldn't find much to be happy about 'because you've failed here'.

He pushed his pay-off cheque to me face down across the table. 'Do you call that failure?' he said.

I pushed it straight back without looking. 'If you call that success,' I said, 'you're not the man I thought you were.' (Some years later he made it clear that he did 'call that success': 'I was financially secure for the first time in my life.' And his move to Leeds because he 'wanted another crack at the European Cup' did, in a roundabout way, set up his claiming of that trophy for Nottingham Forest.)

When I arrived home from Leeds at one in the morning, Penny was just finishing tidying up after a long-arranged party. I'd made many phone calls, and she was very understanding.

The next time I saw Brian was when he'd accepted the position at Forest, after a brief spell with Brighton. He was down at Bisham Abbey prior to his first match in charge, a winning third-round Cup replay at Tottenham in January

1975. I'd asked him to do a piece for 'Football Focus', saying that I wanted to put some pretty straight questions, to which he replied, 'I've always given you straight answers.' He was not, though, prepared for my – true – observation that there were people at Leeds who claimed he knew nothing about football. It was the only time I've known him lost for words. It was momentary, of course, before a typical response dismissive of his accusers. Afterwards, we went to a pub in the village for a very amicable lunch.

About a year later, when he'd brought Forest back to the First Division, I phoned him and was put through instead to his number two Peter Taylor, who'd rejoined him in the Midlands. At the end of the conversation Peter suddenly said, 'Brian says, why do you want to talk to him when he knows nothing about football?' and rang off.

It took a moment for the penny to drop. I rang back, and again Peter answered. 'Tell Brian,' I said, 'that if he thinks I think that, he's off his head – but why should it bother him, anyway?'

Peter and Brian often tried to play people off between them in those days. Brian described himself then as more relaxed and more calculating but admitted that, for all the success, the Championship and two European Cups, it wasn't as exciting as it had been at Derby. Not that it stopped him in a 1987 interview making the observation that, 'Although I was as full of myself as I was in the early days we used to work together, I'd calmed down a bit because I knew I was the best.'

My commentary on the goal that put Forest's name on the European Cup for the first time has resulted in a certain amount of stick from Martin O'Neill and John Robertson, who either greet me with 'That's what I wanted him to do' or introduce it soon afterwards. It was the first time in the final against Malmö – who were coached by an Englishman, Bobby Houghton – that Robertson had attacked on the outside to provide the cross for football's first million-pound man, Trevor Francis, to nod home. It was the 'I wanted' – was I the manager? – the duo picked on.

In his own way, but having learned much from Brian even though they often didn't get on, Martin has proved a worthy successor to him, and I'm delighted to see him back in the English game. He still leans towards the pessimistic in some of his utterances – when he joined Celtic he said he might be out before Christmas – but he does the job brilliantly. He was my choice to succeed Sven-Goran Eriksson as the England manager, but, as had been the case with Cloughie, the Football Association was a little scared of a man who would certainly have done it his way. The chance may still come.

Clough's line on Robertson – who, like Alan Hinton at Derby, was crucial to the balance and style of his two teams (which had many similar ingredients) – is worth recording. 'He was an unbelievable scruff in suede shoes, but when someone gave him a football and a square piece of grass he became an artist and a genius.' It was the 'stealing' of Robertson when Taylor returned as manager to Derby which led to Clough falling out with the man he'd described as 'having an expertise about finding players and a knowledge of football second to none'. That he missed him there was no doubt.

Brian's mood at the City ground became increasingly impossible to predict. Waiting with our production team outside the dressing-rooms before kick-off sometimes produced comments like, 'I don't know why we allow all these television people in here.' At other times he'd be all sweetness and light. He once greeted me with 'Want a cup of tea? Come on,' led me into the dressing-room and told Archie Gemmill, then still a player, to go and get me one. And this was about half an hour before kick-off.

At the end of his managerial career, it all went sadly wrong for Brian, though. I felt most sorry for his son Nigel, to whom I was first introduced together with his older brother with the comment 'Have you met the bairns?' when he was six. When a Sunday newspaper quoted a Forest director suggesting that Brian should resign because of his drink problem, Nigel asked me to read on 'Football Focus' a statement from the family. He always behaved impeccably and in support of his father, and even as the manager of Burton Albion had to put up with joking observations from his dad which I thought sometimes went too far. He was also an excellent player, whose brain was often two passes ahead of his colleagues – if the Almighty had given Nigel similar pace of movement, he might have become world-class. Stuart Pearce, for one, should be grateful to him for the way he was brought into the game as an attacking force which led on to a fine England career.

On the day when Sheffield United sent Forest down to the Second Division – a decline which is only now being halted – Brian was a shadow of his former self. But thanks to his family he looked much healthier, though still more than his years, when Burton's second-round FA Cup tie against Hartlepool featured live on *Match of the Day* on 7 December 2003. In an interview with Ivan Gaskill, Brian added some generous comments about me to the surprising hug and indeed kiss captured by *Grandstand* on the day he retired. My last conversation with him had been a few days earlier when I watched Burton in a league match. The man was no saint, though with his powers of persuasion and his past charisma he might be by now. He used the media blatantly, and for a time believed the image of him that they created; and his failing health may well have saved him from disgrace over transfer dealings. But there was an impish warmth about him which necessitated a response. As I once told him, if I could have played I would have done so for him, either because he'd inspired me or because I wanted to prove him wrong. Many who could play did just that. 'If we achieve what we set out to achieve,' he responded, 'does it matter what happens in between?'

On the Monday after my last *Match of the Day*, I was sitting on a plane about to take off for Riyadh, where I was to talk about sports commentary to Saudi Arabian Television, when my eyes fell on a headline in the *Evening Standard* being read by someone across the aisle: 'Farewell to voices of a golden age'. Taking my own copy from my briefcase I discovered that the voices were Brian's and mine. In thought-provoking style, Matthew Norman had linked Brian's death and my retirement from his game. I was glad I had the row to myself for it was very hard to accept that only one of us could read the article.

17

Revie, Greenwood and Robson

If Brian Clough was the people's choice as the best manager never to manage England – and it would have been fun and probably productive – what about those who've filled the role since Ramsey? The total is now thirteen, including Howard Wilkinson who stood in twice, in 1999 and 2000, and Peter Taylor, once against Italy in autumn 2000. As they say, I was there.

The increasingly voracious demands of the media affected all but one. Joe Mercer, the first caretaker manager in 1974, was a breath of fresh air and his selections played with freedom, but he knew he would only have the job for seven games. Frank Worthington, whose silky style of playing centre forward was viewed with suspicion by many, certainly enjoyed Joe's reign, playing six of the matches. Won three, drew three, but losing to Scotland at Hampden was the record.

By the autumn of '74 Don Revie, the first of Clough's contemporaries, was in charge. He started against Czechoslovakia (with Davies in the commentary box) when the introduction of Dave Thomas, as a substitute – an out-and-out winger on a Wembley stage which had forgotten them – led to a 3–0 win. I'd always got on well with Don, and his use as a pundit by the BBC cemented that relationship. 'Here you come with your questions, Barry' became a standing opening gambit every time I interviewed him. But he was very protective of his Leeds team. When the competition was at its height between Gary Sprake and David Harvey for the position in goal, he objected to being asked in a recorded interview for 'Football Focus' who was his number one choice. Before the producer and I had left the ground, he was on the phone to Sam Leitch, the head of football, demanding that the question and the defensive reaction in his answer be dropped.

That his excellent side didn't win more silverware owed something to carrying that approach too far. The decision, after winning the FA Cup in '72, to take the team back to a hotel in Wolverhampton – not allowing real celebration until after the final league match there on the Monday – in my view cost them the Double. In fairness, the match with Wolves was the only time I have seen a defender, other than the goalkeeper, with both hands on the ball in the penalty area and no penalty given. Bernard Shaw, writing a rather different version of *Arms and the Man*, was the culprit, Ken Burns the referee. But the Leeds team, who were beautifully balanced with a natural left side of Cooper, Hunter and Gray, were that night unbelievably tense.

One day early in his England career, sitting in his office at the Football Association at Lancaster Gate, Revie chatted very openly about his hopes and the players at his disposal. He said suddenly, 'What I need is to find another Billy Bremner and Johnny Giles.' 'Good heavens,' I said, 'don't you think you've been lucky enough to have had such a pair *once* in a managerial career?'

Strangely, his best – that is, most successful – England midfield played together only once, in the 5–1 victory over Scotland at Wembley in 1975: Colin Bell, Alan Ball and Gerry Francis. Ball, 'England's 1966 extra-time hero', was winning his seventy-second cap, and it turned out to be his last. I don't recall what made me think it would be, but I suggested after the match to David Coleman that it would. He thought I was crackers.

Earlier that year Revie had tried Alan Hudson, who against Germany gave a passable imitation of Gunter Netzer three years earlier: he ran the game. But against Cyprus, when Malcolm Macdonald scored all five England goals, Hudson was quiet; and it was that performance which Revie judged the more important, with the comment to me: 'I need players I can rely on to give me a hundred per cent.' He waved away my protestations that Hudson had risen to the challenge of the Germans and that Cyprus really didn't count. To be fair, Cyprus was in England's European Championship qualifying group, and was the only team England managed to beat twice. But the draws home and away with Portugal, and the defeat by Czechoslovakia in Bratislava, where the performance of Marian Masny – dismissed by Revie, but for me the key – foiled England's attempt to reach the quarter-finals.

Revie had his favourites among the press corps, and as time went on became influenced by them – and more conscious of others' criticism. Also, there was much talk of the dossiers on the opposition given to his players. In his twenty-nine matches he used fifty-two players, and at times the team he chose had a balance he surely would not have considered for Leeds United's Reserves.

After England lost their World Cup qualifier 2–0 to Italy in Rome on 17 November 1976 with the team that the opposition captain, Giacinto Facchetti, described as the worst England side he'd ever seen, Revie became increasingly introspective and suspicious. At the Home Internationals that year I commentated on the match against Wales at Wembley when England lost to a penalty scored by Leighton James. On the Saturday following, Revie was again on the losing side, 2–1 against Scotland, and when he came into the interview room at Wembley he refused to be interviewed by me. He claimed that I'd spent the whole of the match with Wales criticising him. I was shocked and saddened by the observation, but told him if he really thought that he should complain directly to the BBC's head of sport. For some ten minutes there was a stand-off, but eventually, after Jonathan Martin had made it clear that it was his decision who conducted the BBC interview and if he would not speak to me there would be no interview, Revie agreed to talk. It was all a far cry from the 1973 FA Cup final when Revie had been a man of stature, accepting the loss with grace.

As England toured South America in the summer, he was making plans to seek his fortune in the United Arab Emirates. England still had two matches to play in what was now a forlorn attempt to qualify for the 1978 World Cup finals in Argentina. Fearing the sack, and knowing how Ramsey had been treated, he found the offer too good to resist. That much was understandable, but the exclusive with the *Daily Mail* for a few extra pieces of silver left a nasty taste. He later took the FA, who had banned him from working in England for ten years, to court and won; but the judge described him as a man possessed by greed.

Even now I find it hard to understand why he failed. Deep down he was a man of simple philosophy: to improve the lot of his family, which at Leeds was extended to include his players. In the wider arena, he brooded too much with too much time on his hands, and missed the support his club players had given him – which was probably greater than at any club before or since.

His successor, Ron Greenwood, began in pragmatic style by picking seven players from the country's most successful club side, Liverpool, and then in November 1977, with four of them surviving, beat Italy 2–0 at Wembley. Kevin Keegan and Trevor Brooking scored the goals. But, enjoyable as it was to watch and indeed to commentate, it was too late to repair the damage of the away defeats in Bratislava and Rome, and England were to be spectators for the second World Cup running. Come Spain in 1982, when Greenwood would have his chance in the World Cup finals, the same two players might – perhaps should – have been the scorers again when England needed to beat the hosts by a two-goal margin to qualify for the semi-finals.

As a reporter for *The Times*, I'd watched Trevor Brooking make his debut for West Ham against Burnley at Turf Moor in 1967. Outside the team, I was probably the first to know about it, because over a tea and chat with Ron Greenwood at the Keirby Hotel he suddenly announced that he was giving a chance to a youngster who would, he said with great confidence, become an outstanding player. 'If only he had a bit more pace, he could become world-class.'

In spite of not having it, Trevor probably did reach that status. He'd won eighteen caps before Greenwood took over the England position, and was chosen by him twenty-nine times in all – a figure limited by injury. He scored five times: the conclusive goal against Italy; against Scotland at Hampden Park (two weeks after heading the winner in the Cup final) which now brought to my lips 'gathering goals in May'; and twice against Hungary in a World Cup qualifier in Budapest – the second of which saw the ball stuck in the angle between post and crossbar. Keegan that day had scored the other, a penalty, in what was a significant win, because on the plane from Basel, where a week earlier a 2–1 defeat by Switzerland had put qualification in considerable doubt, the senior players had dissuaded Greenwood from his intention to resign. Brooking's fifth goal, and the third with my commentary, came against Spain in Naples in the 1980 European Championships. But that was small consolation: England's hopes had already died.

Under Greenwood Kevin Keegan played one more game than Brooking and scored nine goals more; and in part through the fault of the media became the man whom England could not do without. Much of the publicity around the camp in Spain in '82 centred on the captain, who, at one stage, was spirited away to Hamburg, his former club, for treatment on his injured back. Neither he nor Brooking, who was suffering from the pelvic problem that ended his career, had played in the first four matches of the finals. Without them England's record in the first round had, statistically, been the best of the six group winners – three victories, over France (3–1) Czechoslovakia (2–0) and Kuwait (1–0). But a sterile draw with Germany, who subsequently beat Spain 2–1, left England seeking the form and the margin of victory of their opening two matches.

It is all too easy for the commentator, who doesn't have his decisions tested and later queried, but in the build-up to the match I felt strongly that if Brooking and Keegan were fit enough to be given a place on the bench, they should start: give it a go from the kick-off rather than wait until the sands of time were running fast. But I couldn't find many to support my theory. Greenwood's decision to have them on the bench was, I concede, one which all but a few managers would have taken. He was a tactician not a gambler, though to be fair he started with three strikers.

In the end Greenwood was forced to play his hand, bringing on Brooking two minutes after half-time and Keegan with twenty-five minutes remaining. Had Brooking seized the chance he made for himself, and had Keegan, as he should have, nodded home Robson's perfect cross, the manager would have been proved right. As it was, there was nothing but frustration. Would Clough have gone my way at the time? Would Mourinho or Wenger support my thinking, given a similar position now?

Greenwood, whose coaching ability could be summed up in the three words 'Moore, Hurst, Peters', retired to regain the smiling disposition which the demands of the England job had taken away. He had left his club position at West Ham much too soon, to give his protégé John Lyall his chance. He came to the England helm a little too late and was probably too influenced by the eager, and from a fitness point of view too demanding, coach. Many players felt that Don Howe's approach in training was more for the season's start than a season's end. But to listen to Ron Greenwood talking about football was both a pleasure and an education.

Both Keegan and Brooking, though from different perspectives, learned how difficult the job is. Whereas Brooking's playing career had come to an end, Keegan's was to flourish again when he left Southampton for Newcastle – but not for England: the new incumbent, Bobby Robson, decided he was surplus to requirements, which smacked of not wanting such a big personality in the camp. He, too, though, found a great player who, like Keegan, would become one 'without whom England could not perform'. And Bryan Robson, more than Keegan, suffered from injury at crucial times. As I once said to Bryan, standing with him on the Wembley pitch, he again unfit to play, 'You become a better player every match you miss.' He took it in the spirit intended (he played sixty-four of Bobby Robson's ninety-five matches in charge).

Bobby once accused me of being 'impertinent', a word I hadn't heard since my schooldays. We were waiting to board Concorde in Riyadh following England's 1–1 draw with Saudi Arabia. It was a pretty meaningless friendly, save for the sponsored trip and the fact that Tony Adams scored his only England goal. He was one of a posse of Arsenal players selected, which included Brian Marwood. Bobby had been much quoted

Radio Times

500th MATCH OF THE DAY!

Football's back
and so are John Motson,
Jimmy Hill and Barry Davies with
the 500th Match of the Day, Saturday BBC1.
Back feature: unexpected football fans

RADIO TIMES

Quick but too one-footed. The Norfolk House School first X1 circa 1950

A trio of Barry's Bandits

The best decision of my life: my gorgeous suntanned bride, 6 June 1968 at St James' Church, Fulmer, Bucks

Mum and Dad greeting the next generation: Mark's christening in July 1971

Family group at Château de Divonne, Switzerland, for a wedding in June 2006: me, Gigi, Penny, Mark and Miranda

World Cup Line-ups

Mexico '86

USA '94

France '98 (flanked by David Pleat and Simon Betts)

Korea and Japan 2002

Should they have started the match? Kevin Keegan and Trevor Brooking await their chance in Madrid, Spain v England, World Cup 1982

Romario the romantic: after a 24-year lapse Brazil's love affair with the World Cup is on again, Pasadena, July 1994

Smiles mirrored in all generations of the host nation: young South Korean fans at the 2002 World Cup

JEFFEREY A. PALFREY

A man to be envied: one to one
with Katarina Witt

COLORSPORT

In a class of their own: the
Golden Couple, Jayne Torvill and
Christopher Dean performing
their *Boléro* at the Sarajevo
Olympics in 1984

The long pause: Cathy Freeman and the world wait. The opening ceremony of the Sydney Olympics 2000

Congratulating royalty: with Princess Anne and Sir Craig Reedie following London's successful bid for the 2012 Olympics at the IOC Session in Singapore in July 2005

in the press saying Marwood was just the type of player he was looking for, and then in the match brought him on as a substitute with under ten minutes left. In the post-match interview out on the pitch, with English and Saudi media huddled around us, I suggested that, after all he'd said about Marwood, the public at home wouldn't understand why he'd given him so little time. Bobby told me he wasn't going to stand there and justify his selection to me, then tried to do precisely that, without much success. It clearly still rankled with him the following morning when he made the 'impertinent' remark, though there was no demand to write out a hundred lines.

On match day I'd actually been quite helpful to him when, down in the dressing-room area before kick-off, I realised in conversation that he thought that Carlos Alberto, the Saudi Arabia coach, was the captain and full back of the 1970 Brazilian World Cup winners. In fact, he was Carlos Alberto Parreira, whom I knew quite well after meeting him in New Zealand when he was coach of Kuwait. (He was later to end Brazil's twenty-four-year wait by winning back the World Cup in US '94; and return again in charge of his native country, though unsuccessfully, in 2006.) I quickly briefed Bobby and left them to it.

Unlike Ramsey, who also took England to two World Cup finals, Robson had first to qualify for both. He came away from them with his head held high; yet in both he flirted with humiliation. Europe, meanwhile, wasn't kind to him: he missed qualification on his first attempt (1984) and lost all three matches in the finals of his second (1988). But he had huge support from the FA chairman of the time, Bert Millichip, who twice refused his resignation; and he came close to being given the job a second time before the FA decided to look to Sweden.

How Robson felt usually showed, and he tended to see things as either black or white (ultimately both together at Newcastle) with not too many greys. Jimmy Hill once said that he was a lucky manager, which was the quality most needed for success. Robson could justly claim he worked hard to make his luck, and his record for England and for his clubs in four different countries is testament to that. None of his successors (or indeed predecessors) has come anywhere near as close as he did to equalling Ramsey's feat – in Italia '90. Bearing in mind that Alf had home advantage, Bobby would have surpassed him. It was an eight-year reign of highs, lows and a so-nearly, and he was a survivor. Three more contenders would come and go in the next eight.

Coming down from a hospitality suite I bumped into him after England's 2006 World Cup defeat in Gelsenkirchen.

He hailed me from one flight below. 'How are you, Barry?'

'Very well, Bobby,' I replied.

'Wish I was,' he said.

I felt guilty for what had been a standard response, for in his eyes no one could feel well having just watched England lose in the way they had. Penalties again! We chatted for a while, and I left admiring his unflagging intensity for the game and his deeply felt patriotism.

18

Calling Time

O nce it had begun, the 1978 World Cup was, for me, only marginally more fun than that enjoyed by the Welsh referee Clive Thomas.

Argentina was the last of the three major South American football countries to host the finals. Uruguay had done so in 1930 and Brazil twenty years later. So it was about time – but was it the right time? The takeover of the country by a military junta two years earlier, deposing with widely reported brutality the Peronist regime, had raised many doubts; and a combination of Holland and Belgium stood ready to accept the tournament if FIFA decided the risks were too great. (They didn't, leaving the Belgians and the Dutch to wait twenty-two years for UEFA to give them their Championship.)

The main rebel group, the Monteneros, had promised a

ceasefire during what they described as 'the people's fiesta', but Amnesty International told of kidnappings, torture and other atrocities. The first leader of the body formed to run the championship, General Omar Actis, had been blown up in his car. As for the preparation of the stadia and suchlike, military practicality or perhaps insistence at the point of a gun proved more useful than the previous *laissez-faire* attitudes of the Peronists. The generals appreciated that success would enhance, or perhaps hide, their country's status, and were prepared to spend the money to achieve it.

With such a background in mind, I set out with the producer, Bob Abrahams, to contribute to the World Cup preview programme. Spending a day at an *estancia* (a cattle ranch) and trying to gauge the mood of the people in the capital were interesting tasks. There was the usual extreme contrast of rich and poor in South America; from the polo lawns to the slums of a vibrant, open city. There was no obvious atmosphere of fear, although a drive down a main street of Buenos Aires could be an unnerving experience. The journey would be punctuated by the regular squeal of tyres, as drivers emerging from side streets waited to the very last second before checking their racing speed.

Conversations brought a shrug of the shoulders about the departure of Isabel Perón and a barely disguised hatred of the junta led by General Jorge Videla. The Argentine players showed their contempt in various ways when victory had been achieved. The most famous – the result of a bet – was the soapy hand offered to the general by the mop-headed Tarantini, who had just removed it from washing his balls, a story of the dictator's visit to the winners' dressing-room doubtless embellished during the full back's sojourn at Birmingham City. There seemed no doubt that the populus wanted the tournament, and the ticker-tape welcomes and the chanting in the streets 'til dawn owed nothing to political organisation. The junta's claim of the victory was so hollow as to be unworthy of a passing spit.

The tournament began for me in Mar del Plata, a rather dreary seaside resort. The first match was only thirty-one seconds old when I was required to identify a goalscorer, and I did so at odds with the name in the caption on the screen. Happily, I was right: Bernard Lacombe had scored for France against Italy. As a result the Italians were forced to undo their safety belts and come out to play, and Enzo Bearzot, their coach – who sought to awaken his country's football from its defensive mindset – had his first World Cup victory, 2–1. His confidence in giving Antonio Cabrini his first cap, in place of the injured Giacinto Facchetti at left back, suggested almost a gambler's streak. It proved a good long-term investment.

The next day I saw a rather different match in the same stadium as Brazil played Sweden. Clive Thomas wasn't a referee who went unnoticed; neither was he unhappy to be the focus of attention; but he was a good referee and deserved his place in a second World Cup championship. As a Welshman he was, sadly, not from a contending nation, and his status was such that he had a good chance of following the Wolverhampton butcher, Jack Taylor, as a World Cup final referee – not here in Argentina, but four years on, in Spain.

Four years earlier, Thomas had been given two matches,

both at the Neckar Stadion in Stuttgart: Poland's 3–2 win over Argentina in the first phase, and Brazil's 1–0 victory over East Germany in the second. But his World Cup career ended in Argentina. It was said by that most learned observer of the world game, Brian Glanville, that it was because of a rather theatrical reaction to Sweden's Bo Larsson almost putting through his own goal. I believe, though, that Thomas's undoing was his blowing of the final whistle while the ball was in flight from a corner, so not allowing the 'goal' from the head of Brazil's Zico to count. The match ended in chaos, with many on the pitch and off it unsure what had happened. Fortunately I'd seen Thomas's signal, so was confident it was a draw, 1–1.

Thomas always maintained that full time was exactly that, and that he was its arbiter. In many a conversation with him since, he never accepted that he couldn't be that precise or that, in delaying taking the corner, the Brazilians had given him the perfect chance to end the match when the ball was dead. The next occasion would have been after the header crossed the goal line. Most referees would have blown for one or the other but Clive was different, and liked to be. 'It cost you so much,' I said to him. 'Anything else would have been cheating,' was the reply. Arrogant? Stupid? Too honest? Probably all three.

Other referees made worse errors during the championship, but FIFA's Brazilian president, Joao Havelange, probably didn't see them. One such brought the end of France's campaign at the hands of the hosts in the River Plate stadium in Buenos Aires, in what was not only the best football match of the competition but would certainly make the top ten of the best internationals on which I've been lucky enough to commentate. It was stirring stuff in an atmosphere the like of which I'd never before experienced, from the tickertape opening to the delirium at the finish. The football was full of pace and personality.

The French, with twenty-one-year-old Michel Platini, supported by Dominique Bathenay and the flowing Dominique Rocheteau; Argentina, introducing Ossie Ardiles to a British television audience, along with the dark invaders, Mario Kempes and Leopoldo Luque. The referee's clanger was to give a penalty against Marius Tresor, who, losing his footing, fell on the ball in error, and was adjudged to have deliberately handled. Jean Dubach of Switzerland, who that evening should have added a final 'le' to his surname, compounded the error by refusing to give the French a late penalty when Didier Six, running clear on goal was unquestionably pulled back. France lost 2–1, finished third in their group as a result, and like the 'no doubt' Thomas went home after the first phase.

I lasted a little longer but also finished third, leaving the closing stages to Coleman and Motson, and watched the final from my sitting-room at home. I don't recall now whether David said, 'One–nil,' when Kempes scored the opening goal but it was his standard practice, which the public came to expect and, I believe, mostly liked. No one imagined then that this would be his last opportunity. It beggars belief that those who had persuaded him to return now allowed him to quit as a football commentator. He once offered me the demands of the popular *Question of Sport* as the reason. But, while athletics was always his first sport and the one from which he gained his deserved reputation, he surely still had much to offer football. A year or so later, when the game was beset with hooligan problems, David teased Motty over a drink in the bar at Kensington House (then BBC offices, now a hotel) about how he'd 'handed over a game in good shape. Now look what you've done to it.' John took the tongue-in-cheek 'blame' rather seriously!

19

Badminton

The consolation for the disappointing World Cup was a trip to Edmonton, Alberta, for a first Commonwealth Games. I was to commentate on badminton, the start of a sixteen-year relationship with the sport through four more Commonwealth Games, World and European Championships and many All England Championships.

In Canada, the former British number one Derek Talbot was my guide, and there were several others over the years, including the feisty and often giggly Gillian Clark, one of the world's best doubles players; and a man whose playing qualifications weren't quite in Derek or Gill's class, but whose qualities as an administrator had already included the presidency of the International Badminton Federation.

The expression 'shuttle diplomacy' was, I believe, invented

for Henry Kissinger. In sport it would apply very suitably to Craig Reedie. He rose from badminton club player to the chairmanship of the British Olympic Association and to the International Olympic Committee; his contribution to sport was recognised by the award of a knighthood in 2006. I've always been in awe of his ability not only to remember people's names but to know about them and what's happening in their lives – from many a testing name on the badminton circuit to those in the corridors of power in the world of sport. It's a gift which has served Britain well.

My one regret during my badminton collaboration with Craig is that, because of my other commitments, he was never able to introduce me to the white-hot atmosphere of the Asian championships where, in Jakarta in particular, the crowd is a combination of that to be found at a big fight night and a crucial Premiership football fixture. My only experience of it came second-hand, when we dubbed the event for a tape distributed by Trans World International.

We were teamed up again in Auckland in the Commonwealth Games of 1990. Here he reached the highlight of his broadcasting career, for he had the network to himself when a deluge sent all other sports seeking shelter. The executive producer, Martin Hopkins, told him to keep going while a fast car was sent to bring me from the hockey. On arrival I left him, as it were, in the captain's seat, refusing to join in until the start of the next game; better for any future recording not to come in halfway – and a tad amusing.

In some respects, I'd have liked to do the same in Barcelona when I arrived, hotfoot, from the gymnastics after the first

Olympic badminton final – the ladies' singles between Susi Susanti of Indonesia and Bang Soo Hyun of Korea – had already begun. For Craig, helping to bring badminton to the Olympic Games was a lifetime ambition achieved. He also knew well the diminutive Indonesian lady who was the favourite to win badminton's first Olympic gold medal and was prepared to wax lyrical about her exploits. He assures me that at one point I muttered, off-mike, 'Tactics, you bastard.'

It was certainly a tale to tell: a lass from a small village in western Java, a Roman Catholic from the biggest Muslim country in the world, set to become her country's first-ever Olympic champion; the pressure on her must have been immense. She did not disappoint, and neither did her boyfriend, Budi Kusuma, who next day won the men's title, making a double celebration. On their return home a million people turned out to greet them.

I always found badminton a very welcoming sport. I was lucky, because it was a good era with some wonderful players. Many of them, of course, came from the Far East and had strange-sounding names difficult to pronounce. But it's not just because of that that I remember more those closer to home, who between them can boast many titles and medals at World, European and All England championships: Steve Baddeley, Darren Hall and Helen Troke in the singles, along with Ray Stevens and Gillian Gilks, who played both singles and doubles, and wonderful doubles players like Mike Tredgett, Martin Dew, Nora Perry, Jane Webster and Barbara Sutton; not forgetting the doughty Scots of very differing physique, the tall Billy Gilliland and the rather squarer Dan Travers, who came close to bringing the roof down at the old Empire Pool, Wembley earlier than planned, when they reached the final of the All England men's doubles in 1982.

I believe, though, that the Badminton Association of England made a mistake in the '80s in tying the contract for the All England to a newly set-up Grand Prix circuit sponsored by Laing. Unfortunately, they proved unable to guarantee the big names which, as a consequence, led to the sport being scheduled later in the evening on television, to a fall in the audience and to a questioning of the real interest in a sport which has huge player participation.

The Laing Grand Prix did though throw up one memorable and somewhat embarrassing moment for me. It happened on a snowy winter's evening at the Woking sports centre. The first match was meant to involve Ray Stevens, the leading British men's singles player at the time, but he, poor chap, was involved in a car accident on an icy surface coming over Kingston bridge. As a result, a ladies' doubles match was put on first in the evening programme. Nora Perry, always full of fun however tight the contest, arrived totally unprepared to be on so early. Her play was littered with untypical errors. With only a small attendance having arrived on time, my voice in a very open commentary position could be clearly heard. Suddenly Nora stopped playing and called to me, 'You're absolutely right, Barry, I am playing like a drain, but do you have to keep telling everybody?'

Since I handed over my racket and partner, Gill Clark, to David Mercer, British success has reached new heights with bronze and silver medals in the last two Olympics. With a world title to their credit, Nathan Robertson and Gail Emms will be among the favourites for the gold in Beijing. And the sport has been revolutionised: points are no longer only scored on service – they count whoever serves. In the old days it was impossible to forecast the probable length of a match as the score could remain static if rallies were won by the receivers. As a result the sport tended to be shown more often in edited packages.

This was the plan at one of the earlier All England Championships I covered. We were supposed to record the ladies' doubles, scheduled to start at 12.45pm, for a 1.30 slot on *Grandstand*. Late on the Friday evening, the organisers and the BBC producer, Bob Duncan, agreed to change the order of the programme. Unfortunately, nobody told the players.

Twelve forty-five, and there was no sign of them – Bob was tearing his hair out. Urgent messages were sent to their hotel, but it was twenty past one when they arrived. There was no choice but to delay the match another ten minutes and then go live; thoroughly unsatisfactory, as in all probability we'd have to leave the contest at a crucial time so that *Grandstand* could cover the two o'clock race at Newbury. Our 'out time' to hand back from Wembley was 1.57.30. At 1.57.26 the winning shot was struck. Bob proudly puffed out his chest. What a good decision!

The 1980s

'For the last fifty minutes the Heysel stadium in Brussels has been a sickening and bewildering sight'

'Yesterday Boris Becker departed the scene with honour, putting sport in true perspective, accepting defeat with grace'

'Everyone in England will be saying, "Go on, take him on"'

'Tears of joy and a face of disappointment at the other end of the arena'

20

New Zealand's Pom

For three weeks in September 1981 I was seconded to New Zealand's national broadcaster, TVNZ. They had negotiated for the BBC to provide commentary if their country's team made it through to the World Cup finals of the following year, and then requested to borrow a commentator for the opening matches of the final group qualification.

It wasn't until I was on the plane bound for Hong Kong that it dawned on me what I had let myself in for: I was working with people I didn't know, had only a sketchy knowledge of the two teams for the first match – China and New Zealand – and had precious little time to prepare. But I need not have worried. After just one training session I felt very comfortable with the squad in the required task of identification and in the way they greeted 'the Pom'. That the feeling was mutual was made very clear in the book about the team's success written by the manager John Adshead and coach Kevin Fallon. Later in my tour Adshead threatened to fine me for being late for training and then presented me with an All White shirt, which I still have. My squad number was 26.

It was a fascinating trip, which on the second day moved on to Beijing, then a city of cycles by the millions, broad avenues with few cars except official-looking ones, and in the evening countless people strolling about. In preparation for the match I was, surprisingly, given permission to watch the Chinese team. It would have been a more useful exercise if the waiters and others from their headquarters hadn't been allowed to join in.

Another test was the official reception to which Keith McEwan, TVNZ's head of sport, and I were invited. It bore some resemblance to that skit by Michael Bentine in which he plays the role of various ambassadors taking wine with each other with increasing inebriation. The drink was a sort of petrol called *mate* (slivovitz would be the nearest European equivalent to have passed my lips) and at each toast we were required to stand and down the liquid in one. The glass, admittedly small, was immediately refilled for the next toast; for which the wait wasn't long. I slept without concern for the next day's match – or anything else for that matter. Mercifully, the following morning my head was as normal as it ever is.

The first World Cup match ever to be played on Chinese soil proved to be a physical battle from which New Zealand's most skilful player, Steve Wooddin, bore most scars. But the scoreless draw was a good start for the team. The match was played in near silence punctuated by sudden applause as if by order – though the story was that the people had been told *not* to applaud. And then for the masses it was on your bike home and up again early the following morning doing fitness exercises in the street long before their opponents' supporters had even thought about breakfast. When the meal did arrive, however, there was plenty of time for thinking – the bacon taking an eternity to join the forlorn egg looking up from the plate.

In the commentary I had used the expression 'rooting for' to describe support back home in New Zealand. The minute I landed in Auckland I learned from two younger producers that this has a different meaning in their country – not used before the children go to bed, or on television. So welcome, with some amusement, to the Brit! And what a welcome. I was invited to sail on an ocean racer and given a turn at the helm, taken trout fishing at Lake Tarawara, and generally made a fuss of.

Keith wanted me to talk to all his commentators about how the job should be done but, recoiling from the idea, I suggested a get-together with food and drink. So instead of a lecture by the Pom we threw the subject around for a couple of hours – which everyone enjoyed and gained from, including me. (Would that the Beeb had tried something similar.)

Intermixed with the social life were two matches, interviews with me and by me, a role as an early-day Alan Hansen, and 'starring' in a film about how I do the job. I was even asked – and I'm not sure how Alec Weeks would have felt about this – to comment on the television coverage. Having at the end of the previous season at home found myself dropped from the BBC's European final (Cup Winners' Cup, Arsenal *v* Valencia), as well as being given my now usual role at the FA Cup final, it was all a big boost to my morale.

In the build-up to the return match with China, Adshead and Fallon, believing that the Chinese, although no midgets, were vulnerable in the air, spent much time on free kicks and crosses. The reward came when from a near-post flick, Ricki Herbert rose unchallenged at the far to head the only goal. Mount Smart, the home ground – which had a grass bank on one side – was packed and, as everyone had been telling me all week would be the case, the atmosphere was something that football, with the round ball, had never previously experienced in the land of the All Blacks.

The victory and three points out of four further raised expectations for the visit of Kuwait a week later. But they were a notch or two better than China and were thought by the Kiwis likely to be one of the two qualifiers from this final group. (Saudi Arabia, the fourth team, was not yet the force it became a decade later.) Carlos Alberto Parreira's Kuwaitis had skill on the ball but needed much organisation without it. I passed on a few observations to my hosts.

But after a promising first half in which Wooddin gave New Zealand the lead the referee changed the course of the game. He awarded Kuwait two of the harshest penalties I can recall, both for hands and neither, in my opinion, deliberate – a view shared by most of the population of New Zealand, and probably the sheep. The first was saved by Richard Wilson, the second scored – and in seeking the victory the Kiwis were caught out and lost 2–1.

So when I left a team I had felt part of they were on a down; but they made it to the finals – their fourteenth qualifying match bringing a play-off victory over China.

At the draw in Madrid in December I interviewed Fallon (Adshead was on holiday). But his expression when I introduced him to Bobby Charlton said far more than words about what it meant for New Zealand to be among football's elite. In March 2006, while in Melbourne for the Commonwealth Games, I was delighted to be asked to contribute to the DVD telling the story of the All Whites' achievement.

New Zealand's opening match of the finals, in Málaga, fell to me. It was, though, against Scotland, so for the BBC there would need to be not a bias but a Scottish perspective. We were, however, recorded for highlights, while New Zealand would watch it live, so I asked the World Cup editor, Mike Murphy, if, after wrapping up the first half for British consumption, I could add a few words for those watching in New Zealand. He agreed, but then forgot about it and during the half-time interval came on the phone to give me a rollocking over what I'd done. We had a huge row, and then a further one after the match when, feeling some responsibility to TVNZ, who were paying the BBC for the use of commentary, and, I admit, an affection for the team, I again added a few words. It was a little easier this time, for they'd come back well from being three goals behind to worry the Scots seriously at 3–2 before losing 5–2. If I had any chance of doing the final, it disappeared that night in Málaga.

After the Scots and the Kiwis had departed, I once again, as in 1978, had probably the best match of the finals – for drama, if not quite for the quality of Italy against Brazil. It was the semi-final in Seville between France and Germany. Regrettably it was only recorded for the BBC (Gerald Sinstadt was live for ITV). The extra time, after goals in the first half by Littbarski for Germany and an equaliser from the penalty spot by Platini, was a match in itself. France led 3–1 but were pulled back to 3–3; and a decision had, for the first time in the World Cup finals, to be reached via a penalty shoot-out.

This was the match of Harald Schumacher's outrageous and brutal body-check on Patrick Battiston, for which the German goalkeeper should certainly have been sent off – and more suitably given at least one night in prison for GBH. Instead he ended the hero, saving Bossis's penalty, after – as he had throughout the penalty competition – clearly moving towards his six-yard line. I was absolutely incensed at the injustice of it all, and the Dutch referee, Charles Coerver, was given a lashing in my report for BBC radio.

Germany, who had lost to Algeria in their group but qualified with Austria after a needed 1–0 victory against their German-speaking neighbours, got their comeuppance in the final. Italy, the winners, had been dreadful in the group phase and when at the end of that stage I suggested to their long-serving radio commentator, Martinelli, that his country would win the trophy, he thought I needed certifying. My argument was that there'd now be none of the expectation from their fans which so often seems to stifle them. But in truth I did not expect Cerezo, of Brazil, to pass the ball square just outside his own eighteen-yard line and help Paolo Rossi on the way to his hat-trick in the decisive second-phase match that took Italy to the semi-final. France finished third by beating Poland, and two years later succeeded at home in a scintillating European Championship.

I watched that triumph of Platini and his men on the television at home after returning from a tour of South America with the England team. There were, it is true, some consolations for country and commentator for not having made it to France. The 2–0 defeat of Brazil in the Maracana was one, the first victory there ever. The match was covered on ITV only, but I helped out Bryon Butler on radio and happened to be holding the microphone when John Barnes scored his remarkable solo goal. I asked him next day how many times he'd thought about shooting. 'About six,' he replied.

The negatives for all of us on the tour were the comprehensive defeat in Uruguay; a pretty tedious 0–0 with Chile in front of only ten thousand spectators; the fact that people who celebrated only one goal of their 2–0 win in Rio, because a black man scored the other, were allowed to travel on the official Football Association chartered aircraft; and missing a European Championship yet to be matched.

21

T & D

I have always felt that the rules of ice dancing are, shall we say, a little vague. I imagine it's always been that way, ever since it was first included in the 1954 European Championship, which perhaps explains why it had to wait a further twelve years to join the other three skating disciplines – men's, women's and pairs – in the Olympic Games. To be truthful, 'always' to me means since 1983 when, because of a debate about the rules, I became involved in the BBC's coverage of figure skating.

Apparently, Jayne Torvill and Christopher Dean were less than happy with Tony Gubba about an interview he'd conducted with them in Helsinki. They'd just won a third consecutive World Championship and were the red-hot favourites to top the podium again in Sarajevo and become

Olympic champions as well. Never one to chicken out from asking the difficult question, Tony had, according to Chris and Jayne, pushed too strongly that their winning perform-ance had bent, if not broken, the rules. So I was offered the chance to take over the presentation of skating in support of the long-time commentator, Alan Weeks. In the short term my role was to try to bring out the golden couple's person-ality – which, while so vibrant on the ice, melted away in shyness off it – without upsetting them.

After a good lunch with the Beeb's skating producer, Jim Reside, and adviser, Harry Lauder, I accepted the challenge. Harry, who knew everyone in skating and everything about them – he used to run Queen's ice rink in Bayswater – was a lovely chap: short of height but not of stature; a man who would have learned the expression 'ship-shape and Bristol fashion' in his youth and always lived up to it. He reminded me a little of my father, and he was good to have around. He also helped me to appreciate the skill and art of skating. Though I'd watched the successes of T & D, and before them the Olympic victories of John Curry and Robin Cousins, I was initially more attracted by the role than the sport.

This was the skating year that later led Christopher Dean, when receiving an honorary degree from Nottingham Trent University, to update the old joke about a definition of an intellectual – one who can hear the *William Tell* overture without thinking of the Lone Ranger. 'Try this out,' he said, and he hummed the opening bars of Ravel's *Boléro*.

November 1983 saw the first public performance of the routine for the 1984 Olympics at their home rink. It was like

the first night of a predicted hit show, and the BBC broadcast it live just before the Nine o'Clock News. From
Nottingham, packed to the rafters, we followed it to Budapest
for the European Championship, and on to Sarajevo, a city
whose Olympic sites for skiing and bobsleigh were to become
all too familiar as battle sites in an horrendous war of race
and religion, but which now presented a seemingly ideal
example of how peoples of different ethnic origins could live
together.

The skating journey for me was initially on fairly thin ice.
But give or take the understandable tension as the competition went through its first two stages at the Olympic venue,
I had some success in the task of 'getting to know you'. But
they remained guarded on camera.

Regaining the European crown was important, because
Jayne's injury had meant they hadn't been able to defend it
the previous year. It was not only that the Russians, Natalia
Bestemianova and Andrei Bukin, were pushed back to second
place, but the fact that the judges accepted what was a very
different piece from Jayne and Chris's previous programmes.
Skating to *Mack and Mabel* – responding on ice to the love
story of Mack Sennett, of silent movies fame and his leading
lady, Mabel Norman – and then going to the circus with
Barnum, with the full assistance in choreography of Michael
Crawford, had wowed the judges almost as much as the audience. But *Boléro* was more aesthetic. There might have been
questions about the start from a kneeling position and the
finish spreadeagled on the ice. And they had stretched the
requirement of changes of pace, for Ravel's *Boléro* is a

crescendo – 'a progress towards a climax with a gradual increase in volume'. It was mesmeric in its beauty, and for the viewer at home the performance in Sarajevo was much enhanced by the BBC's decision to cover it on one hand-held camera – there had been some concern that the host producer would cut around his cameras too much. Eric Wise did a brilliant job.

While *Boléro* produced feelings of admiration at the perfection of performance, it was the Paso Doble (the original set-pattern dance, the middle of the three parts of the competition following the compulsory dances) which stirred the soul; or perhaps just the male soul. For this was Christopher's piece, the flamboyant, arrogant matador teasing the imagined bull with the twirl and turns of his cape – Jayne. To play the inanimate object was a real test for her; compliant and expressionless, with no eye contact.

The contrast between the two pieces couldn't have been more marked. As Jayne put it, 'If we had the same type of feelings for both pieces it would become boring in training.' 'Like an actor taking on a new character, switch off one, plug in the other,' added Chris.

The Olympic champions were now a bit more relaxed. They'd had a little time to take in what they had achieved, and we were chatting away in their hotel in Ottawa on the eve of the World Championships a month after Sarajevo. At a press conference Chris even chided the assembled company, who briefly seemed stuck for the next question: 'I thought we were supposed to be the shy ones.' But they still were, especially when the media asked the question the man, or more likely woman, in the street apparently wanted to know: would there be a fairytale ending? Of course, because of that I had to ask it, too: were they to be a couple off the ice as well as on? My suspicion was that it wasn't going to happen, though Jayne's expression as we recorded Chris finding out what it was like hurtling down the Olympic run in a four-man bob had certainly suggested otherwise.

How an insurance clerk and a policeman took the world (not only that of ice skating) by storm was alone a fascinating story, particularly as regards Chris. While it now seemed impossible to imagine him as PC Plod, it must have once been just as difficult to imagine the reverse. How did the friendly bobby on the beat come to show such artistry, dancing on a slippery surface? In terms of how his life developed, skating was simply his sport and had been since the age of ten when he was given a pair of skates for Christmas. For him it had always been ice dancing, whereas his partner had been a solo skater and then British Pairs Champion. His employers, once he'd graduated from being a police cadet to the job he very much enjoyed, were generous with the time off he was allowed – until success brought a cordial breaking-point. Jayne couldn't wait to leave the office life.

They were now back in the city that had first seen the unknown clerk and the police cadet in a World Championship six years earlier. This time two thousand would watch their practice and the rink would be full even for the compulsory dances, the first part of the competition, which normally held fascination for aficionados alone. The repetition of the music is enough to dull the brain, and commentating on them impossible: arguably it even justifies the man with the microphone using what should be a banned expression: 'What can I say?' Though it was clear to any open eye that T & D were in a different class from the rest.

Indeed, the only threat to a fourth world title was something which presented more of a problem for me than for them. I had to appear on camera to explain that the refrigeration system at the rink had broken down and fill time for a bit until it became clear that the final competitive performance of *Boléro* would be delayed some hours. We covered it eventually in the early hours at home, and so did Radio Nottingham; such was their fame and the pride of their home city. What the radio commentator said during the performance I can't imagine. Alan Weeks said nothing, for the picture was there for all to see, but without it . . . ?

At the start, Jayne had been the more forthcoming, often helping Chris when his gaze was towards his feet and his words approaching stop. Beneath her quiet demeanour there was considerable strength of character. He was the more diffident – 'suspicious' would be a better word – when, for both, skating was what they did, not what they needed to talk about. But slowly the demarcation lines between 'before and after' and the interview itself began to blur, and over the next decade, when we met at championships in which they weren't competing, trust developed into friendship. He much enlivened the BBC team when he joined us in Sofia for the European Championship of 1991, still competitive, but in a blokeish way, and quick to see the funny side of things. As for his driving of the dreadful Lancia car we hired . . . ! And he was with us for the Worlds in Oakland, California, the following year.

Almost a quarter of a century on I still fail his test of an intellectual or even a further updated version stemming from their rather surprising decision to face the music of competition again and dance – when there would be trouble ahead.

22

Queue to Cue on the Centre Court

'Good afternoon,' I said. Immediately I heard the voice of Judy Jones, the producer's assistant, through the deaf aid in my ear, counting, 'Ten, nine, eight . . .'

'Welcome to Brighton,' I continued, and then with a few more words I led into a videotape recording with which we were starting the programme. I was making my debut as a tennis presenter on BBC television. I met the ten-seconds count comfortably without, I thought, hurrying the last few words. As the tape played I grinned at the floor manager, John Gilpin, a tall, distinguished-looking man who had worked with the best presenters on state occasions and programmes of many kinds, and who exuded control and serenity amid the frequent chaos of television life. To him this was very small beer.

But he had a rather quizzical look. 'You do know you said "Brighton"?' he said.

'Why didn't anyone say?'

'We thought it might throw you.'

I was back where I'd apparently failed my test as a tennis commentator. I was introducing the British Hard Court Championships – in Bournemouth. The *Match of the Day* cameras would be in Brighton at the weekend, which only made the blunder worse. I blamed my mother-in-law, Paule, who was staying with us that week. She was rather fond of Brighton and had asked me several times when I was going there. Each time I explained that I was covering tennis, not football, and that it was in Bournemouth, another of her favourite south-coast resorts. I never did discover how she knew *MotD* was at Brighton. The one saving grace was that the tape recording was quite short and when the producer, Johnnie Watherston, said 'Cue Barry' for a second time, I was able to apologise to those who were watching at the programme's start and assure them that having run like mad I was now indeed in Bournemouth.

It was an inauspicious beginning but I survived with Johnnie's help for several years until the BBC, during one of its not irregular nervous breakdowns about costs and staff, made offers of redundancy which were seized by several of the best producers, three of them Scots with whom I'd worked regularly – Jim Reside and Alastair Scott were the other two. (Johnnie became a gentleman farmer while still being called upon by the host broadcaster of the last two Olympic Games to cover – with his wife, Wendy, also a departed producer – the equestrian events.) All three, though quite different in character, had an ear for words as well as an eye for pictures. Verbal diarrhoea was quickly and sometimes sharply dealt with. Too few have followed their example.

I've often said that my only qualification for being a member of the BBC's commentary team at Wimbledon is simply that, in the days before the All England Club made the Centre Court all seating, I knew what it was like to wait for hours in the queue before making the rush for a few inches of space to be jealously guarded for the day. No one needed to talk of 'People's Sunday' in those days. The local council's demand to remove the standing area from the major courts was, in my view, utterly without justification. Tennis at Wimbledon had none of the problems that were afflicting football.

For two weeks of the year I join a team rich with tennis talent and knowledge, nearly all of whom have graced the lawns in their playing days and many of them with their names on the roll of honour. David Mercer, it is true, cannot be counted among the former players but he was a senior umpire and since giving up the law to join BBC Radio he has covered the world of tennis. He was still a solicitor when he umpired the Wimbledon men's final of 1984, a more than useful extra qualification seeing that one John P. McEnroe was on the court and indeed won the case. Anyway, David was a junior county player, many notches above a man whose service is a weapon which, while having occasional moments of success, is frequently lacking in rhythm and direction – or just lacking.

My agent at the time, Geoffrey Irvine of the Bagnall Harvey organisation, was somewhat taken aback at my reaction to what he described as 'good news': the head of sport, Jonathan Martin, wanted me to join the commentary team. 'He must be off his head' was my first response, and it took a long chat with Dan Maskell and John Barrett for me to be convinced I should give it a try. Even then I only accepted because not to have any role in the championship, when I presented all the other events, was becoming an increasing disappointment. What I wanted was an interviewer's role and eventually the presenter's chair. The former came my way as a result of Gerald Williams's departure to what was then BSkyB, but only once did I welcome the nation to Wimbledon – some twenty summers ago.

With suitable pictures I began, 'Yesterday Boris Becker, beaten by Peter Doohan, departed the scene with honour, putting sport in true perspective, accepting defeat with grace. Today, with St Mary's Church in the background, Ivan Lendl, whose ambition to succeed to the title burns more steadily than that of any other contender here, came early to practise in his new-found position of favourite, eager to prove that he, too, has the character to be a true Wimbledon champion. Hello, good afternoon and apologies for the absence of the usual weatherman [Harry Carpenter], who has an appointment with Frank Bruno and Chuck Gardner – to talk about them, you understand . . .'

I must say I was very happy for the chance to compliment Becker on his manner and his comments. 'Well, basically I lost a tennis match. I didn't lose a war; nobody died. I lost a tennis match.' While his defeat by Peter Doohan of Australia had been on Court No 1, he had certainly fulfilled the words of Rudyard Kipling which greet the players as they make their way on to the Centre Court. And he was still a teenager when accepting defeat after two years of victory, meeting with triumph and disaster and treating them just the same.

My day as the Wimbledon presenter on BBC2 was a particularly busy middle Saturday of the championships. Bad weather in the first days had markedly affected the programme, and the referee was playing catch-up to complete the men's second round. The commentary team, much smaller than today when the demands of the interactive service have greatly added to the number of voices required, was very stretched. Martin Hopkins, the executive producer, was having difficulty finding a commentator for a match reaching its conclusion in the final set between Johan Kriek of South Africa and Scott Davis of the United States.

In a moment of bravado which I quickly regretted I said, 'Well, that's down on the court behind me. You never show where Harry's to be found in the geography of the All England Club and now's your chance. Why don't you come to me and then pan past me and I'll do the commentary.' Of course in the final set at Wimbledon there's no tie-break and from 5–5 it progressed with service being held by both men. The need for a second voice became critical, and eventually Bill Threlfall arrived hotfoot. As is the way of these things he had time for only a few words before Kriek, having broken to lead 7–6, served out to take his place in round three. On the Monday Kriek lost to Ivan Lendl and I was back in the commentary box.

Over the years, my increasing employment there meant fewer opportunities as the interviewer, and presentation remained only 'on the road' – Bournemouth, Queen's Club in Barons Court, Eastbourne, Brighton and Wembley the regular stopping points, with the cups – Davis, Wightman and Federation – intermittently added to the tennis map. Only the Grand Slam Cup brought me back to a studio, as it was linked from Television Centre at White City.

When Jimmy Connors returned to Wimbledon to wear BBC colours in 2005 he quickly proved himself, as Boris Becker had, to be a team player, enthusiastic and helpful to fellow commentators in the box, happy to chat with anyone in the commentators'/producers' room. John McEnroe is more aloof, keeping his opinions for the box and the studio and rarely, if ever, to be seen in the 'waiting room'. To be fair to John, he's also working for the American NBC channel, a fact which accounts for his occasional sudden disappearances from the home airways.

It's no secret that, to put it at its most mild, Connors and McEnroe were not the best of chums in their playing days. Regular reporters on the tennis circuit will probably recall many moments when that was clear, but none, I suggest, more pungent than in the Benson & Hedges final at Wembley in 1981. The arena was like a bear pit, causing Dan Maskell to describe the match as 'disgraceful' and John Barrett to call on the tennis powers that be to take action. Both players were subsequently fined – McEnroe $700, Connors $400, paltry sums even then. McEnroe should have won comfortably but for what I believe was an overreaction by the umpire to John striking the ball into the stop-netting following a long rally at 0–1/40–30, in the third set, which ended with McEnroe hitting a forehand volley into the net. McEnroe was warned for his conduct, and later in the final set he received a point penalty for hitting the ball into the roof. Two games later Connors had won: 3–6, 2–6, 6–3, 6–4, 6–2.

Interviews on court after finals, with the sound carried on the public-address system as well as on television, are now commonplace. Wimbledon resisted the change but the crowd now expect to see Sue Barker with words of congratulations and commiseration. Over twenty-five years ago, though, for the crowd at Wembley to hear the television interview was something new.

'One question too many' was Johnnie Watherston's comment in my ear, and he was probably right. But I was determined that having an audience should not impinge on the editorial requirements of the interview. As a result, I think the only time in my life I was booed by the crowd was for asking Connors if he had any advice to give his defeated opponent. The crowd's reaction remains a mystery to me, even allowing for the fact that they applauded Jimmy's earlier comments that the type of match we had watched brought colour to the game and made them feel they were 'down there playing with us'. But it later became very clear to me why Connors, who in the match didn't miss a chance to act up in a way which placed him in the role of the good guy, dismissed any suggestion that the outcome had been affected by the stop-netting controversy. He'd gained a victory from two sets down against the fellow American who four months earlier had ended the five-year reign of Bjorn Borg. It was a psychological advantage he had no intention of weakening. The following year he not only reclaimed the Wimbledon title from McEnroe but won the US Open as well.

McEnroe might have advised me on how to react to being booed, for this was the year of 'You're the pits of the world', the altercation with the umpire on Court No 1 at Wimbledon which highlighted 'his arrival as a rather different champion'. The club were loath to accept him and for a time declined to offer the membership that went with the name being engraved on the honours board. It's interesting to speculate what might have happened had Fred Hoyle, the referee, decided to default him; what effect that would have had on McEnroe's career. Many believed that the word was 'shits' not 'pits', so one can imagine what 'fun' John's lawyer father might have had with the wrong interpretation. In the twenty-first century McEnroe Jr's attitude would probably be accepted as an essential part of his character, without which he would not have been the great player he undoubtedly was – a comparison with Wayne Rooney briefly flashes through my mind – but a quarter of a century ago there was, I believe, a majority who felt he'd crossed the line of what was acceptable.

What is certain is that McEnroe's manner had an intimidating effect on referees, umpires and linesmen and -women. There were times when I believe he played the role to gain an advantage over an opponent. A final at Queen's in the Stella Artois championship against Brian Gottfried was one such occasion. And he rather conceded the fact that he usually knew how far he could go when, having been defaulted in the Australian Championships, he claimed that he'd believed there was one more penalty point before the umpire was forced by the rules to take the dismissal route.

The style of commentary has changed a lot since the days when Penny and I queued to get in, or, arriving later, joined those eagerly awaiting returns. Then the two leading commentators were Dan Maskell on television and Max Robertson on the radio. Max was extraordinarily accurate, calling every stroke and frequently including observations of slice or spin in the light and shade of a complete picture of the Centre Court contest. But to listen properly required considerable concentration, and it was as well not to be driving at the time. Dan wrote down every stroke with the same detail – 'backhand topspin down the line' – with a shorthand of his own devising but said very little, save for the occasional compliment ('A peach of a shot') or exclamation ('Oh, I say!') until the change of ends. The American NBC network once tuned to his commentary for a couple of games and heard only his reiteration of the score. Their commentator reacted with slight amusement but NBC later received a number of letters expressing approval.

Radio commentary, led by Gerald Williams, moved to a less detailed style with more shot selection and comment, though the change of commentator for different sets sometimes made it seem like a change of match. Television commentary evolved, with the increasing use of replays, to a more American style, to a point where Dan would barely recognise it. But Wimbledon without John McEnroe in the

BBC team is now unthinkable, and the crowd who considered Dan as much an essential part of Wimbledon as the strawberries – incidentally, not a fruit he liked – now thoroughly enjoy the brash American who once so upset their afternoon cream tea. There are, I understand, others who don't like him, but I've yet to meet anyone who has no opinion about him. He offers a real insight into the game, seeing things so early and clearly and – unlike in the film *Wimbledon* – rarely, if ever, says anything obvious or dull. To work with him is a challenge, and the feeling of intimidation that pervaded the court can have a not dissimilar effect in the commentary box. It can be difficult if there's a second expert in the box, for if he or she tries to compete with John the whole contest can become awash with words, not to mention egos. The commentator, aware of what's going on and trying to control things, has a pretty tricky task and may well be thinking of the old adage 'Two's company; three's a crowd' – or occasionally feel that 'John Patrick' is a crowd on his own.

There were just the two of us in the box a few years back when Tim Henman was playing his compatriot Jason Lee. The British number one was struggling a bit, though without ever being in danger of losing. Suddenly, at a change of ends, John turned to me and said, 'There's no doubt about what's going to happen here, so tell me about that little bald guy. Why did he have to give up just because he lost?' It took me a couple of seconds to realise that the subject had suddenly become British politics and he was talking about William Hague; an interesting topic but not one for the moment – well, not for more than a few moments. It was a rather extreme example of the need to be 'on your toes' when working with Johnny Mac. In a rain interval two years ago he told me that I was one of not many who listened to him. 'A big part of my job,' I said, 'is to query, sometimes to learn, and to lead sometimes.'

In 1995, though, in what was probably the best match of the championships in pure tennis terms, Roger Federer against Juan Carlos Ferrero, John failed to listen clearly to my observation to the producer. Twice, following a change of ends, my comment after the remarks of either or both of the old doubles partnership, McEnroe and Peter Fleming, carried over the first serve of the next game. 'Clean ins,' said the producer, Paul Davies. Should the edited version be joined on that serve it would require a sound edit, and those working in the video-tape area at Wimbledon, who have a particularly demanding task, would not have thanked me. The problem was that both times John and Peter's comments had ignored the pictures being offered, and I'd tried belatedly to include, or perhaps justify, them. 'You can't have it both ways,' I told Paul, meaning: if you want words to add to your pictures, it's hard in the time available.

The next day I was scheduled to work with John and Virginia Wade on a ladies' match which was delayed by rain past the point when John had to leave for NBC. When I greeted him in the box he surprised me by suggesting that I hadn't been very happy with the Federer match. With a challenging look he said, 'You seemed a bit grumpy.' Only later did I learn from Peter that they thought they'd heard 'I can't get a word in edgeways'. Not true, though I suspect every commentator has felt that at some stage. People say McEnroe has mellowed, but I'm not sure he's that different from his playing days. However, he's interesting to work with, and, far more importantly for the viewers, interesting to listen to. But the game is doubles (or trebles) not singles.

I hope and expect both American champions who competed in their last Wimbledon Singles final – McEnroe's day, Connors being comprehensively beaten – will be part of the BBC team for many years to come. We were missing a third Wimbledon champion a couple of years back with Boris Becker finding the call of the World Cup on German soil too hard to resist. He was once on the books of Bayern Munich and his skills, especially for a big man, were clearly seen on Court No 1 when he entertained the crowd with a version of 'keepy-uppy' which suggested that he might well have had a successful career with the larger ball.

The Stella Artois championship at Queen's in 1985 had introduced him to a British audience. John McEnroe, the defending champion, was absent, following an altercation about practice with a club member the year before, and Jimmy Connors, the top seed, had been beaten in his delayed first-round match on an outside court. The tournament director, Clive Bernstein, was a picture of despair. Such a well-run and enjoyable event for many years had suddenly lost its two biggest names for reasons beyond his control.

'Never mind, Clive,' I said, trying to cheer him up. 'By the end of this week you could have the biggest story this tournament has known.' I'd watched Becker play in the Young

Masters tournament in Birmingham, where he'd beaten Stefan Edberg in the final – their rivalry ran and ran – and I thought he could win here. That he would one day win Wimbledon was already being said in Birmingham, and by the end of Queen's week many, including Dan Maskell, were prepared to add: 'possibly this year'.

While I waited to interview the Stella Artois winner, I asked for the trophy to be brought to our position. My idea was to point out to the seventeen-year-old German the quality of players whose names were engraved on the cup. He beat me to it. Trying to explain his feelings, he pointed at the magnificent trophy and said, 'Look at all these names. I can't believe I have joined them in winning this tournament' – a kid who felt the history of his sport keenly. It left a lasting impression of the young man's character and a hope that he'd fulfil the dreams of youth.

Two weeks later I was sitting in the Court No 1 commentary box with Bill Threlfall, watching young Becker play the gifted Swede Joakim Nystrom, who was just four years his senior but greatly more experienced. Being paired with Bill was always a pleasure. At the start of my tennis commentary career we were often together and I learned a great deal from the former Royal Navy champion, Fleet Air Arm pilot and, for many years, tennis coach at the Hurlingham Club. He was generous with his knowledge and, as McEnroe observed, I'm a good listener. The comment, often made, that 'You haven't changed a bit' applied more to Bill than to anyone I have met in my life. His style and his voice were instantly recognisable.

I don't know where in his repertoire Bill would have placed Becker against Nystrom, but I can't recall a match with a more exciting conclusion. Becker had break points early in the final set but it was when he faced one himself at 4–all/30–40 that the drama began. His refusal to take anything off his second serve was, it seemed, a youthful flaw which would be corrected by experience. A fifth double fault and Nystrom was serving for the match. But the kid was still going for broke: one backhand crosscourt return was back at Nystrom almost before he moved. Five all. But in spite of a nineteenth ace, the quality of the Swede's returns, turning Becker's pace to his advantage, broke the German again. The contrast in style and character led Bill to remark, 'One icy calm; one very, very ebullient.' Briefly the ebullient one changed style with touch and not punch on a comfortable volley and was made to pay as the calm one covered almost the length of the baseline, but Becker broke back again and then held for 8–7. A seventh double fault had Nystrom in trouble at 15–30. A rasping return to his feet, a volley up, the ball buried. The door to progress was opened and Becker came bouncing through with a verve that wouldn't be matched for two championships, until Peter Doohan caught him on a bad day.

Among my souvenirs is a video-cassette of the profile of Becker I wrote and voiced before his last Wimbledon final: from peeping round the stop-netting to glimpse the ladies' final, in 1985, to sitting in the Members watching the first semi-final between Pete Sampras and Ivan Lendl a decade later. For a set and a half he remained a spectator in his own semi-final against Andre Agassi, bowing to all four corners of the court when he finally broke the American's serve. He then became fully involved in what, for the calibre of the play, Becker considered the best match of his Wimbledon career. I wrote of how the boyish grin had at times lost out comprehensively to the man's grimace and how, after his three finals with Edberg, a win between two losses, his defeat by his compatriot Michael Stich, had been adjudged by some to be a terminal decline – he was bored and had no need of the money, it was said. Later he himself wrote with candour about the effect of that loss, the one-night stand that led to the acceptance of paternity, and the break-up of his marriage to Barbara Feltus. But my preview of the '95 final which he lost to Sampras ended with the observation that the joys of the boy had revisited the man. There was nothing apparent to question that thought when he returned to Wimbledon as a member of the BBC team. He seemed his happy self.

Pete Sampras's is another story waiting to be transferred to DVD. I'd promised Penny I'd do it while researching this book, but somehow didn't find the time to transfer the many tapes that clutter my study. When I have time on my hands and before I cease to know what to do with it! I have my interviews with and previews of Sampras at the start of his Wimbledon career and at the end and many times in between. It may seem very British to be harping on about Wimbledon but that's where I've done 95 per cent of my tennis commentary. I started there as a complete novice, and apart from the occasional appearance in the box at Queen's and for a Davis Cup match in Manchester it has almost all been in SW19.

2007 brought a second trip to the French Championships at Roland Garros but I never made it to Flushing Meadows. If you're thinking you may have heard me at the Australian Open you're right, but it was only up-early and off-tube at Television Centre in London.

Of all my interviews with Sampras, one stands out: the day he played Britain's Andrew Foster in the last sixteen and became a little angry with the crowd. The press who have the first crack – sometimes a very appropriate word – gave him a hard time at their collective conference. The system is that the scribblers get nine minutes, then, assuming the player has been requested, the BBC come next, then NBC, then the second American channel, and then on to other television and radio networks. It's all extremely organised but it can be a bit like a sausage factory. And every leading player has a member of the All England media committee acting as chaperon.

Sampras looked a little shell-shocked when he came into our interview room. Clearly he would be on the defensive. So as he was taking his seat I took a bit of a gamble.

'You can't win, can you?' I said. He looked surprised, even a little aggressive. 'Either you're boring us to death,' I continued, 'or you're upsetting the Brits.' I was smiling.

He responded in kind, then said, 'I like your jacket.'

'So you should,' I replied, 'I bought it in your home town [then Tampa, in Florida].'

The interview that followed was forthright but friendly and relaxed, but neither of us really believed that his comment to the crowd had been, 'Thank you very much, God bless you, hasta la vista, let's get the hell off the court.'

His coach, Tim Gullickson (whose early death from a brain tumour in 1996 was so difficult for Sampras and many others to come to terms with), told me that first year that he felt every player should be allowed thirty minutes of temporary insanity after a match. (I'm sure many football coaches would agree with the sentiment.) Gullickson also said that the important thing is not to make the same mistakes over and over again (I just wish I could avoid that with my scrve). 'If Pete wins this tournament,' he told me before the '93 final, 'it's going to spur him on to the great heights I expect of him. He's going to be on top for a long time and could become one of the great players.'

The haunted look of his early days, when he struggled to live with the expectancy born of winning the US Open at the age of nineteen, slowly disappeared. Fred Perry had said that 'Sampras will be Wimbledon champion by the age of twenty-two,' but to do so Sampras first had to come to terms with grass, which he initially hated, and then find a return of serve to complement his serve-and-volley game.

Rod Laver was his idol, and he shared with him a humility which was still apparent after all his success. 'When people talk about historical things and who's the greatest, it makes me uncomfortable' was his comment to me on the eve of what was to be his last Wimbledon victory. It was the thought that perhaps some kid might one day be inspired by his achievements, as he had by Rod's, which brought a shy smile of satisfaction.

Years earlier he'd responded to the observation made by many that the guys at the top are a bit boring to watch with the remark, 'I don't really want to say anything about the Connors era, but Connors had moments of being a bit shrewd, and that's not the personality I want. I want to let my racket do the talking.' Its eloquence was the character of the man.

Ivan Lendl was never the Wimbledon champion and of those who weren't there's only one player I wished more to take the title. Lendl wouldn't thank me for saying so, for when he was playing he told me, 'The last thing I would want is that people would want me to win Wimbledon because of sympathy. Just like me or like my game.'

'You're very methodical,' I suggested.

'Anything wrong with that?' was the swift reply, with a smile accompanied by the challenge of a thrusting jaw.

That's how it was for over an hour, which may have served to lighten the hotel life he hated. 'I'd play all the tournaments in my back yard if I could.'

The interview produced, I think, an interesting portrait of a man not easy to know yet forthright of opinion and, I suspect, a very true friend to those close to him. The criticism of being a mechanical player did not upset him. 'You have to use what you have in the best possible way. It's more difficult than having natural shots.' He didn't believe he could win Wimbledon the way he wanted to play: 'The bounce is not too good and the technique I have doesn't allow for it. And I'm a bit heavy to move at the back like Borg and Connors did.'

These days golf, which he took up – very seriously of course – and, a lifelong love, ice hockey are his sports, along with exercising his many German shepherd dogs, but I wonder if he ever muses that it was the timing that was wrong. What if he'd been a little younger? He'd have loved the Wimbledon bounce that Tim Henman and others have complained about in recent years. But as one American journalist put it during Lendl's time, 'Thank God for Wimbledon, otherwise we'd be spending all our time writing about him.'

Invariably the top or second seed, he regularly found the luck of the draw placed him in the same half as either Becker or Edberg and when, in 1989, he had his best chance, rain and a postponement to the Monday allowed Becker to escape his clutches. It was against Becker at Queen's in 1990 that he felt he played his best on grass – Queen's plays like a hard court if the weather's good – and Becker was also his opponent when Lendl played the best tennis I saw from him in winning the Benson & Hedges title at Wembley in 1985. I wonder if he still delights in the technical books that used to be his main reading?

A week before Wimbledon '91 I went with Paul Davies to the headquarters of the ATP in Florida, where Andre Agassi was supposed to be practising on a grass court. In fact, most of what was his last day before leaving for England was spent on marketing issues, radio phone-ins and a few interviews, including a brief one with the BBC. That chat apart, he had everyone eating out of his hand. The charisma was as obvious as it was infectious but we returned home wondering what we had.

It wasn't a lot, but from it, with the help of bits of the Agassi video, Paul and the VT editor produced a piece for the Wimbledon preview for *Sunday Grandstand* the day before the championships started. He brought the finished product – apart from my voice on it, that is – to my house late on the Saturday evening. As he was putting the video into the machine, which was just above floor level, below the television, his knee, which was in need of a cartilage operation, locked. He was in agony as we watched his work and there was very little conversation. Fortunately, the pain eased enough for him to drive home.

I went to bed having no idea how the script would go; the piece was some distance from how I'd imagined it. But early on Sunday morning it was done in half an hour. When I presented it for dubbing at Television Centre in the afternoon, Paul had to admit that my part wasn't what he'd expected, either. But he liked it and it worked, and because of poor weather the piece was given two more showings in the early days of the championships. I was very happy about that. I always enjoyed being pushed into writing a good script, and it's a cameo for which I have much affection.

That year Agassi, resplendent in shining white after much debate as to whether he'd abide by the Wimbledon rules, departed in the quarter-final, losing to David Wheaton in five sets. But the following year he was the Wimbledon champion, beating Goran Ivanisevic in five more gruelling sets, his return of serve finally trumping the Croat's many aces. We hadn't yet reached the time when the champion was taken up to chat with Des or Sue, so the interviewer's role was mine down in the sausage factory. Martin Hopkins had said, 'Give it all it's worth,' but as Agassi took his seat his 'minder' from the media committee, Lord Kindersley, said to the floor manager, John Gilpin, 'Three minutes only.' 'Did you hear that?' said Gilpers to me with an extra air of authority to make clear that he was in charge. 'Sorry, what?' I replied. 'I was talking to Hoppy.'

Almost immediately Des was leading to me and we were off, live, on a very chatty interview, the baby-brown eyes flashing with delight at his success. It lasted for just over six minutes, with Gilpin playing his part, trying to wrap me up but knowing full well I'd ignore him. At the end he showed me the stopwatch with a flourish. 'I'm sorry, I really didn't think it was that long,' I said, apologising to Andre. 'For you, no problem,' he replied. But as I left the chair for the next interviewer in line, the champion turned to the noble lord and demanded cuts in the interviews to follow.

Andre Agassi's tennis career was like no other: a roller-coaster ride which more than once threatened to come off the rails but which reached rare heights as he became only the fifth player in the history of the game to lift the trophy at all four Grand Slam events, with eight wins in total at those venues. A wonderful eye, a reaction time without equal; a surprise packet to the end, dissolving in tears as he went to his chair at the 2006 US Open and the next minute battling through them to give a farewell speech of eloquence and sincerity.

He'd wanted to go out as Sampras had, winning the final, but time had caught up with him as he tried to play through the back-pain that had for some time been shouting at him to stop. Instead, he lost in the third round to a man called

Becker – Benjamin, not Boris – and then first by the crowd and then by his peers in the locker room was given a reception of heartfelt appreciation worth many times more than the silver trinket of victory. The best player of his time? Probably not, although he was close. The most exciting, and the biggest star? Undoubtedly.

What a contrast with the Agassi who came to Wimbledon for the second time, following a first-time drubbing in 1987 by Henri Leconte, from whom he extracted just five games. He having shown no interest in returning to SW19 for the following three years, there were many who thought him a phoney. As I'd put it in the cameo, 'the glitzy product of garish Las Vegas with a video proclaiming rock 'n' roll tennis, and stating that image was everything'. And the image was being marketed to millions: 'the baby face which launched many more than a thousand kits'. Time proved that – unlike many a politician – there was a great deal more depth to AA than his critics perceived. His departure leaves a very big hole.

The interviewer who followed me in the factory the day of Agassi's triumph was Bud Collins, he of the pink and blue trousers or any other mixed colours of the rainbow, a regular part of his image which, as a writer and television interviewer for NBC, has plenty of tennis substance. I'm sure he would have claimed his full time from the champion. We swapped the seat many times, and when it comes to questions he certainly takes the biscuit. Perhaps his most memorable was to the surprise Kiwi finalist of 1983: 'Chris Lewis, what's a player like you doing in the Wimbledon final?'

Andrea Jaeger's style was rather different. At eighteen she'd been runner-up to Martina Navratilova; after retiring from the game, she became a TV reporter for an American cable channel, Home Box Office. She once said to me as we waited for the interviewee, 'I've questions one, two and five, but I can't think of three and four.' I was never that organised; but then it does help to listen to the answers, doesn't it? Later she listened to a higher calling: she became a nun.

It was always a challenge, a battle against time in the factory but I enjoyed it. Initially John Rowlinson, then the BBC editor at Wimbledon but from 2002 director of television at the All England Club, thought I wouldn't be able to crack it. 'Very good at the considered interview, but this is different' was his initial feeling. I'd like to think I found the happy medium.

I only had Tim Henman in the chair a couple of times and after no great moments of drama but he, of course, is the man I most wanted to see win Wimbledon. I know it's thought by many that he didn't quite have the resolve, but he was incredibly unlucky not to put his name on the roll of honour, and not only because Sampras, in his prime, twice barred his way at the penultimate hurdle. Henman's year should have been 2001, but that was the year of Goran Ivanisevic. The irony that the Croat was given a wild card into the main draw must have been very hard for the Englishman to take.

There was a period when Tim was the best half-volleyer on the circuit and among the top five as a volleyer. He had a delightful game to watch but one which made huge demands on him because it offered few cheap points. Viewed from afar I think going to work with Larry Stefanki was a mistake, because there was a time when Tim had a more than reasonable serve and was a better player when he went for it and for the rest of his shots. I also think, and again I'd run contrary to his view, that Henman Hill, well-meaning though it undoubtedly was, proved more a minus than a plus. And at times the Centre Court crowd has tried too hard for him: it became a sort of collective heart-on-sleeve. I always felt he needed first to win one of the other three Grand Slams to take some of the pressure off. And while to make the last four at both Roland Garros and Flushing Meadows in 2004 was remarkable, the Australian Open was the one that offered him the best chance, especially in 2002 when, with the draw opening up, he lost in the fourth round for the third year running, this time to that doughty competitor Jonas Bjorkman.

There used to be anxiety in the commentary box when covering his matches but no British sportsman has had to live with the same pressure as our Tim lived with when the green of the All England lawns was the colour of hope. Though the record books don't include him among the Grand Slam winners, surely his record in the modern world of competitive tennis – six times a semi-finalist in Grand Slams – justifies him as Britain's best ever (Fred Perry was of a different era). Now the hill has for the most part become a mountain and it may just be that following Tim's path Andy Murray, clearly a very different character, and with a game which can win on any surface, will climb it – if we give him the breathing space. And if one day there is a need to recall his Wimbledon and Grand Slam debut – against the Swiss George Bastl on Court 2 – the commentator may just strike a chord.

For the record I have long since apologised to Lord Kindersley. The club afforded me the opportunity by inviting me to be the guest speaker at one of their two annual dinners. For Penny and me that led to the bonus of a day as guests in the royal box the following year. David Mercer, doing his homework as ever, checked the list delivered daily by the club and Paul Davies's cameras briefly presented us in our pomp! The best line, though, wasn't David's but a surprised John Lloyd's. 'What's *he* doing in there?' he asked incredulously. 'I've never been invited!' Friends leaving 'saw you' messages on the answerphone seemed rather more impressed.

23

Heysel

Liverpool, the holders, were trying to win it for the fifth time. Juventus had never won it, but if they did so now they'd become the first club to have their name on all three European club trophies. That was the scenario of the thirtieth European Cup final in May 1985 at the Heysel stadium in Brussels.

It was Joe Fagan's last match in charge of Liverpool, the club that had led England's domination of the competition since their first success eight years earlier. The Football League had been represented in seven of the previous eight finals and had been victorious each time. Phil Neal hoped to become the fourth winning Liverpool skipper, following Emlyn Hughes, Phil Thompson and Graeme Souness. And there was a little local issue at home for his team to deal with. A week before,

I'd reported from Rotterdam as Everton had added the European Cup Winners' Cup to their victory in the League Championship. Should Liverpool lose in Brussels, not only would it be a season without a trophy for the first time in a decade, but their city rivals from across Stanley Park would alone carry the English flag in the next season's European Cup competition.

Liverpool were the marginal favourites, but the Italians, led by their country's best defender, Gaetano Scirea, and including in their line-up a magnificent Frenchman, Michel Platini, a mercurial Pole, Zbigniew Boniek, and the master of the half-chance, Paolo Rossi, were a considerable threat. Goals had been hard to find in recent finals – six of the last seven had been decided by a solitary goal – and matches which promised much had often failed to deliver. But surely not this time; the cream of European talent was on show.

Brussels was hosting the final for a fourth time, having been the venue for Real Madrid's successes in 1958 and 1966, and for Bayern Munich's draw and 4–0 victory in the replay against Atlético Madrid in 1974. Eighty television channels were covering the match, twenty-nine of them taking it live. Each club was offered 14,500 tickets, 11,000 places being on the terraces. The Belgian Football Association had 23,000 – the stadium's capacity had been restricted to 52,000, down from 58,000, for reasons of segregation. All such facts were on my crib sheet, with notes on the players. I hoped few of them would be needed.

During the day there was the usual chanting by rival supporters but in Grand Platz and elsewhere, and later, outside the stadium, they seemed to mingle well in a good atmosphere. But this was the evening when what other European countries dismissed as 'the English disease' claimed thirty-nine lives. The tragedy actually occurred before we went on air, though the grim details only became clear as the evening wore on into night.

Bobby Charlton, John Shrewsbury, the producer, and I watched with growing concern as fans with Liverpool scarves first tried to provoke some Juventus supporters, then broke through flimsy supposed segregation barriers to engage in fights; and finally gave chase as their prey ran for refuge. Quite suddenly John said, 'This could be very nasty; someone could be killed here.' He relayed his thoughts to the editor and producer in London, and suggested they try to extricate themselves from what had seemed a harmless agreement that Jimmy Hill should be the last guest with Bruce Forsyth on *The Terry Wogan Show*, which immediately preceded the football. In the end Jimmy was left with the very difficult task of turning from light entertainment with lots of joking and ribbing to welcoming viewers to the story of impending tragedy. His guests in the studio, Terry Venables, then the coach of Barcelona, and Graeme Souness, then playing for Sampdoria, found themselves discussing matters far removed from a game of football.

Three or four times I tried to scribble a few words to say when the studio handed over to what had now become their reporter at the scene of a disaster. I abandoned every one. But somehow some clarity as to what was needed came to me as Jimmy said, 'Over to John Motson.' . . .

'For the last fifty minutes the Heysel stadium in Brussels, the capital of Belgium, has been a sickening and bewildering sight. As a result there is, for certain, serious injury when a wall collapsed – and may be worse. At the left end of the stadium were supporters of Liverpool and Juventus. They were divided by two long poles over which it was easy to climb, under which it was easy to move. After a while supporters of Liverpool moved into the Juventus area. For a while there were scuffles between the rival supporters and a great deal of the threatening, animal-like behaviour which we have become all too accustomed to seeing at home. And then many of the Juventus supporters decided the time had come to move away, and they moved away at such a pace and in such numbers that in moving down towards the track which surrounds the pitch at this Heysel stadium a wall collapsed and certainly there were people pinned underneath it. I should say that it was a small wall of no more than four feet in height . . .'

I was very conscious that among the viewers would be families and friends of the people in the stadium, and treated the information about the growing number of fatalities with caution. The risk of the Chinese-whisper syndrome was considerable. Our position was roughly in the middle of the stand. Bruno Pizzul from RAI, Italy's national broadcaster, was just to our right. BBC Radio, with a team of Peter Jones, Mike Ingham, Emlyn Hughes and their producer, were a few rows behind us. Mike occasionally went to check on the growing number of corpses being collected behind the stand and we were very grateful for the eyewitness accounts passed to us.

It would have been quite wrong to use Bobby Charlton in that way: as it was, Italians, finding the scene impossible to comprehend, seized on a familiar English face and questioned him in the commentary position. 'It is not normal,' said one, and of course it wasn't. But we knew that fighting among rival supporters had become all too common in the English game and the failure to stamp it out was now reaping its gruesome retribution. Bruno Pizzul was barely able to do his job for the many agitated and tearful Juventus fans around his position.

For an hour and a half the BBC output ranged between on-the-spot reports, studio discussion and going to the newsroom where the information given to John Humphrys, it seemed to me, varied very little, if at all, from what had already been said. Meanwhile, we were told, UEFA officials continued to debate whether or not the match should take place. I believe they came to the right decision, though the delay after the two captains had addressed their supporters over the stadium tannoy system probably owed most to waiting for the riot police to arrive in force. Not that they used much of it: stone-throwing and bravado from Juventus supporters was allowed to continue long enough for a banner to be revealed which made it clear that those supporters who had come to the match with the direct intention of causing trouble were not only from one side.

I didn't need the editor's instruction not to get excited commentating on the match; after what had happened it was hard to concentrate on two teams kicking a football about. One of my former flatmates, tuning in late and not knowing why the match was still going on, thought that I must be ill. The penalty that decided the match shouldn't have been given, for Gillespie's trip on Boniek as the Pole was put clear by Platini's pass was outside the area. Ten years later, when I interviewed the Frenchman for the Euro '96 preview series, he remained dissatisfied that Juventus had won that way. But I was glad it was given and hoped it would prove decisive. Hard though it may have been on the Liverpool players, I had no wish to see an equaliser. The thought of extra time was utterly abhorrent. The match was being played simply to prevent further violence.

The BBC rightly decided not to show the presentation and came off the air almost immediately after the final whistle. We walked the couple of miles or so back to our hotel in silence.

While I have only ever felt the need to watch breakfast television when staying in a hotel, preferring at home to be awakened by *Today* on Radio 4, I've always had a respect for those who manage to organise their body clock to work on it. The day after Heysel, though, I found myself making my debut after just forty minutes' sleep. To my horror I discovered on my arrival in the London studio that Robert Maxwell, owner of the *Daily Mirror*, had been invited on to the programme to discuss the implications of the disaster. Before going on air he assured that excellent presenter Nick Ross that he'd had no involvement in his newspaper's presentation and then promptly spent well over a minute praising it.

In contrast to the previous evening, when I'd been keenly

aware of the need for balance between reporting and giving my own opinions, I said categorically that I hoped English clubs would be pulled out of European competition before UEFA acted, and that the time had come for the removal of passports. Sir Arthur South, chairman of Norwich City, supported me on the point against Maxwell's argument about 'freedom of the individual'. Regrettably, it took some years for the government to take that action. Much worse, the immediate lesson of Heysel, the availability of the pitch as a place of sanctuary, to which I had referred in commentary, was ignored. It took four more years and a second tragedy, with even greater loss of life, at Hillsborough for that lesson to be learned.

From Television Centre, Maxwell and I were taken by car to the studios of CBS, one of the three major American networks (this was some time before the arrival of the pro-Republican Fox TV). He wasn't too impressed when I suggested to him that he should be less dogmatic and more responsible in this second broadcast. I found him a loathsome man and was glad that I had no need to 'enjoy' his company again.

It is certainly true that the Heysel tragedy owed much to the failure of proper segregation, allied to the frailties of an old stadium (which has long since been rebuilt). But its true cause was of human making, and that problem we seem no nearer to solving. The segregation of people at football matches is still considered normal practice. Why is it the only sport where that is the case?

24

The Finger of the Devil

Jimmy Hill was talking about something else at the time. Fair enough: the ball was some fifteen yards to the right of the halfway line and the man in possession was facing his own goal. Did I realise that at the time? Or was it only when BBC 2 presented *Goal Night* and I had to go in to Television Centre and add a few words at the start of my commentary? Difficult to say, for it's over twenty years since it all happened. Did anyone notice the slightly different beginning? By then everyone knew what had happened, and quite a few knew what had been said. It won the day in the Azteca stadium and on *Goal Night*, too; and I've had no cause since to change my belief that it was the best goal I've ever seen, notwithstanding the attempt of his fellow Argentinian, Lionel Messi, to produce a carbon copy twenty-one years later.

From the moment when he turned, leaving Beardsley and then Reid, increased speed slightly past Hoddle, he was heading for goal. On he went, past a seemingly mesmerised Fenwick and then Butcher, who at least had the intention to tackle.

'He's got Burruchaga to his left, Valdano to his left – huh, he won't need any of them,' I said (as he dummied and rounded Shilton before sliding the ball home). 'You have to say that's magnificent. There can be no dispute about that one: that was pure football genius.'

Somebody quoted me as saying 'sheer' but I was glad when I checked that I'd said 'pure', for it was the right word to contrast with what had happened a few minutes earlier. 'The hand of God', Diego Maradona later claimed about his flip of the ball over Shilton. 'The finger of the Devil' would have been more accurate, for photographs proved that he'd lifted the ball over the goalkeeper's advancing fist. But the feet and the body movement for his second goal were certainly made in heaven.

His brother, apparently, deserves some of the credit, having berated Diego five years earlier for a run at Wembley when he'd shot early and wide instead of rounding the keeper. Ray Clemence was a little luckier than the man with whom he'd had such competition for the England jersey.

To prove it had been no fluke the devilish maestro scored a similar goal, one of his two in the semi-final against Belgium. But now the run was shorter and flatter and from the left – and not quite as good. Even so, I defy any defender looking from the goalkeeper's viewpoint to say which way he was going to go. For me Diego Armando Maradona in the 1986 World Cup disproved the belief that one man doesn't make a team. Argentina had some good players – Valdano, Burruchaga and Enrique, to name but three – but without their captain they wouldn't have come anywhere near winning. And if you're thinking that he had a quiet final, look again and note who made the winning pass after Argentina had allowed Germany to score two goals from corners, which threatened to take the match into extra time.

My own extra time in Mexico '86 came a month before the tournament. I was asked by *Radio Times* to spend a week looking at a capital city which had been hit by an earthquake the previous September, assessing the damage and the mood of the people. It was a task which took me from the Damnificados, interviewing a factory worker in the 14 square feet of his tented home for a family of six, to the president of the Mexican Football Association in his beautiful house, with office adjoining, in the Lomas district of the Paseo de la Reforma, the main artery of the city; from government figures to the family of fire-eaters on a bridge over the Circuito Interior at Thiers; and on to the coach, forty-five-year-old Yugoslav 'Bora' Milutinovic, whose task it was, as one Mexican travel agent put it, to provide the 'drink' that would make the people forget their problems.

History suggests that the people's relief was transitory, but though the tented village had few creature comforts it was not lacking in television sets, and Bora's team offered more than one glass of tequila. On my first evening back in Mexico

City for the finals, I went with John Boulter, the former Olympian and British 800 metres champion, who now worked with adidas, to Bora's home for supper. Bora was interesting and entertaining when we met again on his World Cup coaching tour, which took him and his Mexican wife to Costa Rica in 1990, the United States (1994), Nigeria (1998) and China (2002), all of whose football teams benefited from his presence in four more World Cup finals.

It was the power of television, and in particular of Guillermo Canedo, boss of Televista Méxicana, which persuaded FIFA to offer Mexico a second World Cup just sixteen years after its first – thus making it the first country to host two. The original choice, Colombia, had decided they could not fulfil the role. But Televista would have many problems to solve after the earthquake, which struck many buildings in the most populated district of the city. When the tournament began there were still many technical difficulties. No one suffered more than Canada, whose debut match in the finals, against France, wasn't seen in their home country. Never has the usual, but often unsung, expertise of the BBC's engineering depart-ment been so needed and so appreciated.

The tournament itself was generally of a far better standard than the altitude and heat had suggested, though midday kick-offs like England's quarter-final – high noon in both senses – bordered on the suicidal. But then when was priority in such matters given to the players? It produced the most entertaining Russian side I can recall coached by Valery Lobanovsky and including nine of his club side, Dynamo Kiev, who that year had won the European Cup Winners' Cup so convincingly and entertainingly. With the clever Aleinikov and the pacy, direct Belanov, they put six goals past Hungary, and were extremely unlucky to go down 4–3 to Belgium in the second-round knock-out stage.

There was much criticism of refereeing in the finals; FIFA had insisted on offering chances to officials from around the world and giving knock-out matches to some far above their experience. Even worse was the quality of running the line. The Russians suffered twice, and the first was a defining moment in the match. In the twenty years since then, the problem has been exacerbated by the increasing number of matches, and by the changes in the interpretation of offside in which the law, to borrow from Dickens, has become 'a ass'.

In Queretaro I commentated on a match which, more than any other, qualified for the cliché 'a game of two halves'. For almost forty-four minutes Denmark played superbly against Spain. They scored once, from a penalty when Berggreen was felled by Gallego, and should have scored more. They had qualified with maximum points, beating the Scots by the only goal (in spite of the prodigious efforts of Gordon Strachan), scoring six against Uruguay, and comfortably beating the Germans 2–0. They were now fully justifying the label of, at least, dangerous outsiders. Morten Olsen as sweeper and captain was a calming influence leading from the rear; Soren Lerby, a skilfully combative midfielder; and up front they had the penetrative Preben Elkjaer and the hugely gifted Michael Laudrup.

Then Jesper Olsen, who had scored the penalty, receiving

the ball in the right back position from his goalkeeper, Lars Hogh, returned it to him in a manner that was as inaccurate as it was unnecessary. Emilio Butragueno, living up to his nickname, 'the Vulture', swooped to equalise, and in the second half, took his personal goal tally to four as Denmark's talents died in a 6–1 defeat.

I had my share of the many spectacular goals in the tournament. One caused a little bit of 'showboating': I gave a passable imitation of a Latin American commentator. Not in the torrent of high excitement that would have accompanied the identification of the scorer, but by holding the third syllable of his name, 'Negrete-e-e-e-e-e-e-e', as his superb volley flew into the Bulgarian net and took Mexico through to the last sixteen.

I commentated on three England matches, the first of which, following England's defeat by Portugal, should have seen the end of England's campaign. But Morocco missed the chance of a memorable victory which would surely have brought the conclusion of Bobby Robson's reign. His namesake, the captain Bryan, whose selection had been much questioned because of injury, fell and had to be carried off. His right shoulder, which needed an operation, had again popped out of its casing. Soon afterwards Ray Wilkins, in totally uncharacteristic style, threw the ball in the general direction of the referee and was sent off. England were in chaos but survived in a dull, goalless draw to stay in contention.

The sight of the manager – head in hands, brow furrowed, eyes cast down – told the story of his and England's predicament. Behind the scenes there was much debate, not to say argument, about team selection. But from despair came delight and what happened in Monterrey a long time ago not only gave Bobby Robson a second World Cup at England's helm but proved to be a major turning-point in the life of one Gary Lineker, a fact he readily acknowledges. His hat trick won the day against Poland, the first two goals classics in passing movement and finishing and accompanied in commentary by howls of euphoria from Jimmy Hill. The side, with a midfield of Peter Reid, Trevor Steven and Glenn Hoddle, with Beardsley, much the best partner for Lineker – unselfish and so adept at creating space – was, once the first goal had settled them, unrecognisable from the first two matches. It was good to be able to pay them well-deserved compliments, after having had to chastise them for 'crass errors like that'.

The same day Morocco, against less historically vaunted opponents, Portugal, found their nerve and won 3–1, then, back in defensive mode, failed only narrowly in the next round against the Germans. A thunderous free kick, through a bad wall, by Lothar Matthaus was decisive as extra time beckoned. These days there's no need for African teams to fear anyone, especially with so many of their players playing in Europe; perhaps the World Cup in South Africa in 2010 will at last bring the success so long awaited.

So via England's comfortable 3–0 victory over Paraguay to the quarter-final in the Azteca stadium, twenty years after the dismissal of the Argentine captain, Antonio Rattin, at Wembley and with a media backdrop of references to the more recent Falklands war. It was a match of magnificence and malevolence, marred for me not only by the manner of the first goal but by the fact that, like the referee and linesman, I didn't spot the handball. Some of the replays were cut in, unseen by me, for me to commentate, with the voice from London in my ear saying, 'They're going up for the ball now – there's the hand,' and so on. Another twenty years on, when the goal was featured in a World Cup highlights programme from Berlin, there was Lee Dixon saying, 'Everyone saw it except the commentator.'

That moment of commentating-to-forget was quickly followed by one I shall always remember. And there are other moments: of Lineker scoring, and then of John Barnes – 'Everyone in England will be saying, "Go on, take him on."' He skinned Giusti once more and crossed another beauty, and it seemed Gary had scored the equaliser. But it was not to be – nor was it four years later; just a little closer and again with a side under Bobby Robson of confusing character.

25

Maestro

Few things during my time at the BBC gave me greater satisfaction than working on the *Maestro* series. Its format was simple: an interview, illustrated by video recordings, with a sportsman or -woman who had been retired for ten years or more. It began in 1979 with Julian Wilson talking to Sir Gordon Richards, followed by Desmond Lynam with Tom Finney and then Fred Perry, and Peter Alliss chatting with Henry Cotton. Then for four years the chair was occupied by Frank Keating of the *Guardian*, whom I succeeded in 1985 for another four years. Jeff Goddard produced the whole series, and it was very much his baby.

The series could and should still be running now – I'm amazed how often people have asked me when there's to be a new one. But in 1988 the controller of BBC 2 decided, for two reasons, that it had run its course.

His first reason was that the questioning was insufficiently sharp. Jeff and I felt that, while there were some difficult questions which had to be asked – and they were – a programme entitled *Maestro* did not set out to prove that every champion had feet of clay. The closing titles made the style clear: 'so-and-so was talking to Barry Davies'.

The second reason was, if accurately reported, possibly the most stupid remark ever to emanate from the lips of a television executive (though there have across the years been a few competitors). 'Too much nostalgia,' he pronounced, 'doesn't work on television.' What makes it even more difficult to accept, or believe, is that the same controller has since produced some memorable historical programmes presenting genius on canvas. Save for his own rather too frequent appearances, they were classic compositions which were deservedly much praised. I stretch a point to make a point that he had little appreciation of sport, save for its boosting of the ratings. Even the government – at least in the ministry's title – accepts that sport and culture belong together.

The most disappointing thing is that so much good archive material sits in the BBC vaults crying out for use, and the huge number of subjects is left untapped. The interviewees in our next series of four programmes were intended to be Jack Peterson, Harvey Smith, Herb Elliott and Ray Lindwall, and Keith Miller and Ken Rosewall were just two waiting in the wings. Even so, I remain grateful for some fascinating days spent with characters fully deserving the programme's title and, even more, for what I learned from my producer.

Jeff Goddard had been at the BBC for many years. Frequently he was the producer running the videotape operation at major championships, a position very much the meat in the sandwich between the senior editor and studio producer on the one side and the individual assistant producers editing events ready for the replay on the other. Time is on nobody's side, opinions are not usually lacking, and the man in the middle is regularly the fall guy. To point out how often he is the saviour with the quick decision cuts little ice.

The pressure can take its toll, and for the often seemingly rather tense Jeff to be earning my plaudits may surprise a few. But he had a musician's ear: he was among the arbiters whittling down the contestants for *Young Musician of the Year*. Sounds could offend, emphasis was vital, cadence a basic requirement, variety a need; and he found in me a willing pupil. More than once, in the dubbing theatre a single line had to be repeated more than a dozen times.

My immediate predecessor on the programme, Frank Keating, had interviewed the likes of Tommy Farr and Denis Compton, Stirling Moss and Mary Rand, Fred Trueman and Bobby Charlton, Mary Peters and Henry Cooper. He wrote the scripts but he didn't narrate them; instead Jeff used an actor. But I wanted to play all three roles and Jeff had no other thought; though over time he offered many and I am eternally in his debt.

This was back in the days of film, and the arrival of the video camera was regarded as a growing threat by many cameramen. They feared that they, with their art of getting a shot right first time, were about to be superseded by mere artisans who would simply use a little more re-useable tape. (In fact, just about all of them converted, some a little grudgingly.) *Maestro* was a low-budget programme, shot in one day, and as the light began to fade the producer would start to regret that he hadn't taken that needed exterior earlier and the reporter felt the pressure as the roll-take rose towards the maximum. Those rather tricky questions which might, if proffered earlier, have blown the interview off course had still to be asked. We always made it, but usually only just.

I guess Jeff and I had a good awareness of each other's space. There were always debates, of course, some lengthy, as the programme came together, but I've always believed that the editor, whose name closes the titles, should have the last word – whatever the programme. I can remember only one occasion when I pushed way over my line. 'But he didn't answer the question,' said Jeff. 'His face did,' I replied, leaving it clear that when England's cricketers won a run-chase to beat the West Indies at Port of Spain, Trinidad, Colin Cowdrey, the captain, gave no specific instructions for the resulting charge.

My time in the presenter's chair coincided with the programme being given an international flavour. We began in style, arriving in the late afternoon in Barbados, where I was to interview one of that country's greatest sons, Garry Sobers. I hadn't met him before, but we saw him in action the following afternoon during a formal meeting of the island's tourist organisation.

It left me with much foreboding, for this wasn't the personality that shone through his cricket. He seemed rather gruff
and full of himself. I told myself that I didn't have to like him
to obtain a good interview, but I knew it would help.

Jeff's plan was to have dinner with Sobers the night before
– only because of the journey was the extra day permitted –
and do the interview early the following morning. It worked
like a charm, for we had barely finished our aperitifs before
Sobers, Jeff and I were talking like old friends. The day after
the interview we visited his mother's house (his father was
killed in the war), and it wasn't hard to imagine her trying
to persuade her six sons to come to the supper table and
leave their Lilliputian cricket – a game played with a ball
made of tar on a half-size pitch, with the batsman down on
one knee wielding a miniature bat. It was easy, too, to see in
the mind's eye, at a slightly later date, those eager contests
of tennis-ball games, the secret of why so many West Indian
players of his time played the ball on the up and often so
late. Garry Sobers is a proud man, and he has every justification for being so.

Dinner with Arnold Palmer couldn't be fitted into his schedule
and as the morning of our one filming day at his club in
Pennsylvania moved on I became increasingly frustrated. Jeff
was, too, though both of us tried not to show it. The previous
day Palmer had failed for the first time to qualify for the US
Open. From a position of comfort the strokes slipped away
as he battled with a contact lens which had become stuck in
his eyelid.

I possibly didn't help his feelings by asking why, when the British Open, as the Americans call it, always welcomed him with open arms, he had to qualify in his own back yard. 'That's a good question' was his terse response, but at least he was more animated on the point than for the rest of the conversation, which produced only pat answers amid a constant string of telephone calls. There was a problem at another of Arnold's golf clubs, in Florida, run by his brother, and it was taking about ninety per cent of the great man's attention. He had to be a great man, because everyone in the world of golf said he was as a person as well as a player. But, as one of his countrymen might have put it, I sure as hell hadn't found him that morning.

He arrived after the lunch break. Walking the course in the sunshine we found the man, though to be truthful we didn't quite find the player. We set up a few shots which looked good in the televised programme, but it took a long time for the ball to go in the hole. It was a shame we couldn't start again the next day, for there slowly developed an understanding and a warmth which too soon was taken by the sunset. I had two further regrets. I stood side by side with a legend on the sixth fairway of his home course, and only one of us had a club in his hand; though if I'd had one I'd probably have been shaking in fear of being asked to use it. And as we left he gave me a personalised signed photo to 'Maestro Barry Davis' – yes, without the 'e'.

Stanley Matthews I had met a few times. As a kid I once saw him play in his heyday, though at Highbury that afternoon, against an Arsenal team reduced by injury to ten men, he was played out of the game by Don Roper, who had begun the match as Arsenal's outside left. That boyhood memory suggests that wingbacks were not entirely an invention of the '70s. I also saw Matthews beat Billy Meredith's record by becoming the first player over the age of fifty to play in a first-division match. It was for Stoke City against Fulham at Victoria Road. My report for *The Times* included this paragraph:

> Forget the past, forget the magic of his name, and consider simply his performance on the day. It is true there were periods when he seemed not to be in the game (but such was always his way). It is true that he beat Langley, a mere stripling of 35 years and 364 days, only twice in man-to-man combat. But he had three priceless gifts to offer – his reading of the game, his ability to pass the ball accurately and his positional sense.

He claimed in the interview that he'd retired too soon, seeing himself in a midfield role in the way Leeds United adapted Johnny Giles, who had played as a winger with Manchester United. Whether he would have had Johnny's ability to, shall we say, protect himself is another matter.

There was no problem fitting in the night-before dinner, for we were in Lake Placid, scene of the 1980 Olympic Games, and of Robin Cousins's gold medal, where Stan was doing something he loved, helping to coach kids and, I am sure, being well recompensed. We didn't expect any problems with the programme: we were dripping with archive and the only real test would be to find a few different lines from a well-known story. Then suddenly, in the middle of the main course, Stan said, 'Now, Barry, we really don't need to go over the 1953 bit all over again, do we? Everything has been said about it and it's Morty's [Stan Mortensen's] story, not mine.' Of course, we had to include it and I persuaded him the next day that he should pass the credit on if that was the way he felt. But I confess I felt a little guilty when he later thanked me for not dwelling on the point when I said, 'And you had that winner's gong at last,' for before moving on to another subject I had counted to five, just long enough for the cameraman to close in on the moistening of the eyes.

The next day we found a side to Stan's life which was not so well known: how the manager of Port Vale, on a pre-season tour of Czechoslovakia, met a lady who worked in the cultural department of the US embassy in Prague. Strolling with Stan and his second wife, Milla, around Lake Placid I couldn't help wondering how two people from such different walks of life, and with such different interests, had come to share what was clearly a love story. She was more prepared to take my point than he, but then the boy from the Potteries unknowingly acknowledged the difference with a simple observation. 'When we come back to England [they had lived in Malta, South Africa and Canada for a long time] she goes to see the ballet and I go to meet up with my pals like Jackie Mudie.'

She died a little less than a year before Stan, who carried on his extraordinary fitness regime, including fasting one day a week, almost to the end of his life. I hadn't seen them for some time but I have no doubt that he was lost without her. She was a charming lady.

And he? Well, let me just record that when he came to the old Football Association headquarters at Lancaster Gate as guest of honour at the launch of Bryon Butler's *Official Illustrated History of the FA Cup*, he signed my copy 'To my pal Barry'.

Watching Calum Best give his sensitive oration at his father's funeral, I had a picture in my mind's eye of the two of them kicking a football around in the garden, the son then about three years old and with golden hair, when we talked to the father for the series. There are many who knew George much better than I did, and I cannot say that he said anything in the interview that he hadn't said before or didn't say many times after. So, other than recording the time he forced me to admit on air that the words of my commentary had just been stuffed straight back down my throat, I have nothing original to offer about him.

That occasion was at the City Ground, Nottingham, after a match, between Forest and Manchester United, in which he had consistently tried to beat the extra man. He did it again as he came outside the last defender, to be well wide of the near post with a much more difficult angle for the shot. I bemoaned the fact and then watched as the ball brushed the paint on both post and crossbar for a wonderful goal.

Elsewhere in this book I have written a little about painting word pictures and, at risk of self-indulgence, and in tribute to an undoubted maestro of his art I'm very glad I knew, there follows the opening of a programme broadcast in 1985:

> More words have been written and said about George Best than about any other British sportsman; few have done justice to his talent. There was an unfettered joy about the way he played. He combined grace with courage, pace with unbelievable balance. He was balletic and yet at the same time aggressive, warming to the heart and yet clinically cold in his application. He could be as frustrating to colleagues as he was to opponents; the little boy who claimed it was his ball. But he was the master of the unexpected, and for every mazy dribble which ended in chains there was another which would suddenly break free – [he was] the most gifted of Saturdays' Heroes and the most tormented; a confusion of self-destruction and blurred images.

'I know at the end of it all,' he told me, 'people will remember me for what I did on the field. I actually think I was the greatest player of all time.'

Ron Clarke, that great Australian distance runner, was another subject in the *Maestro* series. There could be no doubt that Mexico, when he was in his prime, was a totally unfair venue for him and his like, as it gave enormous advantage to athletes living at altitude – as results proved. Because of that, his career is remembered more for his many world records. He told me, however, of the time later when he was persuaded

by one of his heroes, Emil Zátopek, to run in Prague.
Afterwards the great Czech Olympian accompanied him
through the airport customs to the plane – an illustration of
Zátopek's standing in his home city, even in the days of austere
communist rule following the Russian invasion.

As they shook hands to say goodbye Zátopek forced a
small package into Clarke's hand. Such was the Australian's
concern about what he might be smuggling out to the West
that it was not until the plane cleared Czechoslovakian
airspace that he took the package from his pocket and opened
it. He was staring at an Olympic gold medal accompanied by
a signed message: 'You deserve one of these.'

Zátopek had won four and one silver.

The most single-minded of the interviewees was Reg Harris,
the multi-world-champion cyclist, closely followed by John
Surtees, the only man to be world champion on the two
wheels of a motorbike and then the four of a grand prix
Formula 1 racing car. Both had kept many of the relics of
their success, the machines they 'drove' to victory. In John's
case they included the Ferrari presented to him by Enzo
Ferrari, with the hammer marks on the inside of the cockpit,
to give a little more room for his thighs, the proof of authen-
ticity. Both, too, successfully filled the void when their racing
careers were over, Reg by setting up a business in polyurethane,
John by restoring historic houses.

One of the most memorable moments of the Surtees
programme was provided not by him but by Murray Walker.
Jeff had found some wonderful old footage of a TT race in

the Isle of Man which Surtees had won, but it had no commentary. Murray, whose father had taken part in TT races and whose own love of two wheels remained greater than that of four, for all his wonderful career as the central man of the TV coverage of grands prix, whatever the channel, was delighted to turn back the pages of history. Jeff emphasised that it was a dated piece and required the commentary style of the time, in the hope of restraining a little Murray's undying enthusiasm – the quality that made him the commentator he was. But as I exited the lift on the fourth floor of the BBC's old Lime Grove studios (now a block of flats) in Shepherd's Bush, the voice of motorsport could be clearly heard at full throttle of excitement. I entered the operational part of the dubbing theatre, and there, through the glass, was Murray, standing up looking intently at his monitor, giving every impression that the race was happening now. I looked at Jeff, who, with an expression of resignation, said, 'Yes, I know. I've tried four times; but we should be able to take it down a bit in the final dub.'

It was obvious from the outset that the *Maestro* programmes would prove an archive source, when the need arose for obituaries. At the time of writing, parts of three programmes have been used. But only once has the complete programme been repeated as a tribute. The Maestro was John Curry.

I was asked to say a few words of introduction in which I described him as 'a sensitive man who conquered his self-doubts and those of his critics to achieve his aim'. That meant completing the triple crown of figure skating in 1976 – European, Olympic and World titles. But in truth it was the

status that success brought him which led to the achievement of his true aim, setting up his Theatre of Skating in
New York. 'I get much more out of that than anything I
achieved myself,' he'd told me.

We'd recorded the interview in 1987, the year he was diag-
nosed with Aids. He died seven years later. John was a complex
character, who admitted that he found himself difficult to live
with and I'm sure he viewed me with much suspicion when
we first met. The scars of an interview he gave shortly after
his Olympic triumph were, considering how much attitudes
had changed since, surprisingly still apparent. The journalist
who 'outed' him claimed that Curry had used his Olympic
performance to make a statement, something John strenu-
ously denied. He relaxed sufficiently as we chatted and he
liked the finished programme. Later when, at his invitation,
Jeff and I went to see him at the Windmill Theatre in Sonning,
Berkshire, he greeted us like old friends. He probably should
have been a ballet dancer; he said he'd been influenced at
an impressionable age by seeing Margot Fonteyn and admitted
that he'd have loved the chance to be Nureyev. But, in a
remarkable foreshadowing of the fictional story of Billy Elliot,
his father refused to let him take lessons. So his artistry and
grace were brought to figure skating, and thirty years on he
remains an icon for the champions who have followed him.

Of the remaining ten Maestros, seven appear elsewhere in
this book. That leaves an Englishman, an Irishman and a
Welshman.

No man was more worthy of being given the initials MCC

than Colin Cowdrey. I interviewed him at his old school, Tonbridge, where he'd made the XI as a twelve-year-old. He lived with the expectations of others for the rest of his life, and this sometimes produced diffidence and regularly caused battles with confidence. We met at a difficult time, shortly after what had been presented as a very one-sided divorce, and I make no apology for, having raised the issue, accepting his request that this was a private matter. He did not take the chance to present the other side and that was his decision.

At times he was as charming and as fluent as his glorious cover drives, at others the man who could shuffle around in the crease for a couple of overs. But he was enormously good company and so humble about his contribution to the game of cricket. I was delighted when, a little while later, he came to my local cricket club in Datchet with two of his sons, Chris and Graham, for a benefit match for Derek Underwood. He was also kind enough to sponsor my son's application to join the organisation that bears his initials, and of which he was then chairman.

Many All Blacks, among them Wilson Whineray and Tremayne Rodd, consider C. M. H. (Mike) Gibson to be the best rugby player ever to emerge from the northern hemisphere. As one who considers the high point of an undistinguished rugby career (which, for the record, includes once playing at fly half when the scrum half was England's John Williams) to have been an impromptu passing session with the great man, I'm happy to add my vote.

Gibson was attired in a British Lions' tracksuit waiting for some colourful running shots when we had a problem with the camera. 'Come on,' he said. 'Can't stand around all day.' And away we went. Fortunately, there wasn't time for tackling practice, for he was a fly half who tackled hard. Or was he really a centre? That was the debate. For sure Carwyn James, the coach of the '71 Lions, who won in New Zealand, got the best out of him, a fact duly acknowledged.

The interview came at not an easy time for a solicitor who was a sporting icon in Ulster, especially as his elder brother was a leading judge. But it was a particularly pleasing time in the company of Mike and his wife Moira and their children, Jan and Collin. There were no photographs to capture those magic passes, but many a Christmas card since.

The Welshman was certainly born with music in his blood and poetry in his soul. Cliff Morgan thrilled as his country's fly half and inspired as a broadcaster both in front of and behind the camera and the microphone. In the programme which began and ended with his presentation of 'Sport on 4' (a chair I borrowed a couple of times) he waxed lyrical about rugby and about life. On commentary he said he enjoyed someone 'who threw a line across the pitch which tells you something you didn't know about'; and on players talked about 'the responsibility of those with talent, to those who watch, to set an example'. On both points I couldn't agree more.

26

Cue the Tram

When Jayne Torvill and Christopher Dean left the so-called 'amateur' circuit for further if different success following their Olympic and World double in 1984, competition between television stations resulted in the over-hyping – by ITV, I have to say – of British hopes. Karen Barber and Nicky Slater were unlucky to be contemporaries of T & D, and were promoted as their natural successors at world level. A little later their style might have been better received by the judges, and their Chaplin routine remains a favourite of mine.

Then came Joanne Conway. ITV supported her off the ice and exaggerated her performance on it. To be fair, so did some of the press corps; Howard Bass in the *Daily Express* wrote that it wasn't a question of 'if' but only 'when' she would win the world title. In Prague, for the European Championships of 1988, when I was standing in as commentator for Alan Weeks, I had to resist some pressure from an editor in London who, having read the morning papers felt I should build up Joanne's chances of winning a medal. She finished ninth. A rather more down-to-earth opinion came in that year's World Championships in Budapest. Doing a little extra work for Australia's Channel 7, I found myself having to respond to their presenter's introduction of Conway: 'Now, Barry, isn't this the Brit who always falls on her arse?' But that was as unfair to her as were the efforts of those who, in some cases for commercial reasons, wanted to push her to the top before she was ready.

Her best chance to establish herself came at the European Championships in Birmingham the following year, the start of a new Olympic cycle. Joanne was lying fifth after the short programme and came out for the free with the best wishes of all. Sadly, she gave a wretched performance, forgetting her programme and skating around as if she was in a dream. Robin Cousins, who had begun to help her, said she lacked bottle. It was a harsh assessment but was surely thrown down as a challenge to her to apply herself, conquer her nerves and fulfil the potential she undoubtedly had. But it backfired. Joanne's mother took exception, Robin ceased to be Joanne's coach, and she never achieved the success she hoped for but seemed unable to strive for.

Robin's namesake, though not a relation, Steven Cousins, didn't make it to the international rostrum, either, but he was always a genuine competitor who gave his all. The judges were sometimes a little hard on him. Knowing that he was struggling with the triple lutz, they tended to mark him down for his approach to the jump, even if he achieved it. There were others whose approach was every bit as long but who seemed not to suffer in quite the same way. He also had to work hard with his triple axel, but rarely pulled out of it. He had a charisma on the ice which certainly went down well with the girls, and now serves him equally well on the ice-show circuit. Steve kept the flag flying for a long time. He was always positive, even on a bad day, and was good to have around.

With Jim Reside and Alastair Scott as producers, the presentation of the skating programmes was always fun and often innovative. We tried to be a little informative and put the venue of each championship in context; and they never missed a chance to feature the local public transport. Trams, especially in Prague, were a particular favourite, cueing me to start as the tram made its move to be clearly in vision at the link's end. In Cincinnati, in 1987, it was the city's famous paddle steamers. In Budapest the following year I was dwarfed by the equestrian statue of Arpad, Hungary's founder in 907.

The opening links for all the programmes had to be done before the event began, with any adjustments needed made out of vision: 'one day's use of a hand-held camera', said the budget. The format caused a few problems from time to time, not least when ITV brought their full outside broadcast van on site. On one occasion Nick Owen's introduction had a backdrop of gently falling snow. On the BBC it was a sunny day!

At the European Championship of 1988 in Prague the opening link on the first day shot from the Charles Bridge over which the Czech King Charles I used to ride in his carriage in the fourteenth century – now, of course, with tram in middle distance – ended a little differently, because there was no Alan Weeks to introduce. The previous November a phone call from Jim to the sports room in Broadcasting House, where I was enjoying a spell as guest presenter of *Sport on Two* and *Sports Report* (an ambition achieved) brought the news that Alan had had a heart attack. Mercifully, it was a mild one, but he would be resting for three months in the hope of being fit for the Olympic Winter Games in Calgary. I would have to do the commentary in Prague. In any other circumstances I'd have said, 'No way,' but now there was no choice but to give it a go.

I spent hours watching tapes, including two very boring ones from the International Skating Union, trying to recognise the jumps – each, incidentally, named after the first skater to perform the move. The axel, the only one for which the take-off is forward; the loop, with take-off and landing on the same foot; the lutz, turning the opposite way to the shoulder angle of movement – too complicated. Then there were the edges: were they correct for take-off and landing? And what about the number of turns? And the lifts and thrown jumps in the pairs competition? It was a million miles from presenting and then listening to Alan.

I survived, mainly because of the help given me by a Norwegian lady called Marit Rasmussen, who had a small role with her country's association and had paid her own way to come to the championships. (I'm glad to say that working for the BBC eventually led her to a job with the ISU, so a favour gained was able to be returned.) She produced the skater's planned routine learned from hours of watching practice, often very early in the morning. The guide, just for me, was a sheet to which she pointed and which had all the jumps written out in one column with 'single', 'double' or 'triple' written in the next column and 'good', 'bad' or 'indifferent' in the third. Now it is called the Grade of Execution, and every skater is required to present his or her programme for the judges; it's then typed out and copied for the media. But the skater isn't required to stick to it, so it isn't quite as easy for the commentators as it may appear.

Strangely enough, and this was a sure sign of changing times, the only criticism Alan offered when I asked him was that he didn't believe I should have said when a planned triple jump became only a double. He said nothing about my criticism of the Hungarian judge, who, as I put it, 'appeared not to notice when the Hungarian ice dancers, Engi and Toth, fell right in front of her'. One of the better parts of the new judging system, which made its Olympic debut in Turin in 2006, is that any fall is now a mandatory one-point deduction.

Alan and I first met when he was the announcer at the Brighton ice rink. As a student, I was writing for *Ice Hockey World*; that sport, incidentally, was his first love and remained his greatest. He had a wonderful voice, and covered many sports for the BBC – not least, though it was often forgotten, football. He had presented *Grandstand* and introduced the programme that led on to blanket coverage of snooker, *Pot*

Black. But for a man of his quality and experience he was very insecure, and this led to his being rather protective of his position. It took me some time to convince him that I wasn't after his job – a concern which understandably resurfaced following his heart problem.

He was a creature of habit and could be upset by changes in his routine. My naming of the skater's music, which I thought a good idea, led him once to announce a couple as 'skating to a selection of music'. But that moment apart I'd like to think I was some support to him during that period and we – Alastair, Jim and I – eventually persuaded him that a glass of good red wine was, in spite of protests by a man who used to enjoy what he called 'a social occasion', just what the doctor ordered. I used to bully him about writing a book. He never did (I understand now how he felt about it), and sadly, having retired after the 1996 World Championships in Edmonton, he was allowed precious little time to enjoy it with his wife, Jane. His farewell to me at London airport after that trip to Canada proved to be just that, and I'm grateful that he chose the moment to say that he'd enjoyed working with me and wished me well as his successor.

Robin Cousins, Bristol-born like Alan, worked with him well before I became involved in their sport, and was alongside him in Sarajevo. The demands of *Holiday on Ice* and more recently ITV's *Dancing on Ice* (which, incidentally, I had to turn down) sometimes got in the way, but Robin has long been the BBC's regular expert. Although he hung up his boots a couple of years back, he's still very much involved in the world of skating and the theatre. His views are forthright and often passionate, qualities which promise to sharpen the blades of British skating – something much needed – with his appointment as honorary vice-president of the National Ice Skating Association. If you wish to debate an issue with him it's best to be well briefed, but he's fun to work with and his authority and contacts are everything you would expect from an Olympic champion.

Curiously, not since 1984 has the reigning men's world figure-skating champion become the Olympic champion. The Worlds are always the last competition of the skating year, so at the Olympics the world champion is of the previous year. In Cincinnati in 1987 the Canadian Brian Orser won the world title and established himself as the favourite to follow Scott Hamilton, of the United States, who held both titles when he retired after the Sarajevo games of 1984. But the pressure on the home skater in Calgary proved too much. Mistakes in the first two parts of the competition, the compulsory figures and the short programme, left him with too much to do in the free programme.

The figures survived till 1991, before being cast into history, a questionable decision for some as they were the basis of the sport – all the best still practise them – but good for the spectators and for television, which drove through the change. The remark of one onlooker watching the repeated patterns required in Calgary still makes me smile. 'Is that all there is?' he said to his wife. Clearly he expected rather more from being a part of 'the Olympic experience'. As for television there would no longer be the danger of a leading contender blowing his or her chance out of the camera's gaze. That it rarely happened owed much, I think, to the judges employing Horatio Nelson's principle. In Calgary, though, some of the figures were covered; not a pleasurable experience, as for much of those games I was battling with flu.

Skating producer Julie Griffiths, who has fought hard to keep the sport on BBC screens, has often bemoaned the fact that skating's musical repertoire is so limited when there is such choice available. At the risk of being a little cynical I might add that for many performers the music is simply background. Bizet's *Carmen* is one of the pieces most often used, and in the '88 Olympics choosing it probably ended the hopes of America's Debbie Thomas, for Katarina Witt, the defending champion, had made the same choice. At a time when the artistic mark in the free programme carried the greater weight, there could be only one outcome. The East German may not have been the greatest jumper the sport has known but for artistry she was in a different class. And, as was clear when she was interviewed by Sue Barker in Turin, she retains the looks and the charm, finely blended with a tinge of arrogance, that made her a star.

Katarina would have been pleased that her Olympic crown passed to another artistic skater when Kristi Yamaguchi won in Albertville four years later, but two of the judges preferred the free programme of a charming little (only four feet nine) lady whom I christened the 'Nagoya Jumping Bean'. Midori Ito had won the world title the year after Calgary, and in Munich in 1991 produced a wonderful and endearing 'What happened next?' moment. Leaving a jump too late, she hurdled the small barrier cut-out made for a low television camera, and disappeared down a corridor. Rushing back as fast as her little legs would carry her, she continued her programme to a huge ovation mixed with much hilarity.

The fact that the skater is giving a performance which requires artistic merit invites the criticism that it is not truly sport. But that argument is completely destroyed for me by the physical demands and bravery involved in filling four and a half minutes with jumps – including quadruples, these days – spins and other movements covering the full ice surface. Two things can, though, work against the sport ethic: the unnecessarily elaborate costumes of some male skaters – exacerbated by the fact that nowadays most are appearing in shows when they are not competing – and, more importantly, the suspicion that results are preordained. The new scoring system is designed to help prevent that, but there remains a reluctance to judge on the night, to allow someone to come out of the field to claim the crown.

27

Born in LA

The scene would have delighted that wonderful comedienne Joyce Grenfell; jolly hockey sticks everywhere. They were in the hands of all shapes and sizes of children of both sexes: some from the early years of the senior school, more from the preparatory and other schools in the area. It was a sunny autumn Sunday morning in 2001. Proud parents, having forgone the weekly lie-in, hugged the touchline to watch their offspring put through the coaching sessions. Two scratch teams integrating some senior pupils of Cranleigh School would entertain us.

A swift move down the left, pass, return, pass, return; defenders struggling, a shot just wide. The clock had been turned back to 1988: Imran Sherwani and Sean Kerly, with their captain then, Richard Dodds, and Richard Leman, were proving that class can beat the years. Leading the other team from the rear was a certain David Westcott, QC, and the left wing, formerly of the Foreign Office, now from the City, was one Mark Precious, whose day had come in Los Angeles in 1984.

Their presence here was a reminder that Great Britain's Olympic hockey triumph had been ten years in the making: preparations for Moscow '80, bronze in Los Angeles in '84, silver (for England) in the World Cup in London in '86, and Olympic gold in Seoul in '88.

Westcott had originally planned to retire after the 1980 Olympics, but that was the year when politicians decided to use sportsmen and -women as frontline troops. Margaret Thatcher followed the American president, Jimmy Carter, in seeking a boycott of the Games because of the Russian occupation of Afghanistan (a meaningless protest which looks even more stupid in the light of that country's history since then). Other governing bodies resisted but, regrettably, the Great Britain hockey board accepted the dictum from Number 10.

The players' get-together was organised by Steve Batchelor, whose run down the right wing and cross to Sherwani had produced the third goal of the Seoul final and left at least one watcher wondering 'Where were the Germans?' There have been several such happy reunions of hockey Olympians, and I have been delighted to be on the guest list.

When I first came across them, in LA in 1984, happiness was hardly the first word to come to mind. Welshman Bob Cattrall and England's Paul Barber briefly came to blows during a training session before the hockey media. The manager, Roger Self, was to learn four years later, when his side's status attracted the newshounds as well as the sports writers, how difficult such incidents can be. But for now it was just a passing moment which, I suggested, showed a quality of aggression which could be useful for his side, if controlled. Many a goal or point has been won on the back of irritation reaching temper, though too much and the reverse applies in increasing measure. Self knew it well, but seemed surprised at my observation.

The four journalistic musketeers of the game, Bill Colwill of the *Independent*, Sydney Friskin of *The Times*, Chris Moore of the *Telegraph* and Pat Rowley of the *Guardian* – all an enormous help to the BBC commentators – noted that the players selected for Moscow but made to stay at home had an extra urgency in what was, in fact, Britain's first participation in Olympic hockey since Munich in '72. And, ironically, they were only invited after the withdrawal of the Russians.

New Zealand, the last champions from a full Olympic tournament (Montreal, 1976), were the third victims of a run by Britain's 'unprepared reserve side', which arrived umbeaten in the semi-final. There waiting to meet them were West Germany, who had lost one match in their group, to Australia, the overwhelming favourites. In the three major tournaments in eight years those two countries would bar the way to a British triumph and only once would both be beaten. Now a loss to West Germany, by a solitary goal, in a double containment contest was followed by a backs-to-the-wall but stunning 3–2 win over Australia, whose expectation of gold had foundered on a disputed goal by Pakistan. As Bill Colwill put it in 'The Great Britain Story' in Hockey Digest, the team wanted to make a point about the selection mockery, and they did by winning bronze. It was just the start.

The sixth World Cup had been awarded to England because the Hockey Association, the oldest such body in the world, thought it would be the best way of celebrating its centenary. Only in the last twenty of those hundred years had the sport, at club level, abandoned its policy of playing only friendly matches. A county championship had been established in 1957, but leagues and a club cup competition arrived only as the sixties became the seventies. The administrators and the players were all still amateurs. Yet as early as 1971 an application was made to the world governing body, the FIH, to host the tournament, which ranks second only to the Olympic Games.

No venue had been proposed and one wasn't found until nine years later. Then, with other options still under consideration, Tarn Hodder, chairman of the HA's executive committee, announced that he had signed an agreement for the tournament to take place at the Willesden Recreation Centre in London NW10.

It was, to put it kindly, a surprising choice, and I have to confess that, when covering a match there between England and the USSR just one year before the World Cup, I found it an unbelievable one. It was a view not helped by a damp, grey afternoon, nor by the Russians playing in a not untypical, boringly defensive fashion, but the Centre was dull, dreary concrete with nothing to commend it.

A year later it had been transformed, and it offered ideas and a standard of presentation that future World Cups sought to emulate. For two weeks in 1986, in the most balmy English October anyone could remember, Willesden became the world centre of hockey, a sport which from every point of view was bathed in sunshine. It was, to borrow one of David Coleman's favourite expressions, 'quite remarkable'.

In the days and weeks leading up to the opening match Willesden was an oasis of endeavour in which many people had every right to take pride. But the success of the tournament owed most to the setting up of World Cup Hockey Ltd, a company independent of the Hockey Association; the chairmanship of a man whose playing skills had carried him no higher than the position of Third XI goalkeeper; and his ability to galvanise board members chosen for their varied areas of expertise.

Phil Appleyard was outwardly an avuncular figure, but he had vast international experience as a consultant in the fishery business and could, as one of his team remarked, be as hard as nails. The aim was a five-star event and he wouldn't take no for an answer. He was, said Roger Dakin, the communications and public relations director, 'absolutely brilliant at convincing people to do things'.

What John Wilmott, the stadium manager, did was very clever. He used the tournament's cartoon character, a top-hatted World Cup Willie, to mitigate what he called the 'horrible concrete'; and he built a carpeted scaffold staircase from the tented village to the pitch, which ensured a comfortable walk past all the commercial enterprises, the Century

Club and bars and restaurants. An extra stand was borrowed from the world of equestrianism. The public found a new sport, and the media found an operation, run by Jolyon Armstrong, which was prepared to consider its every need.

When the England players came in on a day off before the semi-final, each was presented with a note of his media appointments; it was for all of them suddenly a different world. (*Blue Peter*, though, withdrew their request for their presenter, Peter Duncan, to face a Sean Kerly penalty stroke when one of Sean's chips hit a strut of a groundsman's machine and left a noticeable dent.)

There are many behind-the-scenes tales to be told. The fire linings of the tents had to be replaced just forty-eight hours before the start when Brent Council insisted on setting its own standards. Wilmott's number two, Frank Taylor – a man very much of the old school – upon being told on the morning of the final that there were too many flies in the cooking area, replied, 'Oh? How many am I allowed?' One of the gas cylinders in the cooking area promptly blew up, and briefly the final was under threat. It was also Frank who liaised with the police over the design of the one-way traffic system – and was later booked for turning the wrong way. I don't know if he was responsible for the application to Brent Council for '10,000 black bin liners and seven spades'; back came the reply that they could only provide green bags and shovels – which were, of course, accepted.

Looking back, it seems almost that a script was written to ensure that both the hosts and the sport of hockey would make the most of it. Only on the last page did things go a little awry, when a storm hit north-west London on final night, perhaps to ensure that it wouldn't seem to have all been a sporting fairytale, a figment of the imagination, leaving anyone who returned to Willesden early the following week to wonder if it had ever happened.

The tournament began at high noon on a Saturday; facing the home side were New Zealand. Some 6,000 spectators found Willesden on the map, which was very good for a hockey match but not for a stadium which could house double that number. England had to win to get things off to a good start. They did, with Sean Kerly, the best-known hockey player in the country, scoring twice in their 3–1 victory. Jim Duthie, out of the squad because of a broken leg, was sitting beside me and had me hastily correcting my shout of 'Goal!' The ball had been too high. Covering hockey off-tube can be a nightmare if the camera doesn't capture the umpire's signal: close-ups of scorer or goalkeeper can lead the commentator astray. The ball hitting the backboard is a rule of thumb, so hearing that sound is helpful. We, though, were 'live' from a perch between the trees, with a commentary box on top of the World Cup Willie-branded scaffolding.

Come Monday, the press representation had grown. The papers were full of the fact that it was England *v* Argentina again, just three months after England's defeat in football's World Cup, and four years after the Falklands conflict. Only the hockey made good copy, with Imran Sherwani scoring the winning goal against an Argentine team who were made welcome – a crowd reaction very different from that in the Azteca stadium.

Wednesday produced a cold shower in the Indian summer, but Russia's defeat of England, disappointing though it was, gave extra urgency to the second Saturday meeting with Pakistan, whose supporters helped swell the crowd to capacity. It was necessary for England's second-best-known player, goalkeeper Ian Taylor, to show his quality, but victory in the end was comfortable. The semi-final place was assured two days later with a win over Holland. It should have been 2–0, the replay confirming the belief Jim and I had expressed that the umpire was wrong to give Kerly offside when seizing on a rebound from Paul Barber's penalty corner. (It's hard to believe, but it is now over ten years since umpires were relieved of that sort of problem, the no offside law being introduced, initially as an experiment, after the 1996 Atlanta Olympics.)

That result denied the previously unbeaten Dutch a place in the semi-final, because later that afternoon Russia beat Pakistan to take second place in Group A on goal difference. Australia headed Group B, scoring twenty-four goals in their five matches, with West Germany second. Every England success, and even the dip against Russia, brought an increase in the media's coverage; the BBC began scheduling previously unplanned daily highlights.

Now England faced Germany and though it was a semi-final, not a final, the media seized on a comparison with twenty years before at a somewhat more famous London stadium barely ten miles away. The similarities bordered on the uncanny. Again England had to play in red, with Germany in white; again there was a late equaliser to take the match into extra time with the score at 2–2; and, again, the hosts won. This time, though, the outcome was one goal fewer and the scoring sequence reversed.

England scored first, through Kerly, and then snatched a second chance from the jaws of defeat when Paul Barber, in an extraordinary, not to say thrilling, conclusion had a sequence of three penalty corners which went air shot, block (by Blocher!), goal. Early in the second half of extra time Barber, the man from Slough, provided another friendly bomb – just inside a post. That Germany hit an England post as the final hooter blew proves simply that it was not their day. For the BBC the momentous decision to go live and stay live, in spite of having their request for England's semi-final to be played second turned down, had been thoroughly vindicated. There was no 'Football Focus' in *Grandstand* that afternoon when, instead of Gordon Banks, Bobby Moore, Bobby Charlton and Geoff Hurst, the story of the day read 'Ian Taylor, Paul Barber, Richard Dodds and Sean Kerly' – another world-class backbone.

Come Sunday the weather had broken and so had the spell: at half-time England were 2–0 down against Australia, the best team in the competition. Jon Potter's goal – from speed of thought and action – gave new life to a spirited attempt at a comeback, and team and crowd alike glimpsed a repeat of twenty-four hours earlier. Alas, it was not to be, though Australia's coach, Richard Aggis, said afterwards that the last six minutes were the longest of his sporting life.

This time it was silver for England. But for ten of their players Olympic gold was to follow two years later, in Seoul in 1988.

28

The Substitute Who Wasn't

Q: When is a substitute not a substitute? A: When he's playing in Hannover in 1988.

It was a bizarre opening day of the European Football Championship. The initial problem was that Sepp Piontek, Denmark's coach, refused to allow the media to watch his last training session. How fearful some team bosses can be (perhaps he knew this would be the last hurrah for his gifted team). It shouldn't have made any difference to me, and I didn't believe it would. I knew most of his players, and also the Spaniards who would provide the opposition in this second match in Group One following the opening game, a 1–1 draw between West Germany and Italy.

The fact that the commentary position had room for only two seats, which were occupied by Jimmy Hill and me, leaving producer Mark Schofield hidden behind a large pillar, was a second irritation, but I was hoping for a good beginning to the tournament. Spain's two defeats of Denmark, by 6–1 in the Mexico World Cup, and 5–4 on penalties in the 1984 European Championships, gave them a psychological advantage.

There was a penalty now which should have given Spain a half-time lead, but Michel, whose goal in the fifth minute had been matched by the brilliance of Michael Laudrup twenty minutes later, offered over-confidence and under-force, allowing Rasmussen to parry the ball for a corner. I felt justice had been done, believing that Michel had looked for the challenge by Sivebaek, and I said so. Jimmy Hill agreed. But at half-time the studio panel said they didn't know what we were talking about, claiming that it was clearly a penalty. At the time I was doing a report for radio, but Jimmy heard the studio and wasn't best pleased. Over the talk-back I asked John Phillips, the editor in London, what had been said. His response was to tell me I should have been listening, rather than making a bit of extra money working for radio. I protested that I was only doing as instructed and wasn't being paid, but by now the teams were on their way out and there was no time for further discussion before Des Lynam linked back to me.

The second half began, and I soon became aware that Denmark had made two substitutions because there were numbers 12 and 13 on the pitch, Lars Olsen and John Jensen. I soon spotted that Jensen was replacing Helt but couldn't fathom who had gone off for Olsen, and neither, bobbing backwards and forwards round the pillar, headphones off and on, could Mark. I was also less than convinced that the new 'other man' actually was Lars Olsen. Jimmy's mind was still on the penalty incident.

In the BBC's Dusseldorf headquarters for the championship, they were aware of the problem and among those watching the match was John Motson. He kindly offered four suggestions but quickly corrected himself on each as the supposed missing player came into view. Eventually, after what seemed an eternity, I worked it out; only the shirt had changed, not the player. John Sivebaek, once of Manchester United, had simply picked up the wrong number. Twenty minutes into the second half Lars Olsen did arrive, replacing the captain Morten Olsen, who was suffering from blurred vision. He wasn't the only one.

Spain won again, 3–2, and were better than the score suggested. At the end Jimmy, trying to console me, wondered aloud whether anyone watching would have noticed the confusion. Mark left me be, and I walked back to the hotel alone. (These days the fourth official's board, though it can be a pain to work, makes it much easier, but the golden rule is to check as the players return for the second half and not to be distracted by *anything* else.)

An hour later Mark and I were on our way to Stuttgart for the next day's match, between England and Ireland. We had earlier agreed that I'd take the first driving stint of the longest journey between venues at the tournament. So Mark's debut driving an automatic, a very comfortable Mercedes, was delayed until it had just started to rain, which, on German autobahns, has always seemed to me to be the cue for increasing speed. Nearing our destination, with me back in the driving seat, the rain was torrential and the visibility barely ten yards. But in the early hours of a Sunday morning there wasn't much traffic around and, knowing the Graf Zeppelin hotel well, I drove directly towards the underground car park, passing the attendant in his glass booth. He immediately closed the gate, forcing me to reverse quickly. We signalled to him that we were late-arriving guests, and tried again; only to find the gate once more closing on us.

After such a day I had something of a humour bypass and marched into reception, demanding, rather than asking, that the receptionist sort things out. 'What man in the booth?' he asked. I ushered him to the door and showed him. He looked perplexed and went back to the desk, returning with keys. The fault with the gate had nothing to do with the drunken Irishman who had somehow locked himself inside the booth and was now showering us with thanks, literally as well as metaphorically, before wandering off into the night, presumably in search of further refreshment to celebrate his escape. I was still laughing when I fell into bed: a ridiculous end to an arduous day. After about four hours' sleep I was awoken by the early-bird editor, Bob Abrahams, who rang to commiserate with me about the substitute who wasn't.

The state the grateful Irishman was in the following evening isn't hard to imagine, after Ray Houghton's well-placed header had proved enough to beat England. It was one of those days for Bobby Robson's men. They had chance enough to save the day in a one-sided second half, the future *Match of the Day* presenter fluffing his lines more than once.

He wasn't alone. It proved to be the start of the Irish fairytale that took them to a draw against the eventual runners-up – Ronnie Whelan hitting a magnificent 25-yard curler – and almost another against the winners, Holland; and two years on, to an audience with the Pope in Rome.

For England, Holland came next: a much-improved performance with Hoddle restored to the starting line-up, but a second defeat through Marco van Basten's hat trick. The referee might have stopped the move that led to his first goal for a foul on Lineker, and the second was possibly offside – certainly the England defence thought so – but Holland, coached by the man who had come so close to winning the World Cup fourteen years earlier, Rinus Michels, were the best side in the championship and proved it in the final against Russia, where van Basten scored a screamer.

England, already out after the two defeats, lost their third match to Russia, giving what the captain, Bryan Robson, later agreed with me was the worst performance in a competitive match of his England career. His explanation of why a side of much talent failed so miserably centred on the absence of the injured Terry Butcher at the heart of the England defence, and on the belief that Peter Beardsley and John Barnes had given too much in leading Liverpool to the Championship and the Cup final, a pressure neither had previously experienced. He added, 'Many players you expect a lot from weren't a hundred per cent fit.' Injuries, and players not at their best – a recurring theme for England managers and one to be updated with an added twist on the return to Germany eighteen years later.

29

But Frankly, Who Cares?

'Just look at his face' was a 1974 football commentary line of mine, when Franny Lee scored for his new club, Derby County, against his old one, Manchester City, at Maine Road. It applied equally well, fourteen years later, to a different player, in a different sport, on a sunny afternoon in Seoul, South Korea.

I was drawn to this face as I walked around the Olympic hockey stadium. In their semi-final, after being in sight of victory and a place in the final, Great Britain had been hauled back by Australia, for whom Neil Hawgood had equalised to level the match at 2–2. Extra time 'loomed' – a favourite expression of commentators – and to use an original definition it now had for GB a threatening shape.

If they lost, I selfishly thought, the final I'd be commentating on would be 'nothing'. I should have been in the seat for this semi-final – but then Nigel Starmer-Smith, who was, can rightly claim (and did so at the time) that he should have covered the final. He had, after all, followed the team all through its somewhat tortuous journey to this stage. However, before the Games began, Jonathan Martin, the BBC's head of sport, had decreed that Nigel must return home after the semi-final because he was needed for *Rugby Special*. The gymnastics over and the Olympic football not clashing, Davies would take over. Jonathan didn't know how tough a call that would prove to be.

I'd covered all the matches of the 1986 World Cup at Willesden and most internationals since then and I think that, had hockey been consulted, I'd have won the vote. But pragmatism, not favouritism, was the issue here. Jonathan, though, showed a sensitivity he usually sought to hide from his public demeanour on such an occasion by asking me if, contrary to arrangements, I would cover the lesser semi-final. I believe that I had a right to decline, but how could I? Having argued that Nigel and I should have shared the World Cup, I had every sympathy for his position.

So West Germany *v* Holland was mine; GB *v* Australia was Nigel's; and it was going wrong for both of us.

But 'the face' was not about to let that happen. Its expression combined irritation and determination. No despair, just a burning desire to win the day and a fierce belief that the decision lay in his hands. Whether the deal had been struck with the Almighty or the Devil, Sean Kerly was going to succeed. He admitted afterwards to an obscenity-supported shout of 'Don't you lot want to win?' and a brief let-down which allowed Warren Birmingham, Australia's centre half, to go round him 'for the first time in the match'. And he claimed that his motivation was the thought of extra time: 'There was no way – I was completely knackered.' There was a further test of character as the marrying of pace and inspiration was denied by the ball cruelly bouncing the wrong way past the unguarded far post.

Then, with three minutes left, came the winning goal, one which the team's manager, Roger Self, later claimed no one but Kerly could have scored. 'Only he would have had the optimism, the strength, the sheer balls of determination.' Richard Dodds's pass in the circle to Kulbir Bhaura was, as Self put it, 'doglegged' by the recipient. But at full stretch from further away than the goalkeeper or Bhaura, Kerly pounced for his hat trick. The smile on 'the face' meant that GB would play for gold and I would have the privilege of being there.

1 October 1988 was a red-letter day in the history of British hockey and the ultimate triumph of what the captain, Richard Dodds, eloquently described as 'a unity of purpose and mutual self-belief'. Britain beat West Germany 3–1 in Seoul, to become Olympic champions.

'The effort which has gone into this triumph has been quite tremendous, from the management team down to every member of the squad' was my observation after the final whistle, and my summary of their success, if you'll forgive me a small pat on my own back, would not, I think, have benefited much from more time for consideration – and there are few occasions about which I could say that.

'They started slowly [taking only a point from the first match against Korea after being two goals up]; gave us moments of doubt [losing in the last minute to the Germans through a penalty stroke awarded, harshly, but by the letter of the law correctly, for high sticks by Paul Barber]; in the semi-final lived a little on the dramatic side; and in the final were hugely disciplined.'

That last comment was supported by the winning coach, David Whitaker, when we put together *Hockey's Golden Year* for Christmas-time transmission. The 'we' included the VT editor and my producer then and for all the hockey in Seoul, Alan Griffiths, who still blanches at the bill he had to put in for an evening's celebration with the squad after their place in the final was won. 'We were determined that we were going to dictate the final,' Whitaker said. 'We were as patient as they were, perhaps even more. We made them chase us.'

Sean Kerly, who scored five goals in the tournament, spoke of his 'massive relief'; of feeling a bit sorry for the Germans [they'd lost in the final four years earlier as well]; and of his amazement, even three months later, at the huge number of people who had set their alarms for 6am on a Saturday to watch the television coverage, many of them having never watched hockey before. Ian Taylor talked about 'pride, patriotism, lots of Union Jacks, "God Save the Queen" – I love all that sort of thing – and the fifteen chaps who stood with me on the rostrum.' Paul Barber spoke of the greater satisfaction of being successful as a part-time sportsman: 'You lose the guys who'd be hanging around because of the kudos in it.' He, like Taylor and the quietly authoritative skipper,

Richard Dodds, now an orthopaedic surgeon, retired after the Games.

Not so the two-goal hero of the final, Imran Sherwani, who had missed the '84 Olympics through injury, and who later referred to the reward 'for all those puke-making runs up Trentham Hill [near Stoke on Trent, where his father ran a newsagent's], and knowing that we couldn't have done any better'. In the immediate post-match euphoria Richard Leman and Jimmy Kirkwood put it rather more simply; their chant was, 'We gave them a bloody good hiding.' Presumably they meant the West Germans, but it applied to everyone else, too, for as I said in commentary – more than once, I have to admit – GB were on top of the world of hockey.

It was Sherwani's second goal, making the game safe at 3–0, which led to the title of this chapter. Having recapped the detail of Stephen Batchelor's dashing run down the right, the cross that matched it, and the clinical finish, I found myself wondering what had happened to the German defence. So I said, 'Where were the Germans?' But then I thought: Who gives a damn where the Germans were? – we're going to win now. So I continued, 'But frankly, who cares?' It wasn't until I was back in England that I found what a stir the line had caused. The commentary was used at the start of a commemorative disc to mark the team's success, and people have been very generous about it ever since. In a small way, perhaps it helped viewers at home to share the feelings of those who were there in the Sognam stadium, Seoul, South Korea that warm October afternoon. As Whitaker put it, 'It was a moment encapsulated in my life that will never disappear.'

The post-match scenes and the television coverage of them were more than a little chaotic. While the host broadcaster continued to offer pictures, back at the broadcast centre the producer was augmenting them by cutting in shots from the BBC's hand-held camera. During that time, as wives, sweethearts and friends joined the players on the running track surrounding the pitch, there was a danger that, unable to see those shots until the Korean transmission finished, I'd suggest a few incorrect partnerships. 'I'd never have heard the end of it from Nigel [Starmer-Smith]' was my first comment as we moved into recorded mode for later programmes.

Then I acquired a new role as a secondary director, leading the camera crew to possible interviews. 'Go right – the grey-haired dapper-looking man, that's Phil Appleyard, the president of the Hockey Association.' He said something about taking hockey to a new dimension in the UK. The diminutive Colin Moynihan, a former rowing cox who was now the minister for sport, and who had needed all his powers of persuasion to convince a security man that he was indeed a VIP, was promptly lifted into the air by Richard Leman, briefly belying Moynihan's nickname of 'the Minister for Short'. Around Princess Anne there was rather more decorum, but her understanding and enjoyment of the situation was clear and her conversations with the team many and unhurried.

'Quick!' I cried. 'The wives are sitting on the medal rostrum.' And so it went on until Tony Gubba took over for more formal interviews. It is hard to recall a victory which was more enjoyed – even the Korean bow was included – and the rapport with their supporters was very much a family feeling. It was in many respects the best day of my commentary career.

Nineteen years on, if you asked the proverbial man in the street to name a hockey player, the answer would probably be still Sean Kerly or Ian Taylor. That is of course a tribute to two great players, but it also points up the decline in British hockey that followed Olympic gold (quite as bad as English rugby's collapse after winning the World Cup, or the 2006–7 Ashes whitewash after victory in 2005). At one point, the Hockey Association very nearly went bankrupt.

A deal of hard work and much politicking promises to bring a revival. A greatly simplified performance structure (I won't go into the details of the previous arcane procedure) ensures continuity of direction and coaching and will allow preparation over the four-year Olympic cycle and not just the final year, while still accommodating the needs of the separate national associations. In addition heroes of 1988 are in positions of power: David Faulkner is the performance director for both England and GB and Richard Leman is the new president of GB Hockey Ltd, as well as being on the executive board of the BOA.

Women's hockey has offered many interesting contests and some fine players in our national colours, but it also gave me probably my most uncomfortable afternoon in the commentary box. It was supposed to be a celebration match for the Typhoo Tea Trophy, following the GB women's bronze medal success in the 1992 Barcelona Olympics, and we were live into *Grandstand*. But the Birmingham rain came down in torrents, and players I knew well became strangers barely identifiable by their numbers. Vicky Dixon, Kath Johnson, Sandy Lister, Mandy Nicholls and company were a bedraggled bunch. I had never before appreciated how different women can look with soaking hair; even the copper-haired Jane Sixsmith was lost in the flood in the second half (fortunately she'd scored the only goal just on the stroke of half-time and Spain, the new Olympic champions, could find no reply). The only memorable moment of a miserable afternoon – save, of course, for the result – came when Jenny Cardwell, the England manager, arrived at the post-match press conference and announced, 'I shan't sit down – my knickers are soaking.'

After Barcelona, the team had little success, even failing to qualify for the 2004 Athens Games. But in Manchester last August a bronze medal in the European Championship brought qualification for the 2008 Olympics. Youth is on the march, and Danny Kerry, the England and GB women's coach, was very upbeat when we chatted about the future, and he has a jewel in Christa Cullen.

At the hockey writers' awards lunch in January 2008, Kate Walsh, the ladies' captain and 2007 player of the year, looked forward with confidence to Beijing. In contrast Barry Middleton, the men's winner, could only contemplate the difficult six-nation qualifying tournament in Chile – the result of collective failure to take scoring chances in Manchester. Any thoughts of marking the twentieth anniversary of Seoul were at best fanciful. But table conversation with Leman and his later speech of an 'exciting future' – seen in the eyes of the youth winners, Sophie Bray and Liam Doige – made clear GB's aim to be right there in London 2012.

30

Learning from My Children: Gymnastics

It's common for children to develop interests learned from their parents and – when it comes to lots of travel, courtesy of opportunities afforded by their air stewardess mother, sport and the desire to avoid jobs with 9–5 hours – that applies in full measure to my two. Much less common is for the father to follow the children, but I've commentated on two sports as a direct result of my children's participation, and have often been much in their debt.

The first was gymnastics, and my involvement began in 1987 when the publication of the programme for the following year's Olympic Games in Seoul made it clear that the BBC would have to augment its gymnastics team, as Ron Pickering (who of course would be covering athletics) and Alan Weeks (swimming) would otherwise have to be in two places at once. Jonathan Martin wanted me to fill the gap, a selection based on my daughter's success as a gymnast. At the age of ten Giselle was the Southern Area and Berkshire champion, and she later captained her school to victory in the National School Championships before, while at Cambridge, gaining a half-Blue in the contest against Oxford.

Certainly I had inside knowledge of the sport: the angst as back-flips were attempted on the beam, and the hours Penny and I spent choreographing floor routines (furniture pushed to the walls in the living room). I'd also learned something of the politics of the sport because I could hardly refuse the request to become chairman of the county association. But to be press-ganged into commentating was a very different thing.

'I want you to go with the team to Rotterdam to observe the World Championships,' said Jonathan. I was reluctant, not least because it took me out of the football scene, but he was most persuasive, selling gymnastics as one of the top four Olympic sports in television terms – which, post-Olga Korbut in the 1972 Munich Games, was probably true. Eventually it was agreed that I'd go, not for the whole week as he wanted but for one day. I chose one filled by the men's competition because, while I could appreciate the elegant artistry, not to say skill and daring, of the women, I thought, quite frankly, that the men would bore me to tears. I had none of Ron's fascination with weight ratios and geometric movement and, being something of a Slim Jim and of average height, I felt somewhat inferior when faced by these pocket battleships whose forearm measurements would have embarrassed my biceps.

When I arrived, the competition was well under way. I stood at the back of the commentary box feeling a bit of an interloper, even though I'd worked with three of the team in other sports – the producer, Johnnie Watherston on tennis, Alan Weeks on skating and Ron Pickering on athletics – and of course I'd heard both commentators on gymnastics at four Olympics.

I hoped they'd been told I was coming and, more importantly, why. Ten years earlier, in Dusseldorf, Ron had had to put up with me doing rather more events than he'd expected, at the athletics World Cup, and Alan was still a little defensive of his position as skating commentator. The fourth member of the team, Mitch Fenner, I'd met at the Los Angeles Olympics in 1984. He'd been a British national coach at various World, European and Commonwealth Championships, and I recalled him telling me that his club, Bush Harlow, had been British champions eight years on the bounce. If I was to be involved in Seoul, he, it became clear, would be crucial.

At a lower level I was used to observing four events simultaneously in women's gymnastics. With the men there were six. I watched with interest but at first without enthusiasm. Mitch later recalled that I had the air of someone who had been told to be there rather than one who wanted to be. Actually, I think it was more that I was working out how much there would be to learn and whether I'd be able to cope. But by the evening I was rather regretting that I'd have to leave the next day. Over dinner I found myself asking lots of questions about the competition, which was dominated by Eastern Europe, and in particular about the performance of the youngest Russian, Dimitri Bilozerchev, who by beating his two compatriots in Rotterdam established himself as a favourite for the all-round individual Olympic title. He was a showman as well as a gymnast.

During a break in the competition I chatted to Mitch about his role in the team. At times he seemed to be giving something like a running commentary, which was fed into Ron's and Alan's earphones, and they used the information as required. It worked well except that, if they needed his prompt before identifying a move, the commentary was inevitably a fraction behind.

I was still at the 'maybe' stage when Johnnie asked me at breakfast the next morning what I thought. But of one thing I was certain, and I told him. If I was to work in Seoul, I couldn't operate under the system used here in Rotterdam. If Mitch had so much to offer, why wasn't somebody teaching him about commentary? That afternoon, while I was making my way back to the world of football, he was given the proper microphone during a part of the competition which wouldn't be included in the evening's edited version.

I'd said to him the previous day, 'If I say yes, we'll do a deal: you teach me about your sport and I'll help you to become a broadcaster.' And so it has been through six Olympiads; with Christine Still, another coach, joining us from the time the World Championships came to Birmingham in 1993. Where would I have been without their explanations of the seemingly ever-changing gymnastics code?

To prepare for Seoul Mitch and I had one stint together the following March, covering the American trials off a monitor – for the archive only. Seoul itself was everything we could have hoped for.

As we approached the arena on the first day we were walking in the road – there wasn't a vehicle in sight. 'Sidewalk, sidewalk,' shouted one of the students employed as helpers. We obeyed but I went up to him and tried to explain that the English word was 'pavement'. Every day of the competition we tried to teach each other a few words of our respective languages. A short while after the Games, student riots in the South Korean capital were put down in brutal fashion. Before the riots we'd sent and received photographs of our commentary team. After them I heard no more.

The Soviet Union dominated the men's competition, winning five of the eight gold medals, but the overall champion was not the favourite but another Russian, Vladimir Artemov, who quietly went about his business while the story of the flamboyant Bilozerchev was of a swing too far on the high bar and therefore only bronze. I thought the silver medallist, Valeri Liukin, was the best, though I said so only off-mike. It's interesting to note that the gold medallist's son and the silver medallist's daughter may well both be competing in the Beijing Olympics – for the USA.

The women's individual all-round competition in Seoul was one of the highlights of the entire Games: a drama of expressions off and expertise on the apparatus, the former only slightly less important than the latter in telling the story. It was a challenge to find the right words and a challenge to say nothing. In the end the title went to Elena Shushunova of the Soviet Union by 0.025 of a mark over Daniela Silivas of Romania. Silivas, having completed her floor routine, had to wait, hardly daring to watch, while Shushunova, sitting opposite her across the floor, tried to keep her nerves in check before being the last to vault.

Silivas won three of the four apparatus finals, adding further glory to her perfect scores in the team and all-round competition, but I doubt if they were much consolation. My imperfect summary, trying to match the pictures at the end of an epic sporting struggle, came out like this: 'Shushunova is the Olympic champion. In the end they had six tens apiece, but only one will go away with the gold. Put yourselves in their position. The winner is nineteen years old; the loser eighteen; tears of joy, and a face of disappointment at the other end of the arena.'

On the advice – not to say demand – of Mr Fenner, I have to include here the moment when my love affair with gymnastics nearly came to a speedy and fractious end. At the next major championships after the Olympics, the Europeans in Stockholm, it was decided that the gymnasts would warm up behind a curtain at the end of the arena, perform, and then return whence they came. Gone was the march round at the end of each rotation, gone were the moments of tension – the practice move that failed, the wait to mount the podium, the congratulatory slaps and sympathetic pats. Instead it was what I described, with reference and apologies to David Niven, as a case of 'Bring on the empty horses'.

'On . . . routine . . . off': where would the drama of Seoul have been had it been presented like that? Silivas would have been out of sight after her floor routine. Shushunova would have appeared from the darkness to compete last. Where is sport without the agony and the ecstasy? Nowhere. It is the only time in my career that I've thrown a tantrum. I ripped the headphones from my balding pate and hurled them on to the desk in front of me, sending the beautifully prepared chart of information flying. I said to Mitch, 'If this is where your sport's going, I want no part of it.' Martin Webster, our producer, looked on in disbelief: could this really be Davies? I recovered my composure but protested strongly to the Swedish producer in the break, only to be told that it was what television had asked for. Madness! No commentator would admit that it was his company's idea, but when have authorities ever consulted the troops at the front? Regrettably, the gymnasts still warm up out of sight, but at least once they've competed they stay around. Sport is about human endeavour but also about human feelings. Television needs them both.

The four Olympics since Seoul have offered increasing difficulty and many fine champions; and one record which will probably never be surpassed: Vitaly Scherbo's six gold medals in Barcelona in 1992. But only the women's team competition in Atlanta has come close to matching the drama of my first foray into the sport. The American audience's enthusiasm played a big part, but what NBC later presented as the decisive second vault by Kerri Strug, brave though she certainly was after falling on her first and injuring herself, actually didn't matter, because the United States had already built a sufficient team score to beat the Russians. (The network's desire not to let the facts spoil a good story was later worth a fortune to Strug on the celebrity circuit.)

Regrettably, the World and European Championships on which I've commentated since then have mostly been covered off-tube. It is by no means the most difficult sport to commentate that way, but there's no opportunity for an overall view of the competition.

At the *Sports Review of 1991* a gymnast from North Korea, Kim Gwang Suk, was invited to confirm her expertise on the asymmetric bars, on which she'd won the gold medal in that year's World Championship in Indianapolis, which we had covered from London. I was shocked when I saw her in the flesh at Television Centre. She looked no more than thirteen, in contrast to the age of sixteen she was 'given' and the image presented on the monitor. It certainly did nothing for the sport. The North Koreans were subsequently suspended.

In Beijing I trust the bars will offer everything that is best for gymnastics and for Britain. Beth Tweddle has been a gutsy and determined competitor for a good few years, overcoming injuries and disappointments to achieve a remarkable hat trick in 2006: world champion, World Cup champion and European champion on bars. The Chinese are certain to offer keen competition in Beijing, but I'd dearly like to see Beth join the list of Olympic champions on her favourite apparatus. It includes the great Russian gymnast Svetlana Khorkina, who won twice, Nadia Comaneci of Romania and, in 1988, Daniela Silivas.

The 1990s

'The need to gamble on a margin of one foot'

'Sue, do you think we could have three interviews this time?'

'Collectively they were short of being a great side, but they had one player touched with genius'

'All the lads and lasses are here, and all the smiling and painted faces, all hoping that the summer carnival will continue'

31

'Nessun dorma'

In terms of quality of football, Italia '90 wasn't a great World Cup. But the atmosphere in the country, where the game is important to all strata of society, was wonderful, and the tournament had enough moments to ensure that none should sleep – until the final, that is, which was a nightmare wide awake. The BBC's choice of signature tune was inspired, though whether the source was Brian Barwick, Desmond Lynam or Gerald Sinstadt (an opera buff) remained unproven. But the voice surely offered the definitive version of 'Nessun dorma' from Puccini's *Turandot*. Regrettably for the Italians, the golden disc for Luciano Pavarotti was the only trophy they won.

Of the three World Cup opening matches I covered, this one in Milan was the most dramatic. The preceding opening ceremony included a catwalk with models displaying the wares of many of the famous Italian fashion houses ('I can't understand why your voice isn't trembling,' said Jim Reside over the talk-back circuit). The match was nowhere near as beautiful, but was absorbing and historic, with the holders, Argentina, losing to an African nation. Some of the tackling by Cameroon's players was crude and often calculated. Maradona, whistled by the crowd because of his Naples connection, was the early target. Later they gave Caniggia, a half-time substitute, plenty of opportunity to show his skills as a hurdler as well as a footballer. And they finished the match with only nine men, Kana Biyik and Massing both having been sent off for lunges at Caniggia, the latter succeeding where two others had failed in the Argentine's thirty-yard run. And the goal was a mess from the champions' viewpoint, as both Sensini and the goalkeeper, Pumpido, failed to prevent Omam Biyik's header. Even so, the victory was well merited and the man who became their star, Roger Milla, who was said to be nearly forty, only appeared for the last eight minutes.

My other matches in the opening round included another tale of woe for Scotland – when will they ever end? – this time at the hands of a Bora Milutinovic-inspired Costa Rica. Only Mo Johnston looked like scoring, and their defence was split apart by Marchena's diagonal run and a back heel which set up Cayasso. The Scots recovered a bit of their dignity with the defeat of Sweden, but lost, by the only goal, to Brazil late in the day, when they felt they had done enough for the needed draw. Brazil weren't a good side, though in their match against Sweden I had difficulty convincing Bobby Charlton of that. I felt the Swedes were giving them too much respect, and was a little irritated by it. But Bobby was still seeing the yellow shirts of other days, and I found it a very difficult commentary. They finished top of the group with maximum points, but then fell to Caniggia's goal in the second round.

The Germans began with a rush of goals, four against Yugoslavia and then five against the United Arab Emirates. I saw the second match and I think most of the six goals – Khalid Ismail Mubarak scored one for the UAE – but I did so from four different commentary positions. The San Siro stadium was hit by a storm and the expensive new roof proved no defence. We were first sitting in water and then walking in water, at every new position recapping what had happened and commentating on goals as I recalled them – some of them scored while we were off on our travels. It certainly had its funny side, like some Whitehall farce, but I was lucky as the match was only recorded for the BBC. Poor Brian Moore was live for ITV. At least nobody was electrocuted.

The three German players of Internazionale – the forceful Lothar Matthaus, the captain, the blond striker and some-time diver Jurgen Klinsmann, and Andreas Brehme – were enjoying themselves on their home club soil. The left-sided Brehme, the least vaunted of the trio, was, I believe, crucial to the balance of the side; nominally a full back, he timed his injections as an attacker with great skill. I saw the Germans' last group match as well, when Colombia deservedly held the side that had already qualified. But I caught only edits of a close encounter with the Czechs and the fiery quarter-final against Holland, which Brehme missed through suspension. Although they went on, when he returned, to ultimate victory, when the full back scored the decisive penalty, the Germans were never again quite the side of that opening phase.

I caught up with England for their last group match against Egypt, won by Mark Wright's head from Paul Gascoigne's free kick; and memorable for only two thoughts. The first is how close Gascoigne came to missing the trip. I commentated on the match at Wembley against Czechoslovakia in April when he starred, being involved in three goals in a 4–2 victory. I'm convinced Bobby Robson chose him to get the media off his back, only to find the jewel was genuine; 'daft as a brush' though he was. How sad it would have been if such a great talent had never played in the finals of a World Cup, for this proved to be his only chance.

The second thought had to do with the England supporters' banners. There was one from a place I'd never heard of and I said so, adding, 'But I'm sure someone will soon ring in to let me know.' And they did. It belonged to a soap. Sitting about six places down from my position at the front of the main stand in Cagliari was the BBC's director-general, Michael Checkland, a man who steered a steadier ship than any of his successors to date. 'Is it ours, or theirs?' I shouted. 'Ours,' he replied: so I made known my newfound intelligence.

I saw Bobby's men next in Naples, having between times rolled my tonsils around the new Italian boy, 'Toto' Schillaci, and seen Dragan Stojkovic, one of my favourite players, score the goals that beat Spain – his first, switching feet and swaying wide of his marker in one silky movement before beating Zubizarreta. To be frank England should have been beaten by Cameroon in their quarter-final. David Platt, the hero of the previous match with a spectacular last-second goal against Belgium, gave England the lead after twenty-five minutes. But defensive frailties, greatly increased by the arrival of Roger Milla for the second half, led to the Africans scoring twice in four minutes just before the hour – a penalty, following Gascoigne's trip on the amazing wiggly, wily and wiry Milla, and a drive by a second new arrival, Ekeke. I felt England had hit the end of the road and 'would not come back no more', and said that Cameroon deserved their position. But two reckless challenges and the nerve of the penalty taker combined to find an escape route to the semi-final – Gary Lineker scoring with eight minutes left of the ninety and then again in the fifteenth minute of extra time.

It was an extraordinary match, which for BBC television had an extraordinary start. Forced without warning to do an unscripted trail shortly before the World Cup programme went on air, Desmond Lynam lost his way in his introduction. Standing close by I couldn't believe it and neither could anyone else. What help he got on talk-back served only to inhibit him, for seeing the opening sequence for the first time he'd already ad-libbed some of the words that came later on the typed script. With great style he simply admitted he'd forgotten where he was going and finally, in his ear, he was given guidance. In his autobiography, *I Should Have Been at Work*, he makes no mention of the trail: to his credit, not wanting to offer it as an excuse.

He put it out of his mind until the match was over and then delivered off-camera the brilliant line, 'See Naples and dry.' But he was devastated by the moment and I think it stayed with him. Rarely again did he wander too far from the comfort of his studio. Even six years later, when he was offered an admittedly small studio in the noise of the Olympic stadium in Atlanta, he refused to use it and was allowed instead to present from the greater calm of the broadcast centre. And in 1998 he stayed 'at home' in the expensive studio overlooking the Place de la Concorde, never stepping out into the square or the Champs Elysées.

Two days later I was back in Naples for the first semi-final, where the more usual version of the famous line would apply to Italy. We left early, as Bobby Charlton wanted to see Monte Cassino where some of his father's friends had died in the crucial battle of the Second World War. Unfortunately, the monastery was closed. Bobby insisted on paying for lunch.

Italy led after seventeen minutes with Schillaci finishing a move he'd started, but it all ended in tears. In the second half they became increasingly concerned with protecting their position against an Argentine side which, for the first time in the tournament, resembled the defending champions they were. Having led for an hour, Italy conceded their first goal in the competition, Zenga failing to reach the ball before the blond head of Caniggia. Roberto Baggio had been left out of the starting line-up, being replaced by Gianluca Vialli, but the coach, Azeglio Vicini, now reverted to the attacking partnership that had served Italy well in the three previous matches. To do so, to my amazement he removed his most creative player, Giannini. Much debate followed later over both deci-sions, as well as the absence of Ancelotti. The coach, however, could not be blamed for the failure of Donadoni and Serena to beat the inspired Goycochea in the penalty competition, which made the city that night feel as though it was under curfew. The local team's star, Maradona, led Argentina to the final again, but they were without four suspended players, including Giusti, who had been sent off in extra time, and Caniggia, who had collected a second yellow card in the second stage of the competition – for handball!

The following evening I watched England's semi-final against Germany, played in Turin, on television in the broad-cast centre in Rome. I did so with the feelings of a fan, a patriot and the personally disappointed – press speculation that the concluding matches of Italia '90 would be mine proved incorrect. I'm convinced that England was the better side on the night and would certainly have won the final. At least I had a pretty good idea, when I commentated in Bari, of how the two teams felt in the third-place match. It was notable for Schillaci's sixth goal in the competition, a penalty to add to Baggio's earlier score, and the last of a hundred and twenty-five caps for the brilliant Peter Shilton.

32

A Question of Authority

Arriving in Rome during the group stage of the 1990 World Cup I bumped into Lawrie McMenemy, who was doing some work for Sky News and TV-am. He looked rather lost, and it seemed a shame that he wasn't more involved in the game. We went back a long way, and it was arguably in an interview with me that his career as a knowledgeable and often very amusing pundit was launched. He was manager of Grimsby Town then, and *Match of the Day* covered their away match against John Bond's Bournemouth at Dean Court. The two appeared together afterwards – something which wouldn't happen with today's managers – and Lawrie conceded that Bond's team hadn't had much luck; observing that if John felt like throwing himself off the pier the tide would be out.

Lawrie covered four World Cups for the BBC, and during

that time I got to know him and his family quite well. We worked together in the '77 European Cup final in the 'Eternal City' and when a boys' football club I helped in Northampton decided to surprise me with a *This is Your Life* he was kind enough to make the journey up from Southampton to appear as a surprise guest. At the high point of his managerial career I was the reporter at his team hotel, Selsdon Park in Croydon, before Southampton beat Manchester United. Bobby Stokes, the shy scorer of the only goal, died some years ago, and the thirtieth anniversary get-together in 2006 sadly became a tribute to another member of that team, one of the game's most gifted characters, Peter Osgood. He should certainly have played more for England, and I shall never forget the wonderful goal he scored for Chelsea against AC Milan in February 1966.

It must have been a bit strange for Lawrie staying at the Cavalieri Hilton on one of the city's seven hills where the BBC were housed, but no longer being part of the team. After he lost his job at Sunderland it was felt by the head of football, Brian Barwick, that he didn't have quite the same authority. Either a successful manager or not one at all seems in the main to have been the criterion over the years. But Lawrie's luck was about to change, for his authority was about to be recognised by the pretender to the English football throne. Over a quiet twosome dinner at the hotel later in the tournament, Graham Taylor invited Lawrie to be the number two in his team.

Reading Taylor's column in the *Daily Telegraph* has often made me think how much better a manager he might have been for England had his chance come later. I recall watching a training session at Watford in the days of John Barnes, and being much impressed by how concentrated his players were on what collectively they were trying to achieve. Of course, there were no big names around and his critics would say that that was the problem, dealing with the stars; and that he was too conscious of his position relative to their ability and achievements. He followed a successful manager and a team judged as the best, so unlucky to lose to Germany, the eventual world champions, in the semi-final. But what if they'd lost to Cameroon? His task then might have been very different. His comment after failing in the finals of Euro '92, 'We have become trapped between our traditional game and the feeling that, at international level, we should play a more refined style,' suggests how he wanted to play, and still has a resonance today. After two scoreless draws against Denmark and France – the second the most sterile defensive international I've ever covered (the low point in the managerial career of Michel Platini, whose French team were as negative as their opponents) – England came up against the hosts in Stockholm. There, Taylor made a decision he would surely not make now.

In one of our occasional but always thought-provoking chats in recent years he told me he should have left out Gary Lineker against France and restored him for the third game. But to substitute him suddenly against Sweden after England conceded from a corner to lose their lead was, I thought then and still think, madness. And to replace him with his former Leicester City colleague, Alan Smith, instead of pairing them, made it worse. England had to win the match, and, however poorly Taylor thought Lineker was playing, who on the pitch in a white shirt was more likely to snatch a winner? Instead the match was decided in two flashes of yellow and blue as Tomas Brolin played wall passes with Ingesson and Dahlin to score one of the best goals I've seen. Lineker, who had said he was retiring from international football at the tournament's end, finished one goal short of Bobby Charlton's total of forty-nine – and Graham Taylor lost a deal of goodwill.

Qualification for the World Cup in the United States in 1994 was difficult from the moment Norway and then Holland held England at Wembley. But while Taylor can be justly criticised for his selection and formation nightmare in Oslo – easily unpicked by Egil Olsen's team – and his extraordinary decision, whatever the financial gain, to allow Channel Four to make a documentary on his management, it can also be argued that he was very unlucky. The penalty conceded against Holland when England were two up turned the home match – Keown, at left back, square with Walker, the pass to the speedy Overmars, and Walker tackling when Woods might have saved the day. The appalling refereeing of the Austrian Karl Josef Assenmacher, who allowed Koeman to remain on the field following a foul on Platt, decided the away fixture, as the Dutchman immediately struck from a free kick at the other end to put the match beyond England's reach. In the documentary Taylor was seen shouting at the linesman, 'Tell your mate he's cost me my job' – clearly heard on the microphone he was wearing. It was a job he wanted so much and in which he suffered so much.

That he enjoys his journalistic and broadcasting life is, I

should think, reciprocated by those who listen to him and read his articles. But looking down at the 2006 World Cup from his Radio Five commentary position, he must have wondered about some of the senior men guiding their country's hopes. So might the man, watching on television, who had joined him on the England bench during the times of travail, and who later took charge of Northern Ireland. Lawrie McMenemy's strongest suit was man management.

33

Learning from My Children: The Boat Race

'Watch out, guys, there's a spy in the camp.' It was said with a smile but it made the lunch I'd just come from a bit of a charade. I should have realised that it was a waste of time trying to conceal my Cambridge connections. I'm not sure who was laughing at me most, the jesting Oxford president, Matthew Pinsent, or my lunch companions, Oxford director of rowing Steve Royle and the BBC's rowing producer, Campbell Ferguson, whom I'd asked to keep mum about 'the other place'.

It was the second time I'd become involved in a sport because of my children: this time, through my son Mark. Cricket had been his game at Eton, where the choice had to be made between the square and the river, but at university he could do both – and in time teach his father the rudiments of rowing.

Like many events, Boat Race day had always had a place in my calendar and, like many people, I chose a shade of blue without having a connection with either university. I initially favoured the Dark Blues but with Gigi at Cambridge, and rowing for her college, Pembroke, Penny and I had a good reason for switching to the Light Blues.

Two years later Mark, in his second year at Christ's College, Cambridge, became a member of the university rowing club, and in 1992 coxed in the Isis–Goldie race (Isis and Goldie are the Oxford and Cambridge reserve eights). From a skiff following the racers, Penny and I watched nervously as he steered across from the Middlesex to the Surrey station approaching Hammersmith Bridge – 'I hope your son has more courage than I have at this moment,' said our pilot, Donald Leggett, the Goldie coach. A 'push' took Goldie clear, and they won by three and a quarter lengths.

Back at Putney, as the crowd awaited the start of the main event, the result was passed to the BBC's commentator, Gerald Sinstadt, who was, I learned later, kind enough to mention the father-and-son connection. At Mortlake the joy of victory quickly passed, as it became clear that Oxford were winning. That evening at the Boat Race Ball it was pointed out to me that Andy Probert, whose experience of the tideway had won him the senior cox's seat over the novice, hadn't had one of his better days. In the Boat Race the cox is rarely praised for the win but frequently blamed for the loss.

Davies junior was given the hot seat when the two universities raced again a week later on the Potomac river in Washington and the result was reversed, but his third year was to be spent mainly in the lands of the languages he was reading, so he wasn't available for 1993, a year which was a turning-point for Cambridge and which found Davies senior in a seat almost as hot.

The offer of the Boat Race commentary came, as it were, out of the blue, but I didn't accept until I'd talked to Gerald: I wanted to make it clear to him that I had in no way sought to undermine his position. He was disappointed, of course, but there were no hard feelings. We performers have to accept the rough and smooth of others' decisions.

Gerald continued to cover all the other rowing on the BBC, including the Olympic Games, which had in 1992 produced one of his best commentaries when the Searle brothers' charge claimed a thrilling victory in the coxed pairs. Curiously, he later lost the role to the winning cox that day, Garry Herbert, memorably seen sobbing uncontrollably as the national anthem was played at the victory ceremony. Garry had been used as an analyst and had made a few contributions on Boat Race day, but as the year of the Sydney Olympics progressed I felt sure Gerald would be recalled. Some among the rowing fraternity urged me to put my name forward, but in deference to Gerald I waited – too long – to offer myself as a member of the rowing team. I'd hoped to augment the team, not replace someone, and as the rowing was in the morning it wouldn't have affected my commentating on the gymnastics, which took place in the afternoons and evenings.

In the end I felt underused in Sydney. The editor and executive producer saw my main task as trying to fill David Coleman's shoes as his successor at the ceremonies, but I've always regretted missing the chance of involvement in international rowing. (Watching the 2006 World Championships at Eton, the sport's venue for the 2012 Olympics, reinforced that feeling – if not the justification. Masochistic rowing may be, but it's also very inspiring, and Britain has been extremely successful at it.)

Happily, though, I was there when Steve Redgrave achieved his fifth consecutive Olympic gold medal – I have to admit that from my position some twenty yards from the finish I thought the British four would be caught. I'd criticised Redgrave on air in 1996, when he presented the Boat Race trophy to the winning Cambridge crew, for having said in print that morning that 'The Boat Race is to international rowing what go-karting is to Grand Prix' – a view he has long since changed. But I was more than happy to introduce him as 'the outstanding sportsman of his generation' at the Sportswriters' Association's fiftieth annual dinner in 1998.

Four years on from Sydney, I was there again, in Athens, when the British four retained the Olympic title; Matthew Pinsent, now a four-times victor, was in tears on the rostrum. But with a growing crew of medallists available, it had been clear for some time that there would be no seat at Olympic events for me except as a spectator.

When I came to the Boat Race commentary seat, Oxford had won sixteen of the last seventeen races, including the so-called 'mutiny year', 1987, when, following the withdrawal of the Americans because of arguments about training methods, the Dark Blue crew had to be thoroughly rejigged. Race day was a fearsome day for rowing. I use the word advisedly as anyone who was there or who heard Harry Carpenter's exclamation at the flash of lightning and the huge clap of thunder over the boathouses on the 'hard' at Putney will confirm. The Wagnerian conditions played a crucial role as Oxford, drawn on the Middlesex station, responded to their coach Dan Topolski's advice by diving for the cover of the Fulham wall, leaving Cambridge to plough a hopeless furrow down centre stream, before crossing to follow Oxford. Cambridge never recovered and, against all expectations, the Dark Blues won. It made a hero of Donald McDonald, the winning president, and led to an excellent book, *True Blue*, by Topolski, required reading for anyone who seeks to understand the event. It was filmed but, as so often happens, the film didn't do justice to the book. It was poorly directed and sometimes embarrassingly acted, which was tough on the author, who made a brief appearance in the role of the umpire – shades of Alfred Hitchcock – but was sadly unable to control either the crews in the boats or the one filming them.

It fell to Dan and Chris Baillieu to guide the new commentator over the testing course. Both had forgotten more about the race than I could be expected to learn. Both knew what it was like to win, Chris for Cambridge four times in a row during the Light Blues' record run of thirteen consecutive victories. As a coach Dan also knew what it was like to lose, though only three times in fifteen races. Their seats in the commentary hut (located on Putney Embankment, just east of where Beverley Brook meets the Thames) were dependent on the toss; the monitors having been placed so that the output of the onboard cameras would correspond with the chosen stations, Middlesex right and Surrey left. I sat between them, occasionally as the umpire, and with nods, digs and hands on shoulders we endeavoured to convey the story of the event without interrupting each other. In front of us other monitors showed pictures from the boats, the umpire's launch, the helicopter, Bishop's Park opposite the hard – later replaced by a camera on a catamaran which followed the crews down Fulham Reach to the Fulham football ground – and in the centre a larger monitor with white tape round it showed the director's choice of pictures from thirty-five cameras – which of course were the ones seen on home television sets.

At the end of our first collective attempt Dan turned to me and remarked, 'You didn't say anything that would have upset the rowing fraternity.' On paper that looks like damning with faint praise, but it was meant and taken as a compliment. They made a contrasting pair, with Chris at times needing a little encouragement to respond to Dan's more robust style. In a way they represented the two universities' approach on the water: laconic precision and aggressive punch. Both encouraged me, and so did the club coaches and many others as I soaked up as much about rowing and a unique race as I could manage. Every year adds to its history, yet every year is a race apart. For eighteen students who for one day have the attention of as many as ten million people it is simply about writing a three-letter word on their clubhouse board: WON. The four-letter word is unthinkable.

I wanted to give brief character sketches of the people involved in the race, so I needed to get to know what made them tick. Mark's involvement the previous year gave me an early introduction at Cambridge, and besides meeting them at Ely, where the wind can blow bitingly cold across the River Ouse, I became a regular visitor to their Nottingham base ten days or so before the event. The Dark Blues were a little wary at first, but it wasn't long before I became a dinner guest at the Oxford house in Boat Race week, a family home close by the Thames where successive crews have enjoyed the hospitality of the wonderful Mrs Heather Boxer and her helpers.

Much detail of the one-to-one chats was never used and invariably conversations ran on far past the commentator's needs. But it was a rewarding exercise which helped me to understand the individual, as well as collective, elation and dejection at the race's end. I confess I once found myself shouting at the monitor when, during the Dark Blues' run of defeats, the losing president was asked what Oxford had to do to get it right next year. He had wanted the victory so much and had tried his best, but his chance had gone and he'd never have another. I felt for him: perhaps I'd got too close.

The character studies led on to 'featurettes' on certain members of the crew. Some involved me, but they later had their own producer and reporter and many were very good. However, the desire to give the race a big build-up, bringing in star names of rowing to look at various facets of the race, had its downside. For me, looking at the crews downstream of Putney Bridge, and watching the coxes manoeuvre to the stake-boats, speaks far more than any forecast. And the tense moment as the crews sit waiting for the umpire's flag, the coxes raising and lowering one arm, struggling to get the boats balanced and positioned right on the swell of the tide, sometimes offers clues to the outcome.

It did in 1993 when the confident demeanour of the Cambridge stroke, Will Mason, contrasted markedly with the fidgety movement of his opposite number, Ian Gardener, who twelve months earlier had been the novice who calmly brought Oxford home. Now Gardener learned the other side of the Boat Race story, as 'Billy Whizz' Mason led Cambridge to their first win in seven years in the fourth fastest time on record.

In many ways that race has a special place in my memory. Because it was the first and it had gone OK, because of the pace of the build-up – quite a lot of the Isis–Goldie race was seen – and because the winning crew were my son's contemporaries. Oxford president, Matt Pinsent, will have rather different memories. He was another of Davies junior's contemporaries, though from further ago, first encountered as the bulwark if not exactly graceful right back in the house football team at Eton. In Barcelona in 1992 he came up to me and said, 'Mr Davies, you won't remember me but I used to swim in your pool.' For someone who had just, with Steve Redgrave, become an Olympic champion, it was an engagingly modest salutation. A year later his partnership with the

Canadian gold medallist, Bruce Robertson in seats five and six in the so-called 'meat wagon' of the boat was supposed to be Oxford's trump card. But the crew never found a true rhythm and Pinsent suffered the only 'failure' of his outstanding career.

In 1994 the Dark Blues were in disarray. On the Tuesday evening of race week I took their coach, Richard Tinkler, to the commentary box at Wembley to watch England play Wales. So much for informal preparation: the next day he lost his job. On the Saturday Cambridge won by six and a half lengths. Every year had a different tale to tell, though for seven years the sky was light blue. In 1995 it was a personal tale, as Cambridge included five of their losing crew from the December trial eights but not the cox, one Mark Davies, who was much praised for cutting the corner at Barnes on a slack tide to minimise the margin of defeat. The Boat Race is full of such hard-luck stories – for the next three years, for example, injury or loss of form resulted in three presidents missing selection – but at least the Beeb showed much of Goldie's victory, with Chris being generous in his comments while I thought a lot but said nothing.

The umpire's comment on the 1996 race, 'Well rowed, Cambridge; well raced, Oxford,' summed up the frustrations of the Dark Blues in what was the closest result in the Cambridge run, two lengths. The quality of Cambridge's rowing owed much to Harry Mahon, described at the celebration of his life following his death from cancer as 'the best rowing coach the sport has known'. Harry had a very down-to-earth approach to life which, when it was threatened, didn't change.

His approach to rowing was equally straightforward. 'People think it's about arms,' he once said casually to me, 'but it's all about legs.'

Rob Clegg, the Oxford president that year, 1996, was among a group in the '90s who had to accept being three-time losers. Much later, when he'd become a chum of Mark's – being part of something special produces many lifelong friendships with those who, at the time, to quote Dan, 'you have to hate' – we discussed how Oxford would probably have won the race had it been rowed on the Thursday. But Cambridge got it right on the day, which is what counts, and won it in the second fastest time ever. Two years later, in 1998, both crews beat the previous best, Cambridge setting a new mark of 16.19 minutes.

The year between, 1997, it was the umpire who reached new heights: Tom Cadoux-Hudson issued 120 warnings to the Cambridge cox, just over half of them before Hammersmith Bridge and thirty-eight on the crown of the bend to Chiswick Steps. (The Oxford cox was reprimanded just twelve times; the story that he'd been instructed not to risk a clash raised a few eyebrows.) But Cambridge, despite having lost the toss and finding themselves away from their successful station of the previous four years, held their half-length advantage round the outside of the Surrey bend and won again, by two lengths.

In 1999, when the race's twelve-year sponsorship by Beefeater ended, Aberdeen Asset Management assumed the role and, under their chief executive, Martin Gilbert, and chief representative, Douglas Connon, a former colonel in the Gordon Highlanders, they became very popular with the clubs.

Aberdeen's first year almost looked a stunt, for the Cambridge president, Brad Crombie, with several helpers including the presenter, Mr Gilbert, found the cork of the magnum of champagne impossible to remove. Gilbert had to put up with a certain amount of leg-pulling about Scottish meanness at providing a bottle that couldn't be opened, but was understandably delighted at the extra exposure of the Aberdeen brand name. The rules of the BBC charter about advertising were certainly broken, just as the long embrace between the six-foot seven-inch Cambridge bowman, Toby Wallace, and the Light Blues' cox, Vian Sharif, at barely five feet, offered pictures usually reserved for after the nine o'clock watershed.

Seven races and Cambridge had won them all, in '99 by three and a half lengths in a new second-best time, 16.41 minutes. I really did begin to wonder if the Oxford connection that had got me into this – Jonathan Martin and the London race organiser, Duncan Clegg, were both at the city of dreaming spires – would think about a change of commentator. It was certainly becoming difficult for Jonny Searle, who had taken over 'our' Oxford seat while Dan was helping to turn the tide, to find words of consolation. He was a little too quiet for some in the senior production team, but I thought he offered more than a few pearls of wisdom. And his influence in inspiring those who had followed him and his brother Greg into the crews of Hampton school was about to bear fruit.

At the challenge six weeks before the 2000 race, Richard Stokes, the Cambridge president, announced a crew which didn't include himself. But two weeks before the race he was back in the stroke seat. Kieran West, a tower of strength the year before, was now concentrating on delivering that strength to the British eight that, with two other Blues in the boat – Andrew Lindsay (Oxford) and Luka Grubor (Cambridge) – triumphed in handsome style in Sydney six months later. At the Cambridge dinner for the media in Boat Race week, the feeling of confidence was somehow not the same. As Mark pointed out, there was no one, except Donald Leggett, still around who knew what it was like to lose.

On the Saturday Oxford knew again what it was like to win, and Dan Snow, son of Peter of swingometer fame and nephew of Jon, the best news anchor on television, summarised their feelings: 'The win's made my life worthwhile. I haven't been wasting my time for eight months or two years. I guess you have to lose a race to know what it is like to win.' They had pulled away in Crabtree reach through the worst of the rough to win by three lengths.

In 2001, the 147th race saw its first restart. The Thames had less tide than in living memory, and it was thought, after Cambridge had won the toss and opted for Surrey, that the Oxford cox, Jeremy Moncrieff, would cut the Fulham bend tighter and earlier than usual. His opposite number, Christian Cormack, made that assumption and was quickly warned by the umpire as Moncrieff held to the traditional line. There was a clash and the Cambridge bowman lost his blade. Oxford continued but the umpire, Rupert Obholzer, shouted at them to stop rowing; no easy decision with the flotilla of following boats steaming up from behind.

There was a small irony here, for Obholzer had upset the Light Blues with gestures and too much mouth when leading Oxford to victory ten years earlier. Had he not warned the Oxford cox last, he might have disqualified Cambridge. Instead he restarted the crews level – wrongly in my view – not allowing Oxford the lead they had built: half the advantage of the bend had lapsed. Cambridge won by two and a half lengths and was, I think, the better crew. But had Oxford been given their advantage at the restart, the Light Blues would have been made to prove it.

The often-made criticism that there are too many graduates in the boats has to be set against the relative numbers of graduates and undergraduates at the universities and the balance of the two sexes, which has changed enormously. At the time of writing, there have been thirteen female coxes, the wafer-thin brigade. The odds against a female rower becoming a true Blue are still very long but with the British women's success at international level, and the competitive races between the women's boat clubs at Henley, it is not impossible that some day it will happen.

In 2002 Cambridge were caught napping by the umpire's flag and fluffed the first three strokes – the cox still had her arm aloft, indicating her crew wasn't ready. But on the Middlesex station Cambridge were just ahead at the mile and held the advantage through Hammersmith Bridge and on to Chiswick Steps.

Chris Baillieu was the first to spot that there was a problem in the Cambridge boat: Sebastien Mayer, at four, had virtually stopped rowing. Seizing the chance, the Oxford cox called for a push and the Dark Blues, down by a fraction, became only the third crew in the race's history to win from behind at Barnes Bridge on the Surrey station. (Exactly fifty years earlier, in 1952, Oxford's Christopher Davidge had achieved the same feat, in blizzard conditions, and had instantly been added to my list of sporting heroes.) For the Light Blues, carrying the 'dead weight' of Mayer's fourteen stone was simply too great a handicap. Happily, Mayer not only recovered but later rowed in a winning crew.

Looking again at the 2003 Boat Race for this book was an exhausting and a moving experience. The race was truly remarkable, with the advantage of the bends being fiercely contested at every stroke: the best example I've seen of collective fortitude in a sporting event. It was also the first race to take place on a Sunday, the first since 1841 in which both presidents rowed in the stroke seat, the first for a hundred years to pit brother against brother – in this case, brothers against brothers.

The Friday before the race I'd watched in amazement from Putney Bridge as the Cambridge boat and the harbourmaster's vessel collided. The cause of the accident was, in my opinion – and when asked I put it in writing for the inquiry – the lack of a lookout on the master's boat: Cambridge's cox could see little with Tim Wooge, their six-foot seven-inch stroke and president, directly in front of him. Their bowman was the sufferer, being forced to miss the race because of a broken wrist, but it could have been so much worse. His replacement, Ben Smith, was the younger brother of Oxford's Matt Smith.

By the time the boats reached Barnes, Oxford were two-thirds of a length ahead, and seemed on course for victory. But, refusing to give up, Tim Wooge raised his crew's rate to a mind-blowing forty-four strokes a minute, and brought them to within a single stroke of victory. Six months of preparation for eighteen minutes and five seconds on the water to complete four and a quarter miles and to be separated at the finishing line by just one foot . . .

I felt I had to call a winner, though the moments waiting for the official verdict were very nervous. That Chris, Dan and I now and then interrupted each other while looking at the two exhausted crews in the shadow of Chiswick Bridge was, I think, forgivable; that we embellished the same themes, understandable. Not the least remarkable thing was that Oxford won despite giving away a record 7 kg per man.

James Livingston, the only Light Blue survivor from the previous year, competed in two epics, only to be a loser in both; very tough to take especially as it was his last chance. Yet he was still able to say, 'I'm very proud of my little brother [David] for winning such a great event.' His estimate of the quality of the race was rightly shared by Wooge: 'This was a great event for the sport of rowing, of which we ultimately are the ambassadors.'

After that battle of heroes, everyone hoped for something very special in the 150th race, which was also the 175th anniversary of the first race. Alas, it was a big anticlimax. It was decided by a clash just short of the mile post and won by Cambridge, who raced away from the incident to win by six lengths.

Afterwards, Douglas Connon hosted a small reception by Aberdeen, which Penny, Gigi and I attended (Mark was in Australia) and, encountering the Cambridge winners as we left, I found myself lifted into the air like the race trophy by their stroke, Nate Kirk. He'd told me before the race that he'd never been with such a close-knit crew who were so driven; a variation on a familiar refrain, whatever the shade of blue.

It was for me the final act for in February the axe had fallen. The Boat Race producer, Paul Davies, had phoned to tell me that from 2005 the race would be covered by ITV, news which was not yet public knowledge. I found it hard to take in. The race was such a BBC event, a national sporting occasion – to stand alongside the Grand National, the Derby, Royal Ascot, the Lord's Test and Wimbledon – which had been part of the national broadcaster's remit since it was first covered on radio in 1927 (amazingly, the first TV broadcast was just eleven years later). It was difficult to blame the Beeb for being wrong-footed when ITV's head of sport, Brian Barwick, decided to bid for an event in which ITV had never before shown the slightest interest. All the same, it shouldn't have happened.

There was a suggestion that the modern BBC felt the event was elitist (in fact, the crews were drawn from an increasing number of schools and increasingly international, with rowers from Scandinavia, Holland, Italy and France joining the many Americans, Canadians and Germans) and that the director-general, Greg Dyke, wasn't unhappy to lose it. In response, I record a luncheon at Twickenham before the 2004 England *v* Wales rugby match. Our host was Peter Salmon, the BBC's director of sport, and among the guests were the acting director-general, Mark Byford, the contracts manager, Dominic Coles, and the recently deposed Dyke, who arrived a little late. He had barely taken his seat when he asked Coles, 'What the hell happened with the Boat Race?' The only response was embarrassment.

In 2005 I was again invited to the Cambridge race week dinner. I felt that it would be inappropriate because I was no longer involved and I didn't want in any way to cramp the style of ITV and in particular of my successor, Peter Drury, with whom I'd had many conversations about the event. But the club insisted and now on a wall in my study resides a blade with the inscription 'The Voice of the Boat Race 1993–2004': twelve years of many faces and different characters all playing their part in a wonderful sporting contest of great tradition and huge endeavour. It was a privilege to be a small part of something very special.

The voice of the race, is, of course, John Snagge, who was the radio commentator for many years before and after the war; a slightly gravelly voice of wonderful diction and authority. However, his most famous line was born of uncertainty. On a rather foggy race day, he said, 'I can't see who is winning: it's either Oxford or Cambridge.' In 2003 I hadn't been sure, either, but will there ever again be the need to gamble on a margin of one foot?

34

'That's It! She's Done It!'

I am proud to say that in the Wimbledon Museum are two videotapes which include my name. The first is entitled *That's it! She's done it!*, Dan Maskell's regular line when the ladies' championship was won. The second, *Chalk Flew Up*, tells the story of the old No 1 Court. You cannot be seriously interested in tennis if you need telling the author of those words.

Both tapes – I should check that they're DVDs by now – were produced by Paul Davies. I first worked with him on a dead Davis Cup rubber in Manchester, when Great Britain beat Thomas Muster and Austria back in 1991. He has many times since confirmed my impression from the first point of that match that he is a natural in the very considerable skill of directing cameras. It's an art which I believe the BBC

Sports Department have tended to take for granted in recent years. The man or woman in the chair, either calling the shots to a vision mixer or alone pressing the buttons, is on the line all the time. Decisive moments can be reworded but not recreated.

On the history of No 1 Court, Paul teamed me up with Sue Barker, whom I've known since her playing days and who is the only sports person to have given me some credit for a moment of their success. The occasion was the annual ladies' event in the autumn at Brighton in 1981. In the quarter-finals she beat Tracy Austin, the teenage sensation who had just won the US Open, and Sue was understandably full of smiles when she came up to be interviewed. At the end of it, though, she was a little perplexed when I said, 'Sue, do you think we could have three interviews this time?' and added after a pause, 'We usually have the "Well done" and then follow it with the "Hard luck, the chance was there but . . ." Wouldn't it be fun if you came up here on Sunday still smiling away?'

She took my comments in good part, but when she was losing to Barbara Potter in the semi-final they suddenly hit her. She records that she said to herself, 'I can't face Barry Davies,' and that the thought helped motivate her to win. Come the Sunday, after she'd beaten Mima Jausovec, we did the third interview, complete with trophy.

It was at the same venue years later that I followed the instruction of the deputy head of sport, John Rowlinson, to ease her into her new role as a presenter for BBC Sport. I knew, of course, that I was easing myself out of that tennis role at the same time, but we had a few laughs then and in various arenas since. I confess that, egged on by Robin Cousins, I've often tried to hand back from commentary to her in the in-vision position with a line that might crack her up – very unprofessional!

Sue could have had a bigger part to play in the championship video, but she was surprisingly beaten in the semi-final by Betty Stove, who then lost in the final of Jubilee Year 1977 to the lovely Virginia Wade. Virginia recorded on the tape that she was thinking about the huge amount of noise on the Centre Court at the end, and suddenly realised, 'Hey, it's because of you.' Checking the daily commentators' roster on arrival at Wimbledon's broadcast centre, I'm always happy to find myself paired with Virginia. Whoever is playing on court, it will be an interesting partnership in the commentary box, with a match containing a few shouts of 'Yours,' plenty of good rallies, and usually lots of chats at the back of the court – i.e., off microphone.

Telling the history of the ladies' championship, which began 'when one woman ruled the world and every other woman knew her place' – three years before Queen Victoria's Golden Jubilee – was quite a challenge. The researchers had found some wonderful old photographs and then film of the likes of Suzanne Lenglen and Alice Marble and, later, Little Mo (Maureen Connolly), all of which needed careful scripting. Murphy's law governs such things: never enough time when a good phrase enters the brain cells, always too much time when there's nothing particular to say. And ten seconds typed at the computer will take fourteen to read properly in the dubbing theatre.

A trip to the States to complete the last couple of decades of the 'century' had me changing my mind a bit about Chris Evert and Martina Navratilova. At Brighton, where I'd interviewed both of them a number of times, I'd formed the impression that Martina was the more generous when accepting defeat. But at Chris's home in Florida I found a much warmer character than the 'ice maiden' she was called when she first came to Wimbledon. Because of a delayed flight we were two hours late for our appointment, but Chris, having swiftly organised refreshments for Paul, Penny and me – and for the American crew   made no attempt to hurry things along. She described herself as the world's greatest runner-up; laughingly claimed that she lost to Martina in 1978 because she was in love (with John Lloyd) – 'I was 4–2 in the third and 40–15, for goodness sake!' – and wistfully recalled being rushed off the court by Steffi Graf, having the chance of only 'a little wave' in farewell to the Wimbledon crowd.

Whereas Chris by then had retired, perhaps an aid to getting things into perspective, Martina was that year, 1993, trying for a third time for the tenth singles title at SW19 and as such was still pretty much the driven character. Even so, considering her pre-eminence in the Wimbledon Championship story, it was disappointing that she played hard to get before agreeing to the interview. In her own way, though, she was generous to Chris, adding, 'I certainly don't miss those backhand crosscourt passing shots that I saw whipping past me time after time.' And she offered this simple little gem about how she felt on winning Wimbledon for the first time: 'I kept saying, "I can't believe I did it."

You think you can, but until you do, you don't know if you will.'

A couple of years earlier I'd interviewed her after she was beaten in the quarter-finals by Jennifer Capriati. Martina was devastated, and I asked for the studio lights to be lowered to give her time to recover her composure. Later I worked with her and Pam Shriver when I commentated on the first of two ladies' finals, and the programme signed by both is among my souvenirs. And yes, I did get a few words in and posed a few thoughts. There is a soft side to Martina's nature, but it's covered by a pretty tough exterior.

Billie Jean King is another complex character. But she has infectious dynamism and her importance in the development in the women's game is beyond question. The Wimbledon crowd loved her as Little Miss Moffitt, but then not much until her twilight years. She was another Maestro, and I interviewed her when she was commissioner of team tennis and then again in Rhode Island for the *Championship* programme.

She had endeared herself to me with a comment made a couple of years after the *Maestro* programme when, as a member of the BBC commentary team, she joined me in the No 1 Court commentary box. While the players were knocking up I said to her, off microphone, 'Look, I'm not Dan Maskell or John Barrett, so if I say something you disagree with or think needs correcting please, within the confines of the BBC style [of the day], don't hesitate to say your piece.' She watched the match standing up, and her lively approach filled the box. At the end she turned to me and said, 'OK, so you may not

Taking care of my wife Penny: Des Lynam and Stuart Storey doing the honours at the Los Angeles Olympics in 1984

'Oh, I say!' With Dan Maskell in the main Wimbledon locker room before he left for the championship dinner in 1991. It was the last time I saw him

Three men not in a boat: in the box at Putney ready for the 2001 Boat Race with Chris Baillieu and Jonny Searle

Maestros

'Come on, Dad, come and play.' With Calum and George Best

Bet he could have cleared it! Wistfully hurdling at the gate with David Hemery

Two wingers of rather different
standard: with Sir Stanley
Matthews in Lake Placid

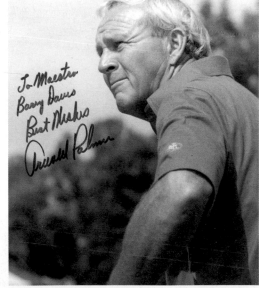

To Maestro
Barry Davies
Best Wishes
Arnold Palmer

If only he could spell my name!
Arnold Palmer dropping a
stroke at his home course in
Pennsylvania

In the midst of protest: referee Ray Tinkler after allowing WBA's 'offside' goal at Elland Road in April 1971

Never knowingly dull: the ebullient Franny Lee that day at Maine Road

'Crazy Horse' Emlyn Hughes with Liverpool's first European Cup, Rome 1977

The conclusion of Maradona's amazing run – the best goal I've ever seen: Argentina v England, World Cup quarter-final, Mexico City 1986

A cracker from Gazza: Spurs v Arsenal, FA Cup semi-final 1991. My words made the T-shirt market

A scene of despair: the Heysel stadium, Brussels, May 1985

Grass marks on the Wimbledon white: the diving Boris Becker in more classic pose on the way to becoming the championships' youngest winner in 1985

Not a German in sight: victory achieved for Richard Dodds (right) and his men. The Olympic hockey final, Seoul 1988

be Dan or John, but you have a real feel for what they're trying to do down there.'

In Rhode Island she had described Martina as 'the greatest player who ever lived'. But although, in the two doubles matches I watched Martina play in her last Wimbledon in 2006, I felt she was still the best player on court at the age of forty-nine, I was pleased that the twenty-first title at Wimbledon eluded her. It left her sharing the All England record with Billie Jean.

The 100th championship, in 1993, was won by Steffi Graf, the fifth of her seven Wimbledon singles titles. I interviewed her many times during the years between the young girl running joyfully through the BBC area at SW19, when she won for the first time, and the rather more serious – sad, even – moments later in her career. I particularly recall one, at a Brighton hotel during the autumn tournament, when we got into a rather deep conversation about Teddy Tinling's thought that a star had to be lonely. I remember her charm, her smile, and the self-conscious swishing of her hair; and the fact that, as the evening sky darkened, my reflection slowly appeared over her left shoulder in the window behind her.

35

Facing the Music

The Sheffield Arena, in the Hallam area of the city, was opened by the Queen in May 1991 and featured a concert by Paul Simon the same evening. Two and a half years later, in November 1993, with a capacity crowd of 12,500 it was a scene of much expectancy, and for four people the sort of nervous tension they hadn't felt for some time. Two of them I had only recently met but the performers were old friends, if now showing just a few glimpses of that wary look of a decade ago.

The first two parts of the competition had gone smoothly, but then came another unveiling totally different from all the others. This was Fred Astaire and Ginger Rogers; at least, the music was and so were the costumes. Last time, the public had known – or in some cases had quickly learned – the tune;

now many could already sing the words, quietly, to themselves. The international body, so their British vice-president, Lawrence Demmy, had assured me and other members of the BBC team, wanted real dancing again, after years of complicated manoeuvres, some more befitting a wrestling ring, others raising the question whether they should be allowed in a public place.

The ballroom was made of ice, and the best in the world were set to perform. Two of the nervous quartet could only watch, hoping his wife and her husband would be properly acclaimed. After ten years as professionals, Jayne Torvill and Christopher Dean had again accepted the challenge to face the music and dance. They need not have worried, because in front of the home crowd and the home judges there was nothing but moonlight and music and love and romance. Once again they were British Ice Dancing Champions. They left Sheffield with a total of ten sixes and nine 5.9s, and enough teddy bears and toys to suggest that the special room in Jayne's mother's home where all the others were kept would need an extension. It was a triumph, and the interview was very different from the way things had started last time round – but all four knew it was only the start.

Copenhagen for the European Championship in February 1994 told a different and rather confusing tale. A 5.2 was among the scores for the first compulsory dance and T & D were only third, behind two Russian couples. Alarm bells were ringing. Were the international judges saying you can't be away ten years in shows and expect automatically to be placed above those who've spent that time honing the precise steps

of the compulsories? Was there resentment of the professionals who had returned?

The original set pattern dance, the next day, was the
rumba. Jayne and Chris were exquisite; a performance for
me to rank with the Pasa Doble of 1984 and 'Don't Send
me Flowers' from *Mack and Mabel*, one of their gala numbers
from even earlier. Overall they were now equal first with
Maya Usova and Aleksandr Zhulin, both couples having 1.6
points. Oksana 'Pasha' Grishuk and Evgeny Platov, third in
the original, second in the compulsories, had 2.8. The Free
Dance was the decider, and the judges preferred Usova and
Zhulin to the British. The Union flags in the arena went
limp, and in the dressing-room area the disappointment was
funereal.

As the final couple started to skate, one of our producers,
Alastair Scott, went backstage and watched Grishuk and
Platov on a monitor. The judges enjoyed their rock 'n' roll
and placed them first in the free dance. Then, on our monitor
in the commentary position, it said T & D had won the
title: but how? Jim Reside, the senior producer, sitting with
Alan Weeks and me, passed the news to Alastair, who in
turn told a disbelieving Chris. Then up came Lawrence
Demmy to congratulate Jayne and Chris with the comment
'I told you it would all work out,' to which Chris responded,
'By default, but what the hell.' The 'how' was for me to
explain. Alan, having finished his commentary on the last
performance, had no thoughts to offer me. Many viewers
probably went to bed that night more than a little confused
after my explanation of how A can beat B but when A loses

to C, B is the winner. But what was for sure was that there were now three contenders for the Olympic title – one British, two Russian.

The 1994 Olympics were the best of the seven Winter Games I've covered to date. For a start, everywhere was a snowy scene: on the drive to Lillehammer where one of the ice-hockey rinks, Haakons Hall, was cut into the side of a mountain; on every type of skiing course and even in the city, which made those of us whose winter sport takes place in rinks really feel part of the overall event – often not the case. There was no need for the artificial here, and the natural applied as much to the people, who were the warmest of hosts. And the sun shone every day, which was as well, for the air, crystal clear, was mighty cold.

I felt we didn't make anything like enough of the beautiful scenes offered by the cross-country events and the even more demanding biathlon. At successive Games we have been loath to show sports which aren't well known at home. It has continued that way but in this lovely Norwegian setting it was an opportunity lost not to make more of something different – the pictures alone would have entertained. I fear it will always be the same, left to Eurosport and a million words, until a British contender appears for those 'different' disciplines.

From the whole team competing in nine disciplines, Torvill and Dean were Britain's only real hope of gold and the European champions had a huge task on their hands. The three weeks' training since Copenhagen had been harsh and not a little argumentative. The advice now was for bigger moves and tricks with the concern that their difficult steps wouldn't be appreciated sufficiently by the nine who would decide the outcome. I found that all rather confusing. Hadn't they been persuaded to return in order to restore the classic image of ice dancing?

There was another story to tell – of the tabloid variety – about the main opposition. The Russian couples' rivalry was far keener than the contest with the British. Maya Usova and Aleksandr Zhulin were married and were the reigning world champions. They had all shared the same coach until Pasha Grishuk made a play for Zhulin and as a result of the affair was left with a bloody nose by the older Usova. The coach, Natalia Dubova, sent Grishuk packing, but, failing to find a replacement to skate with Evgeny Platov, lost him as well and they were now coached by Natalia Linichuk. The ladies, all four, were at daggers drawn. But after the compulsory dances the judges couldn't split their couples, who were placed equal first. Two nights later Jayne and Chris again produced a spellbinding rumba. As in Copenhagen, it all came down to the free dance.

Some comments by Jayne's husband, Phil, summed up the doubt. 'I wonder if the ISU [International Skating Union] have advised them correctly about the free dance?' he said. 'If the judges don't like the pros back . . . if the ISU wanted it for the TV ratings. Three Russian judges!' Jill Trenary, Chris's wife, a former world and United States singles champion, kept her knowledge of skating politics to herself but was equally concerned.

Usova and Zhulin went first and left the audience applauding politely. Having said there was insufficient time to introduce completely new moves, T & D changed their start. Later they included her lifting him, and they ended with Jayne's back somersault over his shoulders. The crowd went wild; a standing ovation. But the rock 'n' roll – speed of movement hiding imperfection – won the day, though only the Russian judge from the old Soviet Union voted for Grishuk and Platov. The Belarussian and the Ukrainian had them third. The British judge alone voted for T & D – for them gold had turned to bronze. 'The audience were our judges,' said Jayne and when asked, 'What now?' she replied, 'I don't know, I don't care, because we're not doing it again.'

Later the chief of the technical committee of ice dancing confirmed that the British couple had been marked down by the judges for an illegal move, the somersault. I asked several times about Grishuk and Platov's long separations – more than the allowed five seconds apart – but he refused to give an answer. It was utterly ridiculous. Why bother to have rules if they aren't applied to every couple?

Afterwards Jayne and Chris gave me a last TV interview – well, actually two interviews, because after ten minutes the cameraman stopped me and said apologetically that he hadn't connected the sound line to his camera. (I suppose he might have chosen a worse time!) They were obviously very disappointed, but took the philosophical route, avoiding any accusation of sour grapes. To come back ten years on and make the rostrum was a terrific achievement – 'How did they manage that?' will be asked many times in years to come – but for them and their supporters the result was a huge anticlimax.

Some months later, chatting to Chris, I offered the thought that they shouldn't have changed but just perfected the routine that had won in Sheffield. He assured me that that would never have been enough. I believe Phil was right to ask whether the ISU had advised them correctly. Perhaps those who did, in good faith, didn't have the backing they thought they had. There were too many subjective views clouding what was supposed to be the main objective: to improve the quality of ice dancing. All I know is that no one while they were away for ten years or since Lillehammer has performed as they did.

After their first retirement I often found myself at odds with the judges' choice of their successors, usually empathising with the audience. I preferred the Russians Klimova and Ponomarenko, the Olympic champions of '92 before they succeeded their compatriots Bestemianova and Bukin (he unkindly nicknamed Dracula), with whom I never came to terms – and not only in the brief period when her name was arguing with my tongue. I liked the French Canadians Isabelle and Paul Duchesnay (she was briefly Mrs Dean), although they could be a bit intense. In contrast the husband and wife Finns, Susanna Rahkamo and Petri Kokko, whose quickstep original dance at the 1995 World Championships in Birmingham was sensational, were always fun. So were the Canadians Shae-Lynn Bourne (Steven Cousins's girlfriend for quite a long time) and Victor Kraatz. Their best number – a free dance – was *The Lord of the Dance*. They finally won a World Championship in Vancouver in 2001. But they had the worst position of all – fourth – in both the Nagano and the Salt Lake City Games.

The unfolding story of the ice dancing took the greater part of my attention during the Lillehammer Games; setting things up for Alan Weeks's commentary, then finding the words of summary over the scores, before, as it were, heading backstage for the post-performance interviews. But there were the two final chapters of a rather more pungent tale to tell: the case of Tonya Harding; the girl from the wrong side of the tracks. Her desire to be Olympic champion led to her ex-husband, Jeff Gilhooly, arranging for her main American rival, Nancy Kerrigan, to be injured and put out of contention. Harding came from a broken family, with an out-of-work father who eventually left the scene and a mother who at the time of the Games was married to a sixth husband. Kerrigan was American chocolate-box, from a happy but not over-rich family background. She had won the bronze medal in Albertville, was doing nicely in the advertising world, and was very much the favourite of the United States Skating Association.

Gilhooly was arrested and later pleaded guilty to planning the attack. Harding, who had won the US Championships two days after it happened, was kept on the American team, the US Olympic Committee capitulating at the threat of being sued even though Harding did admit to knowing of the plot after the attack. She eventually pleaded guilty to hindering the investigation, and was fined $150,000 and given 500 hours' community service. In a way the skating outcome was a bit of a let-down. Kerrigan, whose injury was fortunately just above the knee, recovered in good time.

The short programme produced the highest television audience in the United States for over a decade – and unlike us they weren't even live – but it proved a disappointment for their viewers watching 'the soap'. Harding made a mess of it, and was only tenth. Kerrigan was in the lead. But that wasn't quite the end of the drama. Two days later, when Harding was announced to skate her free programme in the penultimate group, she was nowhere to be seen, leaving me with enough time to bring the British audience up to date with one of those 'It could only happen in America' stories. Then, having arrived just in time to avoid disqualification, she stopped after forty-five seconds, and, in floods of tears, sought the mercy of the referee, leaving more time to be filled with speculation. It transpired that she had broken a bootlace in the warm-up and hadn't been able to find a replacement long enough. She was allowed to re-skate at the end of the group.

She didn't include the triple axel, of which she was capable, but skated well to the theme music of *Jurassic Park* and certainly made a large imprint on the event. Kerrigan offered her best, but lost out to the waif-like but beautiful Oksana Baiul from Ukraine, though the replays the judges can call for in the twenty-first century might have seen the American in the gold rather than silver medal position. Whether Harding would be amused by that thought I don't know, but I suspect that, like the rest of us, she might not have been able to resist a smile at Kerrigan's remark, heard by the television microphones when she was told the victory ceremony would be a little delayed because Baiul was in make-up. 'What for?' she said. 'She's only going to cry again.'

Katarina Witt finished just one place ahead of Harding, bowing out with a very emotional performance of 'Where Have all the Flowers Gone?', a tribute to the city of Sarajevo, which was where she had won her first Olympic title, and which was ravaged by the war in Bosnia. Her natural long-term successor as Queen of the Ice was the thirteen-year-old reserve on the United States team that year. But, although she won five world titles, Michelle Kwan could manage only silver and bronze in the Olympics, losing at the next two Games to two little girls who took the judges' eye, Tara Lipinski and Sarah Hughes.

36

'Everything Comes to Him Who Waits'

The opening ceremony of the 1994 World Cup was somewhat prophetic. Diana Ross, the big name of the show, was anything but supreme in contriving to miss an arranged short-range penalty. (At the end of the tournament, others in more suitable footwear and from the proper distance did the same.) The opening match – the first World Cup starter for three points – was a great deal better than expected and the same was true of the whole experience of a World Cup in a country which didn't understand the game and mostly didn't want to – it was only for the young and the girls. America the beautiful did well by the beautiful game. Over three and a half million people attended the matches, an average of sixty-nine thousand a match. The prophets of doom had forgotten the many immigrant populations who came to watch the game of their fore-bears; the success of the Olympic football tournament ten years earlier; and that part of the American dream which likes to be able to claim, 'I was there.' There were, though, a few occa-sions when a forty-yard clearance to no one in particular drew applause in the belief – short-lived – that yardage had been gained.

Of considerably more importance to me were the few yards I gained in the placing of the first commentary position. Soldier Field in Chicago, the venue for the opening, was rather quaint. It had a tower in one corner, and the main stand was covered by an awning, a rather larger version of the type to be found bringing shade on the sea front or covering the home patio. Because the BBC had invested in small cameras attached to the rear of the commentary positions, for on-the-spot interviews with our team of experts, we were in the back row, where there was likely to be less chance of an outsider blocking the shot.

However, researching the position while I stayed in the hotel doing my homework, Simon Betts – my producer whose back-ground was in events and light entertainment – discovered a drawback: the angle of the awning meant that those in the back row could only see the near side of the pitch. Eliciting the assis-tance of Steve Goodey, our senior engineering manager, he ensured that the position was changed. As a result I had no difficulty seeing Germany's Jurgen Klinsmann, one of the stars of the championship, score the first goal; nor the altercation which saw Bolivia's mooted star, Marco Etcheverry, sent off after being on the field as a substitute for precisely four minutes.

The extreme temperatures and early kick-offs made it a real test for the players, and the travelling over vast distances was demanding for both them and the media. But that was also part of the enjoyment. The chance was there to see quite a lot of the United States: Simon and I were intent on making the most of the opportunity. The football came first, of course, but a World Cup deserves a more worldly view than the regular bread and butter. Here there was jam, and occasionally cream.

The executive producer, Malcolm Kemp, was a New Zealander who had joined the BBC four years earlier on the strength of his coverage of the ceremonies of the Commonwealth Games in Auckland. (Later I would much enjoy working with him on those at the Manchester Games.) His attitude was very much that a happy team would be a successful one, so with everyone called to Dallas the party came first.

From there the schedule took Simon and me to the 'Windy City' on Lake Michigan, to New York and then to Washington in the first three days of the tournament. I found that we were booked to leave the capital to travel back to Dallas at a time which would deny us even a post-match glance at the White House or Capitol Hill. When I asked if it could be changed, Patricia Gregory, who was Malcolm's right-hand lady, said, 'But I thought you'd want to go and watch Nigeria at their training camp.' 'But,' I said, 'that's in Austin! Are you going to fly me another six hundred miles?' Patricia had worked for the BBC from 1970 to 1978 and then had five years with ITV before returning to Auntie in '94 as chief assistant to the head of sport. She was also involved with the Women's FA for thirty years and UEFA for fourteen, but even she had been caught out by the vast distances of the four-teenth World Cup. Simon and I did the tourist bit.

At all the big televised events there is an area set aside for the world's camera crews and television and radio reporters to interview the performers. It's called 'the mixed zone' and as you can imagine there are times when it's a pretty hectic place. When things were a bit fraught in the BBC's World Cup office, a phone call would sometimes be met by Malcolm saying, 'It's a bit of a mixed zone here at the moment.' Sometimes it meant a disagreement with his number two, for Patricia could certainly defend her corner. But over many years I've found her a helpful listener and adviser with a knack of seeing the wider picture.

The most telling move of my opening three commentary games was Ray Houghton's scuttle, right to left, to seize on a poor clearing header by Baresi, then giving himself room to hit a left-foot shot up, over and down behind Pagliuca, Italy's goalkeeper. It gave Ireland a shock victory in New Jersey's Giants stadium. The point of contact was high on the instep and owed a bit to the sock, and for the second time Scotty, as he was known – for there he was born – had Irish eyes a-smiling. There were rather more of his adopted countrymen to be found in New York than in Stuttgart, where six years earlier he'd scored the goal that beat England in the European Championship. The contrast between the Irish and the American city's other main immigrant population had to be seen to be believed – or, better, to be heard.

Only Boston was missing from our itinerary covering eight of the nine cities involved – and I still haven't been there. But it was helpful that we kept returning to Dallas and the main broadcast centre. It offered the chance to test the pulse of the championship; hear all the in-house gossip; and use the Beeb's facilities to phone home. We also, of course, found time to visit the Book Repository, sit on the Grassy Knoll, and ponder the whole story in the John F. Kennedy museum.

I can't say I much enjoyed working with John Fashanu on the first match there. As Nigeria's new-found number-one fan and fixer, he was very one-eyed on an admittedly promising performance against Bulgaria. But seeing the Germans, who were three up in thirty-seven minutes, almost run out of gas against South Korea was, as I put it, 'delightful for the neutrals'. Klinsmann scored two of the goals; his second, flicking the ball up with his right foot then spinning to volley it home with his left, brought me right to the edge of my seat.

I had the chance to watch a video of Argentina's 4–0 thrashing of Greece. Maradona seemed reborn: after weight problems, health problems and a suspension for taking cocaine, he looked remarkably fit. I was looking forward to seeing him in the final group match. But I was to be disappointed: the World Cup career of the best player of his, or perhaps any other, generation came to an end in a cocktail of drugs after he'd reached twenty-one appearances. Instead, Hristo Stoichkov fashioned a first World Cup finals victory for Bulgaria in thirty-two years (eighteen matches) and, as fiery talisman, led his country all the way to the semi-final.

The two journeys away from Dallas were to be envied,

and, though I didn't know it at the time, they marked the start of five matches watching Brazil. The venues offered a marked contrast. I didn't care much for the Pontiac Silverdome, just north of Detroit. Quite why it was necessary to play football indoors in summer is hard to fathom, though it might, I suppose, be argued that it was one of the cooler venues. The match ended in a 1–1 draw through a clever lob by Kennet Andersson for Sweden and an equaliser from the darting little demon called Romario. Among the watchers were the former Brazilian motor-racing world champion Emerson Fittipaldi and the Spanish opera singer Placido Domingo. Sitting next to me was a certain 'Trevor Brookley', whom during a locally used interview Pele extolled for his playing career and his friendship. Mr Brooking smiled ruefully and took the subsequent leg-pulling in good part. We told nobody, of course.

Romario, the 'Pele' of the moment, had also scored against Cameroon in the stadium of Stanford University, whose all-wooden stands would never have passed the safety authorities at home. (Neither, probably, would the Olympic stadium in Rome, the scene of the 1990 final.) The Brazilians looked strong defensively but were helped in their cause by Rigobert Song – later an uncertain defender whose European tour included a stop at West Ham – becoming the youngest player to be sent off in the World Cup finals.

Thanks to the efforts of stewardess Penny Davies, of British Airways, to take her husband and children with her as often as she could on her trips around the world, I already knew something of San Francisco, which played host to the matches at Stanford Palo Alto. But for Simon it was a first visit. 'See you at around half past eight, in the lobby,' I said to him when we checked in late, 'but we aren't having breakfast here.' The following morning we turned left out of the hotel, crossed over to the right, round the corner and there, in Market Street, was the waiting cable car. Up, 'climbing halfway to the stars', as Tony Bennett sings, and then down to Fisherman's Wharf and along for breakfast at the Buena Vista – the full American menu. It was a wonderfully clear morning, with Alcatraz set in the blue of the bay; and breakfast could take all day – well, till close on lunch. Back on the cable car Simon's mobile rang. He passed it to me. It was Motty, early into the Giants stadium in New Jersey for Italy against Norway and wanting to check something about the Nigerians. Now it would be something quite common but then it was a whole new world in communication – 'from sea to shining sea'. No longer any chance of escape, but, as my family can tell you, I resisted long; and then got scolded for not turning it on.

A wake-up call was needed for the start of the second-round matches, whose early kick-off in Chicago led me to remark, 'Some of the defenders are still having breakfast.' It was, partly as a result, a thoroughly entertaining match, which left me wondering whether the German attack, with Klinsmann to the fore, would in the longer term be good enough to hide a defence embarrassed now by the spirited Belgians. The holders just about deserved to come through, but Belgium should have had a penalty for a foul by Helmer on Weber. The Swiss referee, Kurt Rothlisberger, admitted as much afterwards, and was sent home for his honesty.

Sandor Puhl of Hungary, who in the quarter-finals missed the worst foul of the finals, had rather better fortune. A vicious elbow by Tassotti of Italy on Spain's Luis Enrique led, after the video had been studied, to the Italian being given an eight-match suspension, which ended his international career. Had it been spotted at the time, Spain would have been awarded a late penalty with the chance to lead 2–1 and Italy would have been down to ten men. Instead Italy scored almost immediately and went on to give their best perform-ance, against Bulgaria, to reach the final, where Mr Puhl was waiting to greet them. Referees need luck as much as players.

Fortune also favoured the team on the other route, Brazil, whom I followed to their destiny. But before that, in my second match in the second round, I saw Ireland's demise in the city of Disney World, Orlando. The themes were not propitious. Two minutes before the start I appeared to be playing the role of Bashful, sitting under the commentary desk, clutching my notes – there was simply nowhere else for me to go – while Ken Osbourn, our prodigiously efficient engin-eer, tried to sort out line problems which were preventing us from going on air. Meanwhile Simon, suffering from toothache, was doing his best to be Happy rather than Grumpy. Then, in the match, Ireland's goalkeeper found himself cast in the role of Dopey. 'Oh, Pat Bonner,' I said, 'the hero of four years ago, makes a sad error,' as a long distance effort from Wim Jonk, an easy collection, bounced off the goalkeeper's knuckles for Holland's second goal.

Later in the year I introduced a review of the World Cup which included some poignant pictures of supporters carefully folding their Irish flag and a rather wistful Jack Charlton at the post-match press conference: 'See you all again sometime, maybe.' He knew it would be the end, and probably wished it so, but, for all the criticism of the direct style of play and taking advantage of the right to use somewhat tenuous Irish connections to build a team, it had been a fascinating six-year ride; and I'd been lucky to see many of the high points. Jack was a man's man, who played it, coached it and told it in a straightforward manner, not suffering fools gladly. He much enjoyed a good chat over a pint of Guinness, and Chris Lewis, the BBC producer with Jack's team in both US '94 and Italia '90, who it might fairly be said had a touch of the Irish about him, made sure that the boss and his sidekick, Maurice Setters, a ball-playing tackler of the old breed, had opportunities to get away from it all.

Jack had a soft side, too, as was seen when he fell on his knees at the end of the '66 final, and again in 2006's recollections forty years on; and I suspect in many moments on the riverbank, fishing – for him the greatest sport in the world. His achievements brought him not only the freedom to fish just about anywhere in the Emerald Isle but also the official freedom of Dublin.

Would England have been as generous if the Football Association had supported his application to be the national manager instead of not even bothering to acknowledge it? And would he have put up with the suits? At the fiftieth celebration of *Sports Review of the Year*, in 2004, I suddenly spotted him sitting next to Martin Peters on the stage. 'We've been waving at you for ages – thought you weren't going to notice us,' he said in that familiar Geordie accent. Three months after my exit from *Match of the Day*, it was a little thing which meant a lot to me.

In the 'Christmas special' programme I introduced Holland's quarter-final against Brazil with the titles of *Dallas*, the very popular soap of the eighties. Only the faces were changed, the stars of the coming encounter taking over from JR, Sue Ellen and company. But some of the stars in orange were missing – the sulking Ruud Gullit and the injured Marco van Basten – which, perhaps, was why they seemed not quite to believe they were good enough to beat Brazil. But the suspension of Leonardo, for an uncharacteristic moment of temper when challenged by America's Tab Ramos in their second-round meeting, robbed Brazil of a certain balance, and they were vulnerable. The Dutch proved that by coming back from being two goals down with under half an hour left, after the referee had suggested he was ten years ahead of his time by allowing Brazil's second goal by Bebeto to stand, although the retreating Romario, under the rule as it applied in 1994, was clearly offside.

Bergkamp began the counter with his best finals goal to date (he markedly bettered it four years on), and then Winter's head was much quicker than Taffarel's hand. But Leonardo's replacement, Branco, had the last word with a twenty-five-yard daisy-cutting free kick to win the match 3–2. Later, Bryan Robson brought him to Middlesbrough. And Brazil found another left back famed for his free kicks, and a far better one, Roberto Carlos. But the fame of both has lived on their only occasional spectacular successes.

England not being involved, the eight matches of the second round were evenly split between the BBC and ITV, with one live game on each of the four days. Motty and I shared the live ones, Clive Tyldesley and Tony Gubba covering the others for the recorded programmes. It was one each in the same format in the quarter-final. John had the story of the round, as the signs of German weakness against Belgium were exposed by Messrs Stoichkov and Letchkov of Bulgaria. Clive had Italy's great escape against Spain. For Tony it was the longest day, Sweden through on penalties against Romania; and for me the five goals in the Cotton Bowl.

It was Malcolm who broke the good news that I was to cover the final, and he did so with great warmth. This time I'd allowed myself to think it might happen and John Motson's comment, when we all met in Dallas before the quarter-finals, about press reaction in my favour added strength to the hope. There was no special celebration; just the good wishes of the headquarters group and a toast at dinner. I'd just been picked: I had yet to play. But there was much satisfaction in the phone call home.

It is a cliché to write about family support, but the evidence of the reaction to the news is on record, thanks to my far more organised wife and son. Penny's diary tells of the Sunday morning phone call and how she, Gigi and Mark jigged around in excitement, and the bonus that the two of us should be able to meet, for she was arriving in Los Angeles on a trip the following evening. Mark has always been a good letter-writer; the early influence, perhaps, of the need to write those 'thank you' letters. Among his carefully bound collection is a copy of one he wrote to his retired 'House Dame' from his days at Eton, bringing her up to date with news of himself and his contemporaries.

> *Talking of fathers in the paper, the Davieses were cata-pulted to fame this week when Daddy was given the World Cup final, as you may have seen or heard. The news was carried by every paper except* The Times *(confirming Charlie's opinion, of course!!) and even made the front page of the* Independent, *despite the fact that their editor-ial policy tends only to report 'hard news'. We were over the moon as you can well expect. Daddy has waited 17 years to do a major final and we very much hope this will be the start of him being the BBC's Number One, although that depends on the public's reaction and whether the Head of Sport is inundated with hate or love mail!!*

I have little doubt that one day he will be asked to write his autobiography, and he'll certainly be far better prepared for the task than his father! My diaries have sadly tended to peter out around March at best. I've kept a few letters – some in my own hand, more received – including some very close and often amusing ones from my father when I was away at school, but their home is among the memora-bilia somewhere in the loft.

On the Tuesday I awarded myself a day off, which I spent in Santa Monica with Penny, returning in good time for the semi-final. Through their own profligacy and Thomas Ravelli, Sweden's goalkeeper, continuing where he'd left off in the quarter-final shoot-out with the Romanians, Brazil needed eighty-one minutes to score the goal which took them on to the final. 'At last!' was my comment when Romario nipped between two defenders finally to beat the goalkeeper. I couldn't help feeling that Hagi and his Romanian company would have played with more belief than the Swedes. I gave Jonas Thern, their captain, a pretty hard time for getting himself sent off for a needless and rather spiteful tackle on the Brazilian skipper, Dunga, who, although by no means the most gifted in the team, surely deserves a better nickname than the Portuguese slang for 'Dopey'. If he survives until 2010 in his new role as the national team's coach, he could become the first to captain and coach a World Cup-winning Brazilian team.

I'd love to be able to say that the final in the colourful Rose Bowl was the most memorable match of my career, but it would qualify only as an occasion, not as a game of football. Brazil, in the final for the first time for twenty-four years, were meeting the country they'd beaten so majestically in Mexico City's Azteca stadium; but Pasadena offered a pale comparison. It was, though, the hottest match I can remember, markedly more so than the quarter-final between England and Argentina in Mexico eight years earlier. Simon, ever prepared, brought along an ice-box and many small towels to cool his commentary team of three (Terry Venables joined Trevor Brooking and me). Considering the temperature, which touched 100 degrees Fahrenheit, and the number of walking wounded at the end of an arduous month, there could be no complaint except perhaps to FIFA, who, as usual, seemed to put the needs of the players at the bottom of their list of requirements.

What proved to be my only World Cup final was the only one to be scoreless and the first to be decided in a penalty competition. But it wasn't the worst – Italia '90, which I came close to commentating, enjoys that distinction. It might easily have been different in Pasadena: the two attacking stars of the championship, Romario and Roberto Baggio, both missed open goals, and Gianluca Pagliuca had a moment when he dozed off, awaking only when the ball which had gone through his hands came back to him off a post. There was a chuckle in my voice, but I was glad he survived.

Franco Baresi was Italy's man of the final. He'd had a knee operation after their opening match and it was a big surprise that he played. But fate wasn't kind: he missed the first penalty, and the ponytailed Baggio, who'd carried Italy through to the final and now played, virtually, on one leg, missed the last, when, with the tally 2–3, he had to score. But the outcome was probably right and I was pleased for Carlos Alberto Parreira. The pressure on him to end the long losing streak was enormous. As I put it, 'Collectively they were short of being a great side, but they had one player touched with genius.' The close-up was of Romario.

Back at the hotel there was a small pasta party with a few glasses of wine. The next England manager told me I'd had a very good World Cup. The family thought so, too, particularly as regards the final, and noted it down again. But I arrived home twenty-four hours after Penny had left for Bangkok and she wouldn't be back for ten days. It's about swings and roundabouts.

37

The Square Mile of History

Speaking to sixth-formers at Reed's School in Surrey – Tim Henman's alma mater, as cuttings books in the head-master's waiting-room make clear – I was asked by one of the pupils if there was anything in my television life I regretted not having done. She was probably a little surprised, as in some ways was I, when, after a brief pause, I replied, 'The Cenotaph service and parade in Whitehall.'

It was more than a little out of context with everything which had gone before and I offered only a brief explanation. On the short drive home I thought of John Arlott and Gladstone's Midlothian campaign.

But I'd covered the Lord Mayor's Show, the first of three events nearly always together at 'Poppy' time, the second being the Festival of Remembrance in the Royal Albert Hall.

I'd been the commentator on the last Royal Tournament – the decision to bring it to an end having nothing to do with my performance! And I was also the voice on *All the Queen's Horses*, one of the tribute programmes at the time of Her Majesty's Golden Jubilee. I was pencilled in to do Trooping the Colour until it was realised I'd be away at the World Cup. And, but for Simon Betts being changed to cover Whitehall rather than Windsor, I'd probably have reported the Queen Mother's final journey to the castle – and local knowledge would have enabled me to point out that the journey alongside the castle wall by Home Park was not 'the journey the Queen Mother would have been familiar with', because her usual route would have been to turn left, not right, at the top of Datchet High Street to enter the castle grounds at the Frogmore Gate, which is adjacent to the increasingly popular Royal Farm Shop.

Perhaps it was an error to point this out – not in a manner critical of the excellent Brian Hanrahan, I should make clear while chatting things over with the head of events, Nick Vaughan Barrett, for I retained the Lord Mayor's Show for only one more year. I'd thought about opting out the year before but had been persuaded by the pageant master, Dominic Reid, to support a fourth different producer, Julie Heptonstall, who had also been in charge, and expertly so, of *All the Queen's Horses*. She and I saw two lord mayors installed, and her last words to me, of thanks, were on the lines of, 'This show really couldn't go on without you.' That, of course, was arrant nonsense, but a sentiment which you might think would have prompted some communication from her when, just seven weeks before the 2004 show, Nick rang to tell me he was making a change, 'to move the show on'. At what point the committee for the election of the next lord mayor was informed of the decision I don't know, but the usual invitation to the traditional Lighting Up dinner, which takes place ten days before the show, duly arrived and had to be forwarded with apologies. The dinner, incidentally, serves also as a test of the menu later presented at the Lord Mayor's Banquet addressed by the prime minister. At that stage I didn't know that Paul Dickenson was to be my successor. Unfortunately my later email wishing him well and offering a couple of tips were, thanks to his computer's failure, not received until after the event.

I next saw Nick after the Queen's eightieth-birthday walkabout in Windsor in April 2006. He may have been a little preoccupied, but his greeting when I offered my hand was decidedly less warm than that I received from two producers I'd much enjoyed working with, Ian Russell and David Pickthall. I'd been working that day for Radio Berkshire, to whom I'm most grateful for involving me in their coverage of the last two royal occasions in Windsor.

I realise that I may be leaving myself open to criticism here. In response, I hope there are enough producers who would confirm that I'm pretty easy to work with. It wasn't being replaced which upset me – programmes need renewing, as do commentators and presenters. It was the manner and the timing. You may also wonder if, with all the different things I've been asked to do, seeking another was a bit greedy. There I plead guilty, but television is like that: producers and performers should be ambition-driven. It may also be more than reasonable to ask whether I really thought I was good enough to deputise for or replace David Dimbleby. I can only answer that I have the utmost respect for his work and his contribution to broadcasting – and I don't know, because I was never given the chance. But, in different circumstances, I might have been.

From time to time the BBC hold cocktail parties with guest lists designed to bring together people from the many varied sections of its output, mixing producers and performers, the latter group usually including a few household names. On the evening I was invited the best-known were Timothy West and his wife, Prunella Scales, and the comedian Bob Monkhouse. It was an extremely pleasant couple of hours and in particular afforded me the opportunity to thank Monkhouse for a past kindness. He was once a passenger when Penny was a member of the cabin crew. She asked if he'd mind signing our children's autograph books, which she carried around with her on her flights. Not only did he agree but he asked if he could keep them for a little while. He'd found ink-blots on both and used them to draw signed caricatures.

Shortly afterwards I was accosted by a lady who greeted me with, 'I spent most of my "board" talking about you.' She went on to explain that she was a producer in Birmingham and had applied for the vacant position of head of events. She was embarrassingly complimentary, but as Jonathan Martin, the head of sport, who had joined us, swiftly reminded me afterwards, she didn't get the job. What might have been! (Much later Jonathan would be equally generous, with his comments at the Royal Television Society awards.)

So there was nothing after the Lord Mayor's Show for me; no Whitehall on the Sunday morning or Royal Albert Hall on the Saturday evening. Even so, I look back on my eight-year involvement with the Events Department with much affection, and I'm very grateful to my first producer, Stephen Morris, who, like the lady whose name I know not, felt I had something to offer – and he, in 1996, had only my sports commentaries to judge me by.

I vividly recall his encouragement over a drink the night before my debut show: 'If you can do this you can do any event; and you can do it, I've no doubt about that.' He also warned me that it would go by in a flash, and how right he was. Apart from various meetings and getting to know the department's chief researcher, Helen Holmes, my introduction to the show came at the rehearsal hour: five in the morning at Wood Street police station, just round the corner from the Guildhall, the hub of the City of London Corporation.

I'd travelled down from covering a match in Liverpool the previous evening, and had had less than four hours' sleep. But it was in meeting my first lord mayor – the jolly Roger Cork – over coffee and croissants, as we all took in the instructions of Pageant Master Dominic Reid, that I first found the pulse of the show and a warmth for it which was renewed every year.

When I was a boy, my parents rarely missed an early Saturday evening radio programme on the Home Service called *In Town Tonight*. It began with the words, 'Once again we stop the roar of London's traffic.' Now, before the day had broken, I saw it happen as we followed the lord mayor's golden coach from Guildhall to St Paul's Cathedral while he rehearsed what was required of him, both on the journey and in receiving a blessing to be given by the Dean (who for all but the first year of my time was a man called Moses). My commentary position was at Amen Corner, facing the cathedral, but even when it was later moved to close by the Mansion House, which meant that the last pictures television saw of the coach was of it disappearing down Poultry, I still attended the rehearsal – and the sumptuous early breakfast at the Worshipful Company of Butchers which followed it.

That the Butchers are twenty-fourth in line among the livery companies was one of the many things I learned about the City of London and the people who make it work. The leaders are the Mercers and in the Lord Mayor's Show of 1999 I had a special reason for noting that fact. Their Master was one Richard Withers Green, who travelled in a carriage with the Masters of the Grocers, Drapers and Fishmongers, the top four of the 'Great Twelve'. Eleven months later his younger daughter, Miranda, married my son Mark at the aldermen's church of St Lawrence Jewry, the reception being held at Drapers' Hall.

I loved the history of an event which continues the line of lord mayors of London dating back to one Henry Fitzailwyn in 1189, though the tradition of the new lord mayor showing himself to the people before swearing his allegiance to the crown dates from 1215 when King John granted the citizens of the City the right to choose their lord mayor. In a small way, in terms of publicising their chosen charity, I served and came to know eight who held the office at the end of the twentieth century and the beginning of the twenty-first. Their City, though, is but a square mile – the heart of the country's finance. The rest belongs to Ken Livingstone, though why the government couldn't have made Ken's title 'High Sheriff' or something similar, I don't know. The beauty of the show is its variety; a carnival, a military parade and a civic parade rolled into one. Saying 'Yabba dabba doo' in my first show as Fred Flintstone went by in his float may have taken Helen by surprise but she need not have worried that once I started on the cap badges of the London Regiment I'd be sure to mention them all. Her knowledge of the military and the protocol of the occasion were somewhat ahead of those who followed her. Among them was a producer who had his cameras going backwards and forwards over the floats, giving a major test to my system of using flip-top photographic albums containing cards of information, and had to be reminded that he needed first to see the King's Troop, Royal Horse Artillery, at the start of the civic parade.

Only the lord mayor's coach ride is rehearsed; the rest is in the hands of the pageant master and his team of military marshals. Forget the old adage of not performing with children or animals; here anything can go wrong – but amazingly it rarely does.

However much I enjoyed it, I always came away from the show thinking about the float that went by without a word, the service person who deserved a mention left as a number in the ranks, and the many tales left untold. The increasing involvement of interviewers and guests made that more likely and, while I am all for live television, I always wished that the show could be recorded so that there'd be more time for the often fascinating expert opinion, for the best interviews and for more of the show, including the fireworks that follow in the evening. 'Too costly' would be the response, I am sure, but it would provide a good early-evening programme on the Sunday, rather than being crammed between children's television and the afternoon sport on the Saturday.

I began my first commentary with a quote from Wordsworth – 'This City now doth like a garment wear / The beauty of the morning' – and, while not as sunny as on that day, the weather on the second Saturday of November was generally kind. By the end of my stint, in 2004, I agreed with Dr Johnson that, 'When a man is tired of London, he is tired of life.' The Remembrancer, Adrian Barnes, CVO, the Queen's representative in the City, kindly arranged that I should, in the presence of Lord Mayor Gavin Arthur, receive the freedom of the City.

The other two programmes I covered for Events *were* recorded and 'one-offs'. One was the last Royal Tournament, which Jim Davidson, very much a serviceman's friend, presented. The producer, Dave Pickthall, recorded three shows, with Jim doing a number of interviews while I was able to research backstage such things as the organisation behind the musical drive of the King's Troop, Royal Horse Artillery – six teams, each of three riders, six horses and a 13-pounder gun weighing one-and-a-half tons; the whole shooting-match very nearly the length of a cricket pitch. Timing their cross-runs needed both skill and courage.

Later I wrote a script to the final edit but tried to make

it sound as though it was all happening at the time of the broadcast. What gave me a particular kick was that Dave agreed that we should try to do the most dramatic and popular part of the show, the Field Gun Competition, armed with all the timings and the penalties awarded so as to make it a proper race for the viewer. We did it in one take and I felt almost as exhausted as the gallant crews who took part.

The idea of *All the Queen's Horses* came from the Pageant of the Horse on which Simon Betts had asked me to commentate, which was due to take place in Windsor Great Park in April 1999 but had to be cancelled because the ground was waterlogged. Somewhat scaled down and taking place in Home Park, the site of the annual Windsor Horse Show, it became the first of many special programmes by the BBC in Golden Jubilee year, providing what I called 'this tribute to Her Majesty from the world of the horse which she knows so well and feels so keenly'. As with the Royal Tournament I watched a couple of the public shows during the week, and my commentary on the composite programme, which included some wonderful archive footage, was recorded the following week. I hope I was able to suggest that I was there with the presenter, Clare Balding, and her various interviewees in the shadow of Windsor Castle.

38

It's Slippery Out There

The 1998 Olympic Winter Games in Nagano offered me a sort of double whammy: my first ceremony for ten years and my first time as lead commentator in the figure skating. I'd covered two European Championships, those in Paris and Milan, and one World, in Lausanne, since Alan Weeks had retired; but much of Nagano was live.

The approach was a little different. Robin Cousins now had more time to express himself with occasional comments during the routine before analysing the slow-motion replays. From time to time I tried to pre-empt the jump that was about to be attempted, and I had a few letters saying this was more helpful than being told after it had happened. In Nagano we had time to discuss a few points, and it worked well in a relaxed fashion.

The two favourites in Japan were the Canadian, Elvis

Stojko, who had won three of the four World Championships in the years between Olympics, and Michelle Kwan, now a veteran of seventeen, who had just regained her United States title from the precocious Tara Lipinski who had beaten her in both the National and World Championships the year before. Stojko was typically bullish when I interviewed him before the men's competition got under way, but Kwan, playing a little bit the prima donna, arrived after the Games had begun, stayed out of the village and treated the whole thing as if it were just another World Championships. Both eventually joined the list of those who never managed to add the Olympic crown to their World titles.

In contrast to Kwan, Lipinski seemed determined to have a ball, and her approach won the day. In the free programmes both offered seven triple jumps, though of no great height, but Lipinski included two different combinations leaving me to conclude, 'She's stolen the title. Tara Lipinski's come up with the goods.' Beating Sonja Henie by two months, she became, at fifteen years and two hundred and fifty-five days, the youngest individual gold medallist in the Winter Olympics and quickly – rather too quickly for the sport – left the scene for the professional ranks. The loser went back to winning World Championships, only for Salt Lake City to bring a repeat of her nightmare.

'Sarah Hughes: a wonderful performance before a packed house and before her seventeenth birthday' was my summary as another American youngster, not unfittingly from Great Neck, New York State, got it right on the night. Skating first after being only fourth in the short programme she proved too good for the two favourites, Irina Slutskaya of Russia, who took the silver, and Kwan, who won the bronze.

It was as well, I think, that after her skating association and an adoring public had stayed with her in hope of success at last in Turin, failure to recover from injury prevented Kwan from competing in a third Games. There would surely not have been enough in her programme in a new era under a more demanding scoring system. Slutskaya, dominant in Europe, and the current world best, had more than enough but skating last it just didn't happen for her. The winner, Shizuka Arakawa, I said, 'really took her chance . . . So graceful, and looked a picture on the ice. A first Olympic figure-skating title for Japan.' And, I might have added, clearly a grown woman, which was, I believe, good for skating.

The men's championship continued a run of Russian winners begun by the surprising champion in Lillehammer, Alexei Urmanov – Victor Petrenko making it clear that his victory in Albertville was for Ukraine. Ilia Kulik was barely out of boyhood when he gave an astonishingly mature and classical perform-ance to claim the title in Nagano, with eight triple jumps following his opening quadruple toe loop. And that became the required standard. Four years on Alexei Yagudin was im-perious, with bronze breastplate and imaginary sword, performing to *The Man in the Iron Mask*. He was the last to skate and with straight 5.9s for technical merit there had to be a six for artistic impression after that performance. How quickly through his tears he saw that there were four I don't know; nor whether he knew that no individual skater before him at an Olympic Games had been awarded more than one. Soon afterwards we knew that, with the implementation of a totally different scoring system, it could never be beaten.

I think that for the sheer verve of the performance I would place Yagudin first among the Olympic champions I have seen. The men's competition, as usual, followed the pairs. So my comment about him at the time made reference to the drama there, about which more anon. 'Oh, they've got it right tonight, the judges . . . Absolutely for sure. He will stand tall among the list of great Olympic champions.' Much was made of Evgeny Plushenko's fall attempting a quad in the short programme, but his turn was to come in Turin with a total points score of 258.33. In the gala he was as magnificently his extrovert self as he had been unusually cold and calculated in claiming the title.

Ilia Kulik is now married to Yekaterina Gordeyeva, who was but a little sprite when first seen with Sergei Grinkov in the Pairs competition – so much so in fact that it was felt it gave them too great an advantage. She was only fourteen (he was seventeen) when they won their first world title, and two years later they were Olympic champions in Calgary in '88. Married and with a two-year-old daughter, they, like T & D, came back from the professional ranks to reclaim the title in the now open competition in Lillehammer. But in November the following year, while rehearsing for *Stars on Ice*, Grinkov suffered a heart attack and died almost immediately. He was just twenty-eight years old. There have been some wonderful pairs skaters in the twenty-two years I've been involved in the coverage of skating, but they were the best.

I've never understood why the event is always the first to be completed at every major championship. It's often the most exciting, combining skill, daring and artistry, requiring much bravery from the female partner, with so many difficult lifts and thrown jumps. The champions in Turin, Tatiana Totmianina and Maxim Marinin, had come back from a horrendous accident the previous year, she falling headlong from the highest point of a lift when he tripped. And one of the lasting images of the Games of 2006 was the injury to Dan Zhang of China, who fell on an attempted thrown quad salchow.

There followed much debate about why the pair were allowed, after some delay, to pick up their programme from the point of the accident, and it will not happen again – Ottavio Cinquanta, president of the ISU, will see to that. But that was nothing compared with the furore which had engulfed figure skating, its president, and the new president of the International Olympic Committee, Jacques Rogge, after the Pairs competition in Salt Lake City.

At the end of the free programme the judges were split 5–4. Yelena Berezhnaya and Anton Sikharulidze, of Russia, who had won the short programme, presented their classic *Meditation by Thaïs*, superbly choreographed but on the night a little rough round the edges. Their technical marks were down, but for presentation there were seven 5.9s. At the end of their short programme, Jamie Sale and David Pelletier of Canada had lost concentration, he falling on the final pose. Now they offered a contrast for the judges, skating to *Love Story*. The crowd, the majority obviously from North America, loved it and there were shouts for sixes.

In the build-up to the Games the rumour mill, always working overtime at major skating competitions, had suggested that the Russians would support the French world ice dance champions in their bid to add the Olympic title. Now as the scores came up for the pairs, the Russian, Chinese, Polish and Ukraine judges had the Russian pair first: the United States, Canada, Germany and Japan had gone for the Canadians. The vote that stood out and gave victory to Berezhnaya and Sikharulidze was that of the French judge, Marie-Reine le Gougne. I felt I had to go out on a limb and tell the story. 'It is difficult to avoid the conclusion,' I said, 'that the vote of the French judge owes something to the ice-dancing competition which will be decided later in the week.' Robin backed me up.

With both at their best I would have preferred the Russians but on the night I thought the Canadians were better and I have never understood how technical mistakes – Sikharulidze had stumbled on his double axel – aren't seen as marring the presentation. Le Gougne later told the British technical delegate referee, Sally-Anne Stapleford, that she had indeed been pressurised to vote for the Russians because of the ice dancing. The IOC awarded gold to the Canadians as well, and happy smiles were on show as all four skaters posed for the cameras. Le Gougne received a three-year suspension, as did the head of the French delegation, Didier Gailhaguet, with neither being able to appear at the Turin Olympics. For the record the Russian judge in the ice dancing voted for his own couple.

The following July, when an Uzbekistan criminal was arrested at his Italian home on drugs-trafficking charges, a tape was found in which he was heard discussing arrangements of the pairs and ice-dancing results. The United States sought his extradition but after a year in jail he went instead to Russia. Ms Stapleford, who was part of a group which tried to set up an alternative governing body to the ISU and failed, is now persona non grata – not the first, nor probably the last, whistleblower to be so treated.

The French couple, Marina Anissina (who, incidentally, was born in Moscow) and Gwendal Peizerat, duly won the ice dancing in Utah. There was no movement of the top eight from their positions at the end of the first compulsory dance, far from an uncommon occurrence, and once again one which beggared belief (it is ridiculous to suggest that every couple does every part of the competition to exactly the same standard – some waltz better or tango better, and so on). Their choice of Martin Luther King's 'I have a dream' speech as their background I found distasteful and utterly wrong for a sporting event. But the judges placed them first, with a 5–4 split in the free dance over the married Russian couple Irina Lobacheva and Ilia Averbukh (he was once Anissina's partner). But the most disappointed couple were the Italians, Barbara Fusar-Poli and Maurizio Margaglio, then reigning World and European champions who only managed bronze. Four years later they returned from the show ranks to leave a lasting impression at their 'home games' in Turin. Long after the names of the winners there, Tatiana Navka and Roman Kostomarov, who regained the title for Russia, are forgotten, figure skating will remember Barbara Fusar-Poli's 'ice cold in anger' stare when her partner, poor fellow, stumbled in the original dance which they had begun in the lead. As I said at the time, 'In the argument as to whose fault it was, he doesn't have a leg to stand on.'

The viewing figures for figure skating at the Winter

Olympics in Turin suggest the sport may be about to make something of a resurgence on the box at a time when television audiences are falling in North America, the result, I think, of a surfeit of programmes involving big names who can no longer perform as they once did. Particularly impressive in the UK were the interactive figures in Britain – you know, press the red button and get your money's worth (we hope).

Part of the reason for the revival is the promise shown by the British ice dance champions, John and Sinead Kerr. Following the brother-and-sister partnership on their attempt to win a medal in Vancouver in the Games of 2010 will be the carrot for both home watchers and television executives. There has, I believe, always been an audience who watch for entertainment alone, unconcerned that we've moved from the old 5.9 mark to the new 116.5, but it does help if there's a British competitor to follow.

The Kerrs are very different from T & D, know it, and don't want to be compared to them. Their performance in Turin, when they finished tenth, was all the more praiseworthy because the leading skaters all had more difficult and therefore higher-scoring moves. Their decision to join the double Olympic champion Evgeny Platov in Connecticut was a good one and has brought a marked improvement in their technical scores. But their natural effervescence, so clear in their 2008 original Scottish folk dance, has yet to be seen in their free dances. The enthusiasm that flows from the whole family will take them a long way, but the journey will make many demands and the competition is very stiff.

*

The ISU claim that they had already started their search for a new scoring system before the debacle in Utah, but what happened there – the root cause being the questionable judging for many years in ice dancing – certainly provided considerable impetus to their task. Whether they have got it right – with the skaters now competing directly against each other, accumulating marks for everything they do, and each jump, spin or step sequence being given a grade of execution – remains to be seen.

Many skaters like it because they can examine their results in detail and see which areas need improvement, though there have been complaints about inconsistency of marking. Fourteen judges with the computer choosing nine and the top and bottom marks discounted – and the subsequent checking of the correctness of the marks given – suggests greater fairness. It was, though, difficult not to smile at the observation of the American skating critic Christine Brennan, who wrote in USA Today: 'This new system allows the judges to be anonymous, arguably the worst idea ever for a sport known for cheating.'

I think there's another danger, too: that the 'wow!' factor may have been lost. 'Just . . . look . . . at . . . those . . . marks!' said a delighted and excited Alan Weeks, viewing the scores for Torvill and Dean. 'Nine sixes – every one a six!' There's no better definition of what I mean.

39

From Venables to Hoddle

Terry Venables knew from an early age that he was a leader, not a follower. At times that led him to over-ambition, and in his business life he certainly skated on some very thin ice – in that area, at least, he more than met his match in Alan Sugar. But the lad from Dagenham (incidentally, the birthplace of Alf Ramsey, too, which might have been forgotten) has always come bouncing back.

Watching him trying to find the right words during and after England's matches in Germany in summer 2006, his frustration at not being able to do anything about it was all too clear. He had something of that look over forty years ago, as the leader of a young Chelsea side, when I wrote about him for *The Times* that 'His apparent inability to take a grip of his side was probably the most telling factor' of their semi-final defeat in the FA Cup by Liverpool in 1965. They took revenge for 'leaving the stage at Villa Park like child actors who had suddenly forgotten their lines' by removing the holders at Anfield in the third round the following season, but that side, under Tommy Docherty, never quite fulfilled its promise. And neither did Venables.

Two England caps and a Cup winner's medal, with Spurs against Chelsea a year later, 1967, were the only rewards for an intelligent and entertaining midfield player. 'And what did he win as a manager?' is a question often asked by those who accuse the media of being beguiled by his charm and quick wit, which make for ready quotes. I recall sitting with him on an evening which should have given the perfect response, but Barcelona, whom he had led to the championship, lost on penalties in the 1986 European Cup final to Steaua Bucharest, who had spent most of the match seeking that lottery win. 'Mr Venables, how can professional players take penalties like that?' was the first question from the Spanish journalists at the press conference following the match. As England manager ten years on, he suffered a similar fate, though in 1996 only one penalty was missed, and then it was said that he had all the advantages, yet didn't succeed.

Save for the 'Oh no!' moment – 'Poor Gareth Southgate' – I have nothing but fond memories of Euro '96. And even then I'd like to think that, without their possible choice of adjectives, I said what most viewers were saying, or just thinking. I commentated four times on Venables's men and saw the best England performance at Wembley for years.

I also saw two matches involving the team who ought to have been the European champions and, in contrast to their usual guarded approach, they played in an entertaining, attacking fashion. Unfortunately, Italy were forced into that style by their manager's decision, after a winning start, to play about with team selection for their second match in the tournament, at Anfield, where they had a man, Apolloni, sent off. Defeat then by the Czechs left them needing to beat the Germans in their final match. Arrigo Sacchi, the Italian team boss, had said that the fans would either kiss his bald pate or pour tomatoes on it. Unhappily for him, it was the latter; fifty matches in charge, and out.

The meeting with Germany, who had already qualified for the second stage, was enthralling, but hard on Gianfranco Zola. Sent off unfairly in the World Cup match against Nigeria in US '94 (on his twenty-eighth birthday), he now struck the worst penalty I can recall at international level: it barely managed to roll to Kopke. But Italy had many chances, several of them set up by the veteran Roberto Donadoni (now leader of Italy's 2008 challenge to be European champions as well as holders of the World Cup).

It was certainly all go in the Old Trafford commentary box that night: I felt in the second half that I was commentating on two matches at once. While Italy sought the goal they needed, with many attacks that promised but failed to deliver, and occasionally Germany seemed likely to snatch a goal against the run of play, I was being fed the score from the other match in the group – at Anfield – which with a few details I passed on to the viewers. Highlights of that match were to follow the live transmission but it was rightly felt that we should keep the viewers informed.

With five minutes left, as in front of me the Italians became increasingly desperate, I passed on news that the Czech Republic, who had been two goals up against Russia at half-time, only to be pulled back to 2–2 within ten minutes of the restart, were now losing 3–2. Italians in the crowd started to cheer, for a Russian victory, as I explained, meant that a draw for Italy would see their team through. Then in the last minute it all changed: Old Trafford was again full of Italian despair. Not another missed chance, nor a German goal; the Czechs had equalised at Anfield. They were in second place behind the Germans on the strength of having beaten the ten men of Italy in that second match, when Apolloni was dismissed. As well as feeling pretty exhausted, I felt sorry for Clive Tyldesley, who in contrast with the 0–0 I'd watched, had had a six-goal thriller which barely made six minutes on the air – he's had plenty of consolation since. The crucial goal at Anfield that night, incidentally, was scored by Vladimir Smicer, who later had many good days – and some frustrating ones – in the colours of Liverpool.

Among my four other commentating matches away from Wembley, the chipped goal by Davor Suker against Denmark's Peter Schmeichel at Hillsborough stands out, especially after the Croat had only just been denied when he tried a shot from within touching distance of the halfway line. I suspect I made some reference to Pele, but a few years later the comparison would have been with David Beckham, who succeeded in his aim. I don't think it was a great championship:

there were too many matches decided by penalties and too many defenders among the best performers. Matthias Sammer, the German sweeper, good but not in Beckenbauer's class, was considered by many to be the player of the tournament. The prime minister, John Major, described it as 'a wonderful three weeks of football', but although he is genuine in his love of sport I suspect that his observation owed much to the atmosphere, which seemed good around the country as a whole, and at Wembley was superb.

The BBC allowed a lot of time for that atmosphere to come through the airways. Having always believed that a big part of the commentator's job is to persuade the viewer that he or she has a seat in the stand, I really enjoyed the opportunity – which mainly meant letting the singing be heard without too many words from me. It was hard to resist singing along to 'Football's Coming Home', the best football song ever.

The best England performance was unquestionably against Holland, which was lucky for ITV because it was their live match; not that that affected in any way the enjoyment for David Pleat and me. The third of England's four goals is a wonderful piece of archive. Gascoigne wide to McManaman – back to Gascoigne – a teasing run into the box – a flick of the right boot to Sheringham – the feint to shoot, instead a lay-off to Shearer with an invitation to bury it, readily accepted – superb; and at the end of nineteen passes only interrupted by a free kick. This match was a lily that deserved to be gilded.

The tension of the next two games was far greater, and 'lucky against Spain, unlucky against Germany' a simple shorthand version of what happened. Several images remain, among them Stuart Pearce's fierce determination, which I hope will still bring him success in management. He suggested in his book, *Psycho: The Autobiography*, that I overplayed his triumphant reaction to the 'perfect penalty', after his miss in Turin. As he's an old-fashioned guy with a patriotic backbone, both of which qualities I applaud, I think the expression is 'Tell that to the marines!'

Paul Gascoigne's near miss in the crazy first half of extra time in the semi-final when, amazingly, both sides went seeking the 'golden goal' is another vivid memory. He later admitted that he had just hesitated. And Venables's arm round the disconsolate Gareth Southgate is a third.

The player had plenty more to offer, and not only in enjoying the pizza for profit in an advert with Chris Waddle, who had also missed in Turin. But for the manager it was the end of the road. At the time it was the shortest career of any in the role, twenty-four matches and only one defeat outside penalties (by Brazil) in twenty-eight months. As with Bobby Robson, the Football Association rather carelessly lost a manager in his prime. Venables's warning, after the Holland match, of the dangers of getting carried away by a good performance – 'Just when you think you've got things licked in the game, it can smack you in the face' – can be given a different connotation. Partly through his own fault and partly because of the FA's fear of his business life, which, while certainly not giving him a character reference, wouldn't have disbarred him from the football job, the assessment of Venables's true ability has been left for watchers to argue over. His players support him because of his coaching, and in his late sixties he had the chance, I'm sure, to add to his converts.

Although he may have felt let down by the players he treated as adults, he used the reported wild goings-on during a '96 pre-tournament trip to Hong Kong to build a positive team spirit. He was comfortable with players of supposed wayward character, and concentrated on giving rein to what a player could do on the field rather than worrying about what he couldn't. Also, while he supported his players he had no obvious favourites. In Euro '96 he helped turn back the clock for Gascoigne and got the best out of McManaman and Anderton, to name but three, and picked the best pairing up front since Lineker and Beardsley in the combative Shearer and the clever Sheringham. And his team, admittedly helped by the crowd, managed to carry the tempo of the English game into the international tournament arena. His choice in the match against Germany stands comparison with Bobby Robson's side which suffered the same fate six years earlier, though the Germans in Turin were a good deal better than at Wembley. (Pearce, Platt and Gascoigne played in both matches; Gary Neville, the best right back in '96, was suspended at Wembley.)

'All the lads and lasses are here, and all the smiling and painted faces, all hoping that the summer carnival will continue' were my words when Des handed over early to me on semi-final night. It continued till nearing midnight and was, in spite of the result, an evening to relish.

Venables's successor, Glenn Hoddle, was immediately into World Cup qualifying games, away matches in Moldova and Georgia, with a home game against a more traditional foe, Poland, at Wembley, fitted in between. All three were won, and he could enjoy his first Christmas as England manager. I was enormously pleased for him.

To tell the truth I've forgotten now the first match I saw Hoddle play for Spurs, but I remember well that in my *Grandstand* report I gave the score, the scorers and then spent the rest of what in those days was a minute talking about the most naturally gifted English player I'd seen in my days in the commentary box. His father must have been listening or been told about it, for on the night his son made his debut for England he came up to thank me for my comments. The match, against Bulgaria in November 1979, was played on a Thursday because of fog the previous evening. Hoddle scored a fine goal which drew a somewhat predictable line from me of 'What a start for Hoddle!' and over the years I could have been accused of bias in his favour. He should have been in the Hundred Caps Club, but while he always starred for Tottenham he couldn't quite dominate international matches in the way his talent demanded.

Michel Platini once told me that had Hoddle been a Frenchman he'd have been far more appreciated and a first name on the team sheet. Yet I can remember suggesting to Hoddle that maybe he should note how often Platini finished what he started. It was a criticism of Glenn after the bright start to his career that he was not found often enough ahead of the ball. But he was a wonderful player and played many good matches for his country, not least against Poland in Monterrey in the 1986 World Cup and, later, in the quarter-final against Argentina in Mexico City.

His time under Arsene Wenger at Monaco first sowed the seeds of management and his start at Swindon, almost a miracle, and at Chelsea promised much. His honeymoon with England, however, seemed to have come to an abrupt end in February '97 when England lost at home to Italy, a result which put qualification in doubt. There was much criticism of his choice of Matt Le Tissier, but what disappointed me more was the way Hoddle failed to support him subsequently. I'm not suggesting Le Tissier had a good match but he almost scored at the outset, catching the Italians – and, I confess, me – by surprise with a shot from some twenty yards which just cleared the bar, and the chance he had in the second half would not have been a chance at all to a lesser player. It's true that 'Le Tiss' was in and out of Venables's line-ups, but because of the type of player he'd been himself I thought Hoddle should have had greater understanding. As it was, Le Tissier's international career ended that night.

For Hoddle the setback was a prelude to his best moment in the position, a tactical triumph in Rome, where England held Italy 0–0 to gain the point that was needed for automatic qualification for France '98. But a number of things led to his downfall. Dropping Paul Gascoigne from the squad again suggested a lack of sensitivity. It's fair to say he was past his prime and was a difficult case, but if there was to be an Indian summer for the 'daft genius' the World Cup would surely have been the challenge to produce it. Some of the players didn't understand the manager and found it hard that his demonstrations of individual skills were of a higher standard than most of them could achieve. And the press turned against him because of what they saw as his attempts to mislead, especially about team selection.

I wasn't among those who felt he should have played Beckham and Owen in the first match, a comfortable enough victory over Tunisia, believing that it was best to ease them into a World Cup where pacing the tournament is a key to success. But Hoddle's comment that Beckham wasn't focused seemed strange; the player later claimed that it was because he went to see his girlfriend, Victoria, instead of joining a golf day. Then it all went wrong against Romania with Dan Petrescu's ridiculous late goal – words nearly failed me as he poked the ball past Le Saux and Seaman – and, although Beckham scored what later became a trademark free kick to beat Colombia, England were on the route that would be blocked by Argentina.

But for twenty-nine minutes against Argentina, between Michael Owen's breathtaking goal and the Argentine equaliser for 2–2, I believe England played some of the best football seen in the tournament. Unfortunately, Beckham's dismissal for reacting to a foul on him by Simeone led on to gallant failure and another story of what might have been.

Then, of course, there was Hoddle's book (written, unbelievably, in collaboration with the man from the FA, David Davies), the manager's story of the tournament, which told a few tales out of school. In my opinion it should be part of the England manager's contract that he may not write for a newspaper or sign an exclusive deal with anyone, and may not write a book, until after his retirement from the job. Mind you, even Alf Ramsey did an exclusive deal with BBC Television for the later stages of the 1970 World Cup, leaving the football boss, Sam Leitch, apoplectic when Ramsey was seen talking to ITV. The England manager, as I once said on air to Don Revie, is the representative for the country. For the supporters it's 'our team' he's looking after and the media are there to help keep us informed. No one organisation should have special access.

During Hoddle's time in charge I once had quite a long one-to-one chat with him at Manchester airport when the Heathrow-bound plane was delayed. We covered a number of different topics – tennis was one – and we eventually got talking about the subject that brought him down: put simply, the unfairness of life. His beliefs which, of course, included Eileen Drewery's gift for some form of psychic healing, were firmly held. But he apportioned no blame, only showed sympathy for those who have to battle through life under a handicap. His later comments to *The Times* – which originally, I am told, were included well down the article but which became the lead – were, I believe, the result of trying to discuss something which, as we had agreed in Manchester, has defied the greatest brains the world has known. With a poor start to the next qualification – for Euro 2000 – he needed friends with influence in the uproar, which even brought public condemnation from the prime minister. But those who sought his removal for a different agenda had been presented with the opportunity.

Probably my best commentary line of the '98 World Cup

was delivered in the final to a rather small audience. I was sitting high in the stand at the Stade de France between the director-general of the BBC, John Birt, and fellow commentator Jon Champion. As France cleared a late Brazilian corner, I said, 'Petit fancies this.' A pitch-length run and the Arsenal player was in just the right place to score the third French goal. They should have won by more with Ronaldo obviously unfit, not on the first team sheet and then reinstated on a second – a mystery concerning his illness and Nike's influence which has never been clearly explained (not even by Leonardo working for the BBC in the summer of 2006).

Jon later had a better line than mine. In the review of the tournament, shown at Christmas, he referred to Motty's long explanation, just before the final, of the team sheet fiasco as 'One of the great sporting monologues'.

Jon commentated on Michael Owen's great moment in '98, though much to the BBC's chagrin it was heard only in recorded mode as ITV showed the match live. I was a little luckier with the best goal I saw: Ronald de Boer's forty-five-yard pass was plucked out of the air by Dennis Bergkamp, who turned inside his man to put Holland in the semi-final. The sound supervisor only just managed to keep my voice in range.

I also commentated on three other golden goals: the first by Sunday Oliseh which brought Nigeria victory over Spain; the second by Mehdi Mahdavikia against the United States, though described as 'golden' only in Iran; and the third, the World Cup final's first official one in Lens, by which Laurent Blanc beat Paraguay's extraordinary but very fine goalkeeper,

José Luis Chilavert, to keep France on course for the Paris final. Blanc, poor chap, didn't play at the Stade de France because of what I regard as blatant cheating by Croatia's Slaven Bilic, who turned a nudge into a knockout blow in the semi-final. FIFA would have done the game a great service if they had used the video-recording to overturn the referee's decision.

Bilic (now his country's coach) wasn't the only cheat around, but my, how they've grown in number. And so have England's failures from the penalty spot. Hoddle once told me the secret of how to practise them: 'We work the goal-keepers by taking the penalties from ten yards and then make the takers shoot from fourteen. So it looks a little easier when it happens for real.' What a good idea, I thought; I was therefore a bit surprised when I heard the story that in 1998 England hadn't practised for what turned out to be the decisive moments.

2000 and After

'Cometh the hour, cometh the failure...
You have to say, what an anticlimax'

'Will he hell! He left us partly to get
the weekends off'

'Please make sure I wake up in the
morning'

'I'm having my best World Cup ever; I
haven't made a mistake yet'

40

Ceremonies

As Cathy Freeman, having lit the Olympic flame, stood with apparent calm waiting for the machinery to take it up to the cauldron, I was instructed by Martin Hopkins, the BBC's executive producer, at the broadcast centre in the heart of Sydney's Olympic complex, to pause commentary as we were switching from BBC 1 to BBC 2: it was time for the One o'Clock News on BBC 1. I was re-cued with Cathy still waiting (neither she nor I knew that there was less than thirty seconds' gas left in the cylinder beneath the flame).

'Cometh the hour, cometh the failure,' I said. 'You have to say, what an anticlimax.' Then the machinery at last cranked into action. 'In a way, a moving cauldron is making reference to the greater importance of taking part and not giving up,' I said, then found myself thinking: That's stretching things a bit. As the agonising journey neared its conclusion, I added, 'A show big in every sense, but the biggest moment took a long time in coming.'

A few seconds later the cauldron was afire. Life had been given to the Games of the XXIX Olympiad. It was seen on both BBC channels, for the leading item on the news was the lighting of the Olympic flame. But only on BBC 2 did viewers hear the on-the-spot commentary.

Decisions like that are made by the controllers of the two channels. Peter Salmon, the controller of BBC 1, was on his way to becoming controller of sport, and a few days later joined the team in Australia. The first thing he said to me as my new boss was, 'I don't go much on ceremonies.' It was not the most tactful remark, but it went some way, I suppose, towards explaining his earlier action. It might also have been made to pre-empt my first question: how come, knowing what was happening in the world outside Sydney, he didn't suspect what might lead the One o'Clock News?

Setting to one side his decision – which went down like a lead balloon among the team in Sydney – and to be fair to Peter, a lot of people would agree with him about ceremonies and I'm prepared to concede that they're usually too long. But I love them and for years, admiring the expertise of David Coleman covering them, hoped that I might one day succeed him in the role.

I was first given the chance at the 1984 Winter Olympics in Sarajevo and it was Coleman, back in the studio in London, who handed over to me. I was told he'd wanted to fulfil his usual role and then fly home to present the start of competition the following day, but that was thought too risky because of possible bad weather. By comparison with future Games, it was a very simple ceremony, but having watched the dress rehearsal with my producer, Alastair Scott, who took careful timings, I decided to script everything.

I was particularly concerned to get the protocol right and not to interrupt the public-address announcers, though, unlike those in other countries, they said only the bare minimum required and mainly only in their own language. Usually there are three voices: for the two official languages of the IOC – French and English – and that of the host nation. Timing is therefore crucial, and it's important not to say something which is immediately repeated by the English-speaking announcer. The executive editor of the BBC's operation in Sarajevo, Harold Anderson, was worried that I'd sound as if I was reading, but the script was only a back-up and he was happy enough afterwards.

Looking back now at a ceremony which began with army cadets saluting the Yugoslavian flags, and which made much of the cultural diversity of its six republics and two autonomous provinces – Bosnia and Herzegovina – brings a chill to the spine. I recall saying how much the people of Sarajevo wanted their city to be remembered for something other than the assassination of Archduke Franz Ferdinand by Gavrilo Princip, which precipitated the First World War.

When I returned two years later, for the 1986 European Figure Skating Championships, it seemed still to be an example of a successful integration of race and creed, but soon after the youth of the world had competed in the Winter Olympics in Calgary, the region became engulfed in a tragedy of man's inhumanity to man. The Olympic hills became focal points of the conflict, and the Zetra ice stadium was first used as a makeshift morgue and then completely destroyed.

The opening and closing ceremonies of 1984 had featured a group who had represented the country in the Eurovision Song Contest. They were called Peppil I Cri. I had mentioned, in passing, that the strict translation of their name was 'Blood in Ashes'.

At the start of the 1988 Games in Calgary, only the temperatures suggested that these were Winter Olympics. Canada's first woman governor-general, Jeanne Sauvé, who officially opened the Games in her country's two languages (the same as the IOC's), forgot the word 'winter' in moving from the French to the English version, simply saying 'the fifteenth Olympic Games'. Until the teams entered the stadium we were spectators at a much-shortened version of the city's annual festival, the Calgary Stampede, and raucously entertained we were by the Stampeders, the Chuck Wagon Racers, the Mounties and stories of frontier days. The chinook, a warm, dry wind from the Rockies, which can raise the temperature by 25 degrees Fahrenheit in little more than an hour and played havoc with the Games' schedule, would have been welcome, if only for five minutes, on that freezing-cold opening day.

David Coleman returned to commentating on the opening ceremonies in Albertville and Lillehammer. But the sound of a seventeenth-century bell from Japan's famous shrine at Zenkoji – rung by a man whose training as a suicide pilot had been brought to an end by the cessation of hostilities in 1946 – which introduced the Games in Nagano in 1998 signalled for me the start of an eight-year run in the role of ceremony commentator.

Every opening ceremony involves the past, the present and the future; or, put another way, the country's traditions, its culture and its children, who in Nagano were, I think, the most engaging. Dressed all in white save for the sewn-on flags of the competing nations, they gave a delightful performance of Andrew Lloyd Webber's 'When Children Rule the World'. It was only upstaged by the sight of a resplendent Midori Ito, Japan's world champion figure skater, lighting the flame and by a hugely ambitious conclusion. I found it a little scary and ultimately a source of some satisfaction.

At the dress rehearsal I had agreed with Alastair that I should take my cue for the final link from the public-address announcer. I summarised the oaths, rather than giving word-for-word translations, and while I was explaining that for reasons of ecology the doves of peace were simply plastic I heard the cue words. So I began my introduction to the previously announced 'Ode to Joy', the final movement of Beethoven's Ninth Symphony, a little late. It had to be right without rushing; any slip needing correction and I was in trouble.

'Now the build-up,' I began as the PA spoke in French and then Japanese, 'to the really ambitious conclusion to the opening ceremony of the eighteenth Olympic Winter Games: eight soloists of Russian, American, Polish, British and Japanese nationality; five choirs in Berlin, Sydney, Beijing,

New York and Cape Town; eighty-one ballet dancers here in the Minami stadium, the Nagano Winter Orchestra in the city cultural hall. All under the baton of a man born in China to Japanese parents, now the musical director of the Boston Symphony Orchestra. Never, surely, has a conductor had such power in his baton as Seiji Ozawa.' As I said his second name the picture cut to the conductor and he began his mammoth task. I sat back to enjoy the extravaganza, with much relief that there had been no collision with the opening bars of one of the greatest works in classical music.

In the days leading up to the start of the 2000 Olympics it slowly dawned on me how nervous the Australians were about the opening ceremony and the Games in general. Sydney had won the Games by only two votes from Beijing, and it was forty-four years since the Olympics had been brought to the Southern Cross. There seemed to be some sort of collective inferiority complex.

David Coleman was still airborne when the ceremony took place, but had sent a good-luck message via Martin Hopkins. I had learned much from him but, as with football all those years ago, I wanted to do it my way. Light and shade would be important; so would finding the right balance between informing the viewers in advance and letting them be surprised before subsequently adding any necessary information. Being critical if it was needed, not shying from the political issue of 'reconciliation' with the Aboriginal people, which was being much debated.

Unlike David I didn't have, or want, a dedicated researcher, some of whom had found it a pretty testing experience. Information came instead from the sub-editors, from my new producer, Julie Griffiths, and the OB stage manager, Owen Thomas – and through my own endeavours. There was one part of the ceremony which we weren't shown in rehearsal. The organisers may later have regretted that decision as much as I did, for it was the conclusion, and 'on the night' it went embarrassingly and almost devastatingly wrong. The names of the torch-bearers and other key performers were, reasonably enough, kept from us until the performance started for real. The first of these 'names' either wasn't found by the director or didn't turn up: I never did find out which. But it was a confidence-testing moment when having warned the home audience to look for a familiar face at the end of the opening tribute to the horse – crucial to the pioneers who opened up the country – Crocodile Dundee failed to appear.

That little hiccup apart, I remember feeling rather pleased about how I'd handled the start and then hastily saying to myself, 'Steady – there are at least three hours to go.' By the time the machinery was finally prepared to carry the Olympic flame to the bowl above, it proved to be nearer four hours. It was long, and I said so, yet it had so much variety and vitality as to make it a rattling good evening's entertainment.

The salute to youth was a big contrast to Nagano, involving teenagers and twenty-somethings, but not in the least patronising. The tap dancing of Tap Dogs, 'part theatre, part dance, part rock and roll', as I put it, was brilliant, leaving everyone with itchy feet. The ballet of lawnmowers stays in the memory for rather different reasons; the story of Australian development was told with imagination, if sometimes testing that quality in the stadium and the television audience. There was no mention of the penal colony, of course, except with a light touch by me (the Pom had to throw in the googly, didn't he?). But just about everything else was fitted in. The Chinese will have a greater problem, to say nothing of the British. Perhaps for the latter a version of *1066 and All That* could be used.

After the athletes' parade and the formalities of the protocol, with a rather nervous governor-general and a judge who forgot the words 'complete impartiality' in his oath, the public had their wish – at least, the media told us it was their wish. In seeking to celebrate the hundredth anniversary of women's Olympic participation the Australians set a trend by having a torch relay in the stadium; the runners included Betty Cuthbert, Raelene Boyle, Dawn Fraser, Shirley Strickland, Shane Gould and Debbie Flintoff-King before finally Cathy Freeman had her moment, which for her must have felt like an hour.

She had a second coming two weeks later, and on her lap of honour, after victory in the 400 metres, the flag of the Aboriginal nation was carried with the Australian one. Citizenship had been granted to the indigenous population just thirty-three years before, in 1967. Four years later one of their number, Evonne Goolagong, was the Wimbledon champion. At the closing ceremony there were some pointed references to apology and reconciliation in a party show in which Kylie Minogue was the undoubted star.

Although the length of ceremonies could certainly be shortened by the loss of one act – or two – or of a specially written song – or two – especially during the protocol moments, what really takes the time is the parade of the athletes. Some people, including members of the IOC, believe team numbers should be more restricted. But marketing research and television audience figures suggest that the public as a whole isn't complaining. The critical comments tend to come from those who've had to sit through a few and, especially in the stadium, haven't always been sure what was going on.

I would argue strongly against further limiting the athletes' parade, and so would other members of the Olympic Committee. It is, as the president's speech always says, about the athletes and the experience for those who take part is life-lasting. Talk to the British athletes who've carried the flag – Sir Steve Redgrave, Christopher Dean, biathlete Michael Dixon (three times the bearer), Sir Matthew Pinsent and three-day-eventer Lucinda Green, to name but a handful. Lucinda, who was chosen in Los Angeles in 1984, described it to me in a *Sportsnight* interview as 'two hours of wonderfully thrilling egotism'.

The amount of time it took in Salt Lake City in 2002, about which my team of three, unchanged from Sydney, all complained, was not the length of the ceremony itself but the four hours queueing in freezing temperatures to get into the Rice Eccles stadium: and then, having made it, being held for a further half an hour because President Bush's empty car hadn't been driven away to its parking place. Above us was a no-fly zone, and the airport was closed. Around us, in the stadium and outside, the police and the army were much in evidence.

Inside the stadium there was a solitary lift to take approaching five hundred people to the television tribune. At least the climb up seven long flights of stairs warmed the feet. I'd hoped to have a couple of hours at least to collect my thoughts and check a few facts. As it was I scribbled some of the former as we waited and hoped that the latter were right. There were fewer than twenty minutes before the start when I finally took my seat.

After the opening had seen the Salt Lake City banner join those of the previous eighteen hosts, and the dignitaries had been introduced, the American flag that had flown over the World Trade Center on 11 September 2001 was paraded into the stadium to total silence. It was, as I noted at the time, 'a very public grieving', but as the president of the Salt Lake City Organising Committee, Mitt Romney, said, 'This is the first time the world has come together since September 11th, and people of eighty nations lost their lives in that tragedy.' The thought of a precedent being set was rightly turned aside.

It is noteworthy now to recall the adulation given to President George W. Bush as he declared the Games open (no Regan bullet-proof glass from the Los Angeles Games here). How soon from decisions he made – in response to 9/11 as much of America saw it – would there be discord in life around the world. The theme of the ceremony was 'Light the Fire Within', which in sporting terms was presented as the stuff of champions. But it had a wider context with the Olympic flag-bearers – including the astronaut John Glenn, former Polish president Lech Walesa and Archbishop Desmond Tutu – joining sporting figures representing the five continents. A few different conclusions might be drawn about Steven Spielberg as the representative of culture, and, given the current administration's policy, choosing the son of Jacques Cousteau to represent the environment might be said to have been taking the easy way out.

On a personal level, the high point of Salt Lake City was the arrival of my daughter Giselle. I told Martin Hopkins and his assistant, Penny Wood, that she might suddenly appear in the IBC. Penny's immediate reaction was to ask if she might want a couple of event tickets. I responded for the moment by simply saying that she was being looked after but later informed them that she was here as one of the final three candidates being interviewed for the job of director of communications at the IOC (she'd been headhunted in her previous position as head of PR for the Jordan Formula 1 team). There was a very proud dad among a big group at dinner that night.

The decision on the appointment rested ultimately with the new president, Jacques Rogge, for whom this was the first Games since succeeding Juan Antonio Samaranch. It was a few weeks before we knew the outcome. With knowledge of the decision as an IOC member, but speaking as a friend, Craig Reedie phoned and asked if he was talking to the father of Giselle Davies, the newly appointed director of communications at the International Olympic Committee.

Although the Commonwealth Games had twice been held in Edinburgh, the Games in Manchester in 2002 were the first multi-sport event in England since the Olympics of 1948, and now there were seventy-two nations for the seventeen different sports. For eleven days, as July turned into August in the Queen's Golden Jubilee year, Manchester became the centre of the Commonwealth. And until the end, when the skies opened, Manchester and rain were total strangers. To have to follow Sydney gave the sceptics and the cynics full rein. It was, of course, not a fair comparison, which should have been made instead with Kuala Lumpur, the Commonwealth hosts four years earlier (and that would not have proved a contest).

The feeling inside the new stadium on Thursday, 25 July shared something with Sydney. The anticipation was keen and tense, but the rapturous welcome to Steve Redgrave – now Sir Steve, and winner of five gold medals – as he strode out literally to bang the drum, set the tone. The enormous bass drum, a gift from Kuala Lumpur, brought a reaction from drums of every kind – all manner of things that could make a noise – and everything that followed drew a response from the crowd, whose support then and over the next two weeks was crucial to Manchester's success.

Ceremonies can offer many tests. The basic one, of course, is researching the geography: where countries are on the map, and in some cases a bit about their origins and their flags. (I'm grateful to the critic who wrote that the information given during the Sydney parade was far more interesting than any geography lesson he'd had at school.) But sometimes the task is rather more difficult. In Turin at the 2006 Winter

Games there was a sequence entitled 'From Renaissance to Baroque' and another called 'Futurism to the Future', based on the avant-garde movement of the late nineteenth century and ending with the entrance of Italy's World Formula 1 Championship-winning Ferrari. I couldn't resist the comment, 'Futurism to the future 2006: discuss.'

Athens 2004 began with an offering of three iconic periods of Greek sculpture to present the evolution of Greek civilisation and human consciousness, ending with a man kneeling on a cube, a shape not found in nature. Following a fascinating but very detailed explanation by Dimitris Papaioannou, the creator of the piece, at the press conference two days before the opening, a representative from American television commented on the fact that there were no pauses.

Dimitris responded by saying, 'Well, it's an evolution,' and then asked, 'How many pauses do you want?'

'You don't want to know' came the swift reply and he and we were left with a distinct impression of how his work would play in the United States.

'Can you give us the name and some details of the guy on the cube and what he does for a living?' asked another from Stateside. For a second I wondered if Dimitris was going to burst into tears.

The next part of the ceremony was a sequence in tableau form of Greek myths and history with various gods circling above, ending with a representation of the double helix of DNA. It's difficult to see how the advertisements for burgers, medicines and the car deals got a look in; but I bet they did.

Dimitris believed that the first part at least could be viewed without explanation, but, brilliant though the concept was, I had no doubt that it needed guidance and at times quite a deal of it. Besides, had I left it to tell its own tale, back in the broadcast centre it might have been assumed that I'd gone missing, as my battle with food poisoning since arriving in Athens had been barely won.

Over lunch a few months after I'd ceased to be under contract to the BBC, Dave Gordon, the head of major events, first confirmed that he wanted me to continue the ceremony role and then told me of his plan to bring in Hazel Irvine to join me for the next year's Games in Turin and the Commonwealth Games in Melbourne. His idea was that the coverage of the parade of the competing countries should be more structured, with close-ups of key athletes to be followed by a video recording of the chosen star in action.

As we've done for many years, we chatted about the pros and cons of the idea. Being a long-term supporter of Fulham has perhaps helped him in the art of keeping things in perspective, and only occasionally have we had to agree to disagree. It had been clear for some time that he wanted a second voice in the box and I was entirely happy with his choice of Hazel, whom I've always liked and consider a very professional broadcaster. What I learned during our two shows together is that her appetite for preparation is never satisfied. She's still checking and re-checking going into the examination room. The balance between letting the viewer as well as the commentators spot faces and giving illustrated pocket biographies is a difficult one.

Away from the parade, the 2006 ceremonies offered a considerable contrast, again reflecting the character of the two hosts. Turin was classic Italian, if a little complicated and sometimes self-indulgent. The historical pieces were beautifully choreographed and well received in the stadium, but the organisers took a few liberties with the Olympic protocol. Much as I enjoyed Verdi's triumphal march from *Aida*, trooping the Olympic flag needs the accompaniment of the Olympic anthem – and I missed a choir. But everything else was done with style, and what if Luciano Pavarotti was dubbed? He just had to be there.

Melbourne was more down-to-earth and belonged to a different age. The start, with a past-generation tram coming down from the top of the stadium to land and disgorge its passengers into the street grid of the city, was inspired; and the use of the Yarra river, with its seventy-one pontoons holding huge models of the world's fish, was magnificent, with the pyrotechnics more than matching Sydney 2000 which was, of course, the aim.

Two other moments stand out. The first took the Queen by surprise when Kiri Te Kanawa, singing an early 'Happy [eightieth] Birthday to You', suddenly broke into 'Send her victorious', the second part of the first verse of the national anthem – only 'Advance, Australia Fair' had been played on the Queen's arrival. Her Majesty, who was seated, seemed unsure whether she should stand. The Duke of Edinburgh looked somewhat amused by the whole thing and his being so helped to cover possible embarrassment.

In the second moment, there was no covering my

embarrassment. I followed the public-address announcement that the Queen's baton, being carried from pontoon to pontoon up the river towards the stadium, was now in the hands of that great miler Herb Elliott. But the picture on my monitor was of a rather large figure with a full head of hair. Had Herb put on that much weight? Was he wearing a toupé? It couldn't be! For a moment all was confusion, to be quickly followed by confession as Maurie Plant, Melbourne-born and the BBC's athletics fixer supreme, pointed to the name Ron Barassi, formerly a star player and coach in Aussie rules football. Soon after, the familiar gaunt figure of Elliott appeared, little changed from his days of competition. As I said publicly of myself, 'Stupid boy!'

Among the carriers of the baton in the stadium was another Melbourne boy, who in our *Maestro* chat a few years before had told me that he might also have been the Aussie rules star he much wanted to be, but for losing part of a finger. Instead Ron Clarke became one of the world's greatest distance runners and was now returning to the stadium where forty years earlier he had lit the Olympic flame. From the mayor of the Gold Coast the baton was passed to one of his heroes – who had once stopped in a race to help the fallen Clarke, before going on to win – the governor of Victoria, John Landy, who presented the baton to the Queen.

On the eve of the fiftieth anniversary of the first sub-four-minute mile, I was invited to host a special dinner for Landy, who had come so close, so often, to being the record-breaker and who, after Roger Bannister set his historic time of 3 minutes 59.4 seconds, almost immediately lowered it to 3.58.

I've kept the letter he took the trouble to send me after the dinner. In it he said how much he'd enjoyed the occasion and that, although he'd been interviewed many times during his career, he'd rarely spoken to someone so well prepared. Thanks to another Victorian, Ian Jickell, who'd organised the tribute attended by invited Australians at 'Ossies' in London, the Pom was well briefed, as well as fed and watered.

Unlike the bid team of the British Olympic Association who had prepared so painstakingly and presented their case so brilliantly I had made no plans. As the contest at the 117th Session of the International Olympic Committee in Singapore to be the hosts of the Games of 2012 reached its climax, I had no clear thought as to what I would say.

At lunchtime I'd responded to the observation of one IOC member that 'You can lose the vote at a presentation but not win it' with the thought that 'This might just be the first time'. I spent the afternoon cut off from the growing tensions – the media weren't allowed in the theatre where the drama was unfolding – but trying to impart them to the viewers at home. I was alone in a makeshift office with a TV monitor, the only assistance being that of a technical engineer. My task was to find words to describe an instruction class to IOC members on how to use their voting machines (not all the words were complimentary) and then guide the viewers through the elimination rounds.

The evening 'show' was very different and considerably more enjoyable. The world's TV commentators were allowed into the theatre, taking their seats at the back of the stalls.

In front of them were the delegations from the bidding cities, with the teams from Paris and London in the front rows. On the stage sat the members and president of the IOC. The photographers were poised, most of them in front of Paris – had the decision leaked? – as we awaited the verdict.

I've always believed that successive British governments have undervalued sport as a means of encouraging youth, helping to reduce crime, improving fitness and thereby health, and as a means of motivation. I also believe that the minister for sport should be in the cabinet, with his or her department standing on its own feet. So as the IOC president said, 'London,' I was launched on words from the heart, as well as the head, on the opportunity now presented to give sport its proper place, to inspire youth to get involved, and to build something which should make us, as a nation, proud. I have to confess that in the celebratory mood affecting us all I kissed the Olympic minister, Tessa Jowell, on both cheeks.

In the years since, the negative comments have been as predictable as the knowledge that there would be many hurdles to clear; with much confusion, some of it deliberate, about the rising costs of the Games and the regeneration of the surrounding area. For government to fork out and then claim back VAT, which didn't happen for the 2002 Commonwealth Games in Manchester, is surely nonsense. But my faith in Lord Coe and his team hasn't wavered.

I wonder what I'd have said had Paris won!

41

The Patriot and the Foreigner

England has twice parted company with managers (Robson and Venables) who were a penalty competition away from the finals of World and European Championships, and both times appointed successors (Taylor and Hoddle) too soon in their managerial careers. So what is one to make of the change from 'the people's favourite' to the people's unknown?

Kevin Keegan had a passion for football which left no room for perceived personal failure. Sven-Goran Eriksson rarely, if ever, showed passion in the arena of football, offering instead a cool, calm exterior which, ultimately, seemed not to calculate enough. His passion in his private life compromised his public position while, amazingly, improving his bank balance.

My judgement of Keegan is, I admit, influenced by his playing career. Then, save for one famous occasion, I much admired him for his attitude and his determination to make the most of his God-given talent and more than double a not-too-generous measure of natural ability by sheer hard work. The cliché 'giving one hundred per cent' was written for him, and it brought him the love of Bill Shankly and the adoration of the Kop. His partnership with John Toshack, who used to rib me for not giving *him* enough of the credit, was very special, with the 'little' as good as the 'large' in the air.

The one occasion was August 1974, and I was commentating on the Charity Shield match at Wembley between Liverpool and Leeds. Keegan and Billy Bremner were sent off for fighting. With Keegan giving the lead, they both left the pitch bare-chested – an act of defiance which made the front pages. I don't recall now precisely what I said, but I gave them both a pretty hard time. It was one of those occasions when the commentator is out on a limb and can be damned by those who have time for consideration, whatever he says – all part of the job!

I also respected Keegan's wish to widen his horizon by going to play for Hamburg in the Bundesliga, and again he gave it everything, including learning the language – thirty years ago, remember. His reward was to win, and then become the first player to retain, the title of European Footballer of the Year. Subsequently he brought a smile to the south coast at Southampton, while to say he revolutionised Newcastle is an understatement. I got to know him and his wife, Jean, a little better when we worked together on the first European Super Cup final in Monaco. That he could, had he wanted, risk rather more than I in the casino there one evening was for me a credit to the way he had managed his life for himself and his family. The boy had done good financially through sheer hard graft.

His playing career ended rather abruptly at Newcastle, as did his first managerial one, a month short of five years' duration in 1997. He'd come to the job after seven years out of the game and with no previous coaching experience, yet he gave the devoted fans the best time they had had at St James' Park since the days of Jackie Milburn. If the two Uniteds of Manchester and Newcastle had swapped goalkeepers, Keegan's team would have been champions in 1996. In their meeting on Tyneside, Peter Schmeichel carried his team to victory.

Keegan's reaction to Alex Ferguson's gamesmanship – the 'I would love it . . .' speech on Sky – was the most public example of the brittle temperament of one who wore his heart on his sleeve. It was highlighted again when he left Newcastle, and even more so after England's defeat by Germany in the World Cup qualifying match that brought down the curtain on the 'old Wembley'. The result, the occasion (with many of the 1966 winners present), the booing by the crowd, whatever it was, led to his immediate resignation as the England manager, telling his players he could take them no further.

How did the man the public wanted, and whose first match – a win over Poland at Wembley – was greeted so favourably by both the media and the fan in the street, so soon become labelled a poor leader of his country's hopes? Was the flowing, exciting football played by Newcastle just a mirage? Perhaps the most pertinent question should be asked of others as well as the manager: why did Keegan so quickly become disillusioned with the role he began on a part-time basis while still manager of Fulham?

'Don't let the turkeys get you down,' I said to him at the draw for the European Championships in Brussels, and then suggested that he should let others get carried away by the middle match in the group, against Germany. I believed that the opening match, against Portugal, was much more important. I suppose in a way I was saying, 'Take each match as it comes,' a reversal of the usual conversation between a manager and his questioner.

As it happened, a poor-quality match with Germany, which I watched as a spectator, brought Keegan's only victory; but both countries went home at the group stage, England losing to both Portugal and Romania from a winning position. I covered both, and neither made for easy commentary, Luis Figo's long-range shot, which clipped the heel of a retreating Tony Adams, turning the first match after England were two up in eighteen minutes; and Phil Neville's clumsy, nervous tackle and the resulting penalty in the last changing a qualifying position into an ignominious defeat. No one could argue with Keegan's typically honest assessment that, 'We weren't good enough.' What made it worse was the high quality of the competition: France, the eventual winners; the Czech Republic, who left early but were still worthy of inclusion among the best; Portugal, who hammered the Germans and then messed things up in the semi-finals against France; and Italy and Holland, who met in the other semi-final.

That proved to be my last match at such a late stage in

a tournament, and I only covered it because my agent at the time, John Byfield, fought for it in my contract – that is to say, that I should be offered the final and/or a semi-final. Niall Sloane rang me to say that he understood from Bob Shennan that he, Niall, had to offer it to me. His reluctance to do so was clear.

I returned to Holland, after a couple of days at Wimbledon, to commentate on an extraordinary match in Rotterdam, and in doing so failed to comply with Niall's wishes, to 'make sure the Dutch win'. They should have by a country mile, but playing against only ten Italians for eighty-six minutes – Zambrotta 'stupidly' got himself sent off for two 'ridiculously crude challenges' – they managed to miss two penalties in normal time and three more in the shoot-out. The Dutch were the better players, and my frustration was not that far removed from that of their coach, Frank Rijkaard, who resigned afterwards. But Italy rode their luck, predictably defended well, and kept their nerve. What's more, they played well in the final, only to lose to Trezeguet's 'golden goal' for France.

It was a good championship in mainly pleasant surroundings and our hotel in Amsterdam, the Pulitzer, deserves the prize. It is cleverly converted from several old houses of character, deep among the canals, and was a delight – such a change from the regular hotels which, once you're inside, challenge you to say in what country of the world you are staying. But the low point of the trip was one shared by all our team – the moment we heard that the BBC's coverage of the Premiership would cease at the end of the following season. Much against all the rumours and forecasts, the contract had been lost to ITV.

The live match that evening, 14 June, was in Brussels and, ready to commentate on Italy against the hosts, I was among the first into the stadium. The press were quick to seek a quote. Ron Atkinson crept up behind me and started to hum the *Match of the Day* signature tune, and there was some gentle banter from other ITV personnel, most of them seemingly genuinely surprised at the outcome. 'Des will be chortling,' said one of the scribblers, to which I responded, a little too quickly perhaps, 'Will he hell! He left us partly to get the weekends off.' But the thought of going into the season before the next World Cup without the regular Saturday programme, having already missed out on the Champions League, left the BBC team feeling very depressed. I felt sorry for Niall, who'd been very upbeat about how things were going. Now there was much for him and many others to consider.

Inevitably we lost some of the behind-the-scenes talent during the following season, particularly a lively potential editor, Tony Pastor, and a gifted outside broadcast director, Paul McNamara, who for some reason had been mostly kept studio-bound as the *MotD* producer. We were together in Newcastle for one of his rare OB jaunts late in the season, and over dinner on the Friday I offered a willing ear as he told me about his offer and counter-offer. He seemed to have decided to stay, but the following afternoon changed his mind. He was in fine form on the buttons, cutting up the camera shots in a lively match, proving a good provider and tester of the commentator – and he joined ITV because he wanted to direct football. But, judging as an onlooker, his talents still haven't been given full rein.

Neither, in my opinion, have Jon Champion's. I suppose I shouldn't have been surprised that Niall didn't fight harder to keep him at the BBC – Jon and I share many views about commentary – but I was. Like many others in the department, I thought – and still think – it was a big mistake. His commentaries in the 2007 rugby World Cup will, I hope, have removed a few blinkers.

On the plus side was the decision to keep 'Football Focus' going. It survived amazingly well and in spite of the lack of Premiership action it gave football a regular platform on the BBC and did better in the ratings than ITV's *On the Ball*. For that, Andrew Clement, the editor, and his team deserve considerable credit, not least among them the presenter, Ray Stubbs, who rose to the challenge, and in doing so much enhanced his profile in the sports department, which has continued to rise.

There was more than enough to keep me busy – Salt Lake City, the World Cup draw, *All the Queen's Horses* and so on – but I was disappointed that only John Motson, returning to his roots, was offered the chance of radio commentary. The FA Cup and occasional international highlights gave me some football during the season, but covering only the UEFA Cup final in its last two months before the World Cup meant that I arrived in Japan and Korea as probably the least well prepared of all the radio and TV commentators from Britain.

The England team, though, was in pretty good shape and

once more among the favourites. Following Keegan's departure, and with only one point gained under the caretaker
management of Howard Wilkinson in Finland, Sven-Goran
Eriksson had turned things round, starting with five straight
wins. The players liked their Swedish boss and even those in
the media who were against him, purely on nationalistic
grounds, were having to hold their fire. The highlight was an
amazing 5–1 victory over Germany on their home soil, at
Munich. Their performance should not be underestimated in
any way, but even so it probably owed much to a save by
David Seaman, which prevented England going two goals
down, and the timing of their second and third goals on either
side of half-time.

My contribution in the telling of the success story came
after football's Lord Mayor's Show – four days after to be
precise – when England made hard work of beating the little-
known stars of Albania. Before the kick-off there was a
minute's silence in memory of Brian Moore, who had died
suddenly the previous Saturday, the day of a triumph he would
have greatly enjoyed. I voiced a brief tribute to a good friend,
which led into the silence at St James' Park, Newcastle, and
was grateful for being asked to do so.

While waiting for Eriksson, England had played a friendly
match against Italy in Rome, and I was there to see Peter
Taylor do a good job as interim boss. He gave a number of
younger players a chance, and made one decision which served
England mightily well when in the final qualifying group match
Greece came very close to winning at Old Trafford. Like most
of his team-mates, David Beckham wasn't playing particularly

well, his much-vaunted free kicks being consistently disappointing. But from the moment Greece took the lead for the second time, his leadership dragged his country through to the finals. His pride and determination as captain were wonderful to behold. He was everywhere, and fully deserved the dramatic ending when at last he found his range with a spectacular last-minute free kick.

2002 should have been Beckham's World Cup; before the image began to blur the reality. But unfortunately for a very good player, but only a great one in the quality of his crosses and free kicks, a broken metatarsal decided otherwise. His injury and those of others – Steven Gerrard and Gary Neville missed the trip – seemed to confuse the final days of England's preparation, and at no stage of the tournament was Beckham truly match-fit. He had his 'revenge' against Argentina, scoring the decisive penalty, but he left unfulfilled after being unable to lift a listless England team, who offered virtually nothing against Brazil in the quarter-final after Ronaldinho's goal, and that in spite of having a one-man advantage for a third of the match, when the scorer of what proved the winning goal was sent off.

Viewed on television in Korea, it was hard to understand. I am not one for constant shouting by coaches, but some animation was required from the England manager. And the substitution of Michael Owen was bizarre. The defeat was not in my opinion unexpected, but to lose so tamely I found hard to accept. My doubts about Sven's England, expressed in their opening match against Sweden, continued to grow.

I have to say that, as the 'old man' of the Beeb's commentary team, I was amused to be asked to cross the China Sea between Japan and South Korea three times (the most) and also set the hat-trick test of covering all three nations from the Far East – China, Japan and Korea. But it was a terrific World Cup and I thoroughly enjoyed it.

I began in Oita, Japan, with a condemnation of Roy Keane, who had quit the Irish cause on the eve of the tournament. Whatever the training facilities or the rights and wrongs of the arguments, I could find no excuse for him. His country needed their best player, and he turned his back. Matt Holland's finely struck equaliser against Cameroon was the perfect team response; and from that point on Ireland were unlucky not to win their opening match. The same was true when I caught up with them again in the second round against Spain in Suwon, though the equaliser now came much later, a ninetieth-minute penalty by Robbie Keane after Ian Harte had earlier missed a similar opportunity. They dominated the extra time, only to fail three times in the spot-kick competition.

My companion in the commentary position for both those matches should have been Paul McGrath, but his disagreement on the journey to Japan with some of the players' wives led to his quick return home. That caused much confusion for Hiroumi, our Japanese interpreter, a rather nervous lady who tried so hard to be helpful. She met me at Narita airport when I arrived alone off the British Airways flight, and was perplexed that, with a wait of three-quarters of an hour for our train, I didn't leave her for some imagined VIP area but instead invited her to have a cup of coffee. Was it a loss of face that we had missed the earlier train?

In Oita, she met Trevor Brooking, who instead of covering the recorded opening match in Seoul had flown over to replace Paul for the first live game. And that, the following day, led to a scene straight out of the Keystone Kops. Hiroumi was again at Narita, this time to meet Trevor Steven, but when he presented himself she refused to accept that he was Trevor because she knew him from the previous day in Oita. He subsequently had us in stitches describing how he chased her up and down escalators trying to convince her who he was. It needed phone calls to and from Simon Betts to sort things out. It was hardly the best of introductions for Trevor to BBC organisation.

His opening match in Saitama was pretty testing, too, for having led against Sweden through Sol Campbell's header, England were awful in the second half. 'An utter shambles' was my description at one point, but it wasn't easy for a former England international immediately to be critical. We were only recorded; ITV were live, and welcome to it. Looking back I'd have preferred a rather better match for what turned out to be my last England commentary at a championship.

Trevor, though, became a very welcome and easy-to-get-on-with member of the Simon, Ken and Barry show. We chewed the fat over years gone by, Everton's heyday under Howard Kendall, and the 1990 World Cup when I wanted to see Trevor used as an attacking right back – wing back, as it became known – in the style of Germany's Berthold and Brehme. But Bobby Robson preferred his Everton teammate Gary Stevens, Trevor only coming on as a sub in the semi-final meeting, and then in midfield. He reckoned it probably saved his legs a little that I wasn't in charge. Although the new team player impressed us in his new role twelve years on, Niall subsequently saw him, too, as one to come off the bench.

While England journeyed on to high points and ultimate disappointment, our tour took in the best of the United States team; the worst of the Uruguayans and the frustrations of the French playing them; the failure of a Danish linesman which helped Croatia beat Italy and badly let down England's referee, Graham Poll; and the joy of Japan as Junichi Inamoto's goal beat Russia. Then, before the full force of the Korean story burst upon us, there was the amazing seven-goal thriller, of brilliant goals mixed with defending which was in danger of requiring emergency resuscitation for Alan Hansen, between Brazil and Costa Rica. The performance of Edmilson, in theory playing in Hansen's old central defender position, was notable in both categories, and his bicycle-kick conclusion to a move he began, and in which, with passes with Rivaldo and Junior, he was twice further involved, was surely the goal of the tournament.

Our mid-twenties student Korean interpreter was called Kim, as are several million others on both sides of the 38th Parallel. To avoid confusion we christened him Sergeant Kim, which, as he'd done a stint with the United States forces stationed in his country, seemed appropriate. By the time of the quarter-final I'd made him a brigadier, his last promotion thoroughly justified by his procurement, somehow, of a day pass for me to interview the Korean coach, Guus Hiddink, when having travelled twenty-eight of the thirty miles from our hotel to the stadium I discovered I'd left my accreditation in my room. Kim and two of his student friends gave us an insight into what their team's success meant to their countrymen, and he also taught me a few expressions which I was able to use in my commentaries.

It's true that the hosts had fortune on their side and that one or two decisions went their way. But I hold no brief for the conspiracy theorists and, while sympathising with the Spanish over a dreadful linesman from Trinidad, I felt that the Italians had no one to blame but themselves. The reaction to Ahn Jung Hwan's 'golden goal' against Italy and the conclusion of the penalty competition against Spain are pictures well framed in my commentating gallery.

42

The Final Whistle

I have been asked many times why I left *Match of the Day* just six weeks into a new season. The answer is very simple: my contract came to an end. It had been extended to cover the Olympic Games, and then a little more until the end of September so that the closing ceremony in Athens wouldn't bring down my curtain as well. Actually, I had little doubt that I'd still be doing some work for the BBC past the last day of September. The only question was whether I'd be doing any more football; and that family debate ran for half a year.

I went to the European Championship in Portugal in June 2004 thinking that I'd probably accept the offer to stay two more years with *MotD*. This time my producer, Chris Lewis, was from the Football Department, and because of Niall Sloane's belief that he had to have an English expert with the England team, in spite of the fact that its manager was Swedish, I worked a lot with Mark Lawrenson. Chris had a patter which would have been the envy of a top comedian – even if the old jokes, recycled, were the best ones! He rejoiced in his goalkeeping for the Dennis Waterman Charity XI, of which he was the co-founder. Mark, no slouch with the one-liners, readily kept our goalkeeper/producer on his toes and the banter between us, which had our engineer Ken Osbourn frequently looking skywards, made for a good trip. In commentary Mark was sharp, sometimes witty, and always fun to work with.

Covering the hosts three times, including the opening match in the spectacularly sited Draga stadium in Porto, looking down from on high over the Douro river, was some consolation for not being invited to watch England. But it took the Iberian contest at the end of the group fixtures to bring the Portuguese crowd to life. They were rewarded with a first victory over Spain for twenty-three years. The French were a discordant bunch when, after they had rather luckily beaten England, I commentated on their match against Croatia in Leiria; and Italy were still stifled by their manager's negative thoughts in Guimaraes. As in the World Cup, Giovanni Trapattoni sought to defend a 1–0 lead by removing two strikers in the final twenty minutes, and paid the penalty. I'm afraid he had no sympathy from me when Ibrahimovic scored for Sweden – just irritation.

Porto was our base for most of the tournament, though unfortunately our hotel was forty minutes away from the fascinating old town. At the start we only had coverage of the rest of the competition on Portuguese television, but our worthy engineering officer Ken played around with a few wires and things, and bingo, we were with Gary Lineker and the boys. But watching our coverage I increasingly thought that unless I changed my style, which I was reluctant to do, I had no real future with *Match of the Day*, other than as a bit-part player. I was past the nation's retirement age; perhaps it was time to move aside for the younger generation.

A case could be made – and was in some quarters – that, with Wayne Rooney's untimely injury, Sol Campbell's disallowed goal and the penalties, England were unlucky to lose their quarter-final to Portugal. But I believe Eriksson's substitutions played their part in the defeat. Bringing on Darius Vassell for Rooney changed the balance of the team. Joe Cole, or moving Paul Scholes forward from the left, would have been a better option for keeping the flow that Rooney had provided. Philip Neville for Scholes and Owen Hargreaves for Steven Gerrard were designed to save the game.

I watched the match back at home, having asked Niall if he could release me for a couple of days for Wimbledon. In the first week there, the demands on the commentary team are (in terms of numbers) far greater than at the sharp end of the championships. The chance for me to be there came about because mine was the last of the quarter-finals to be played. When I left Porto for the second and last time, I felt pretty sure, after watching them comfortably beat Denmark, that the Czech Republic would be playing in the final. However, where Trapattoni's and Eriksson's negative approach failed, Otto Rehhagel's succeeded for Greece. They worked hard to win the title and those who backed them at the tournament's start at 80–1 would have dined out on it. In truth, though, football would have been better served if any of the other three semi-finalists had won.

I returned to Wimbledon and to the concluding days of family discussion about my future. Gigi was back from Switzerland for the Henley Royal Regatta; Mark and his three girls, Miranda and their daughters, Emily aged two, and Alexandra not yet one, were home for a few days from Australia, where he was then based to establish Betfair down under. On 9 July I wrote to Peter Salmon, declining the BBC's offer of a two-year extension to my contract. For the rest of my career, however short or long, I would take the freelance route. With the youngsters having returned to their respective homes, Penny and I went away with friends to enjoy the delights of Venice.

Three weeks later I was off to Athens, where I covered rather more of the football than I'd expected, including back-to-back semi-finals in the women's tournament, the first of which went to extra time. The Americans eventually beat Brazil 2–1 in the final with Abby Wambach scoring her fourth goal of the competition with just three minutes of extra time remaining. David Beckham is presumably finding out – and his boss, Alexei Lalas, who was in the US squads for '90, '94 and '98, already knows – that the women's game in the States enjoys a rather higher national status than the men's.

My last international was the men's final. I covered it alone from the athletics commentary position in the Olympic stadium which meant that I was low down and roughly level with one of the 18-yard lines. It was a morning match and the sun was still rising over the far post of the goal to my left. As the commentary box was being checked, I chatted with the ever-helpful Dave Bowden, a long-standing friend from the OB stage managers' fraternity, with whom I'd covered many matches and a few different sports. There was a sudden tap on the shoulder and the comment, 'I think you are in my place.' I turned with apology to find Jacek Gmoch, the coach of the Poland team who, thirty years earlier, had finished third in the 1974 World Cup in Germany and whom I'd first met when the Poles held England at Wembley the previous October. He was working for Greek television. The final, with some names to be noted by those involved in the next World Cup, again in Germany two years hence, was decided by Carlos Tevez's eighth goal of the competition as Argentina beat Paraguay 1–0.

Back in England, there remained but three Premiership football matches in my commentating career. I'd spoken to Niall about the freelance position and he said he'd be very happy to use me every Saturday but went no further – not that I expected him to, for neither had the proposed contract. Live commentary wasn't on offer, and neither was there any guarantee that I'd have a part to play in the next World Cup. He seemed surprised when I said that meant the end of the road, and asked me to ring him again in a couple of days. I did, but only to confirm my view.

Andrew Clement, in the *Match of the Day* editor's chair, did his best to give me a main match on the final day, and Manchester City *v* Arsenal did the trick. But just as I was unprepared for what happened the first time, thirty-five years before, so I was at the last.

I'd had a phone call that morning from the news editor of the day, asking if a reporter could talk to me after the match, but I didn't expect anything like what happened. Kevin Keegan interrupted my post-match interview with him to say generous things on air and give me a signed City shirt. Arsene Wenger presented me with a magnum of champagne. In the *Final Score* studio Ray Stubbs and company added more compliments – I particularly liked Lee Dixon's comment that he didn't always agree with me, but . . . In the evening not only did *MotD* do me proud, with Gary Lineker mentioning 'turn of phrase' and Mark publicly ignobling me – along with a few goals and lines – but on the main news Jon Sopel presented a fulsome tribute in words and pictures. I said to Penny, 'Please make sure I wake up in the morning.' It was all more than a little overwhelming. But we went to bed still smiling over Gary's final throwaway line: 'I've definitely now got the best suntan in the Sports Department.'

Come Monday the *Times* columnist, Giles Smith, with tongue in cheek, was imagining that there had been a minute's silence at football grounds around the country. Later in the week Jim White, in the *Telegraph*, suggested how I might have handled the first goal of Wayne Rooney's hat-trick on his Champions League debut: allowing the player's name to hang in the air before adding, 'As Gus Khan almost said, it had to be Roo.' The press have generally been very kind to me over the years. Chris Maume of the *Independent* was thought by some in the *MotD* office to be a personal friend; in fact we met just once, briefly, at a Sports Journalists' Association awards dinner.

His colleague, Brian Viner, I know a little better from Lord's Taverners functions; being among his interviewees is to keep interesting company. He jumped the gun by offering his farewell on the morning of the final match and had a small scoop in naming the team I support. He's a persuasive fellow, for at an earlier date he forced me to choose my All-Time XI. I did so protesting about the many players I was having to leave out and made clear I was simply selecting the best and offered no guarantee of chemistry. The team was: Banks, Carlos Alberto, Beckenbauer, Moore, Maldini, Platini, Clodoaldo, Tostao, Pele, Maradona, Cruyff.

43

Some Musings on Commentary

'Which is the sport you most enjoy commentating?' is the question I'm most often asked. The answer is: the one I'm doing at the time. A bit of a cop-out, perhaps, but as I haven't made the decisions about things like whether I remain at the World Cup or come home to Wimbledon, it's true, and the only sensible answer. Then comes: 'Who do you support?' Well, there are a few clues in this book, so I'll leave that one for the moment. In third place is: 'Which is the more difficult, radio or television commentary?' The answer to that is that the comparison isn't between like and like. The two have the same root, of course, but are very different.

The task for the radio commentator is to paint word pictures, and for me the best exponent in my lifetime was

John Arlott, who had wonderful powers of description. On television, the picture is there to be explained when necessary and added to. For the best I would go again to cricket and choose Richie Benaud.

I viewed him first from the perspective of a would-be leg spinner whose contributions at school rarely got further than net practice, and whose brief appearances since reached their zenith when representing the fathers against the staff. I deceived my son's prep school headmaster, who, with some justification, was proud of his ability as an opener. Although the head needed just one for his fifty, I have no reason to believe that my son suffered for his father's indiscretion.

I admired Benaud also for his approach to captaincy – always positive, always thinking – a feisty competitor but a generous one; and a tactical teaser, which perhaps comes more naturally to a leg spinner than to any other. To this day he believes that a declaration should always offer the temptation to his opposite number to go for it.

Most of that part of his life I viewed from afar, but his second career I've followed closely since he and a boyhood hero, Denis Compton (I was among the kids by the boundary rope cheering on the Brylcreem Boy), were paired with two professional broadcasters in the commentary box, Peter West and Brian Johnston, good cricketers both but at a rather different level. As he progressed to the captain's seat in the box, Benaud continued with his concise, often revealing, sometimes pithy, observations. When explaining, he never talked down to the viewer and his humour could be both quick and dry. Given his undoubted knowledge of the game, it was his timing which most distinguished him: it's the mark of a great commentator as well as a great player, for the best are those who make their own. Cricket, even with commercial breaks, offers plenty of opportunities for comment, opinion and conversation, but when Benaud was at the microphone it was always allowed to breathe.

It added enormously to the honour accorded me by the Royal Television Society in May 2005, a Lifetime Achievement Award, presented to me by Jayne Torvill, that I was following Richie Benaud on the roll and had the opportunity to say a few words about him. I was also pleased that though he was retiring from working in England, because he didn't wish to work for pay-to-view TV, he was still to continue for Channel 9 in Australia, for it gave me the chance to dismiss the joking remark of my colleague Martin Hopkins, 'You realise this means goodbye.' I made it clear that, while I had called an end to my football commentating career, I hoped to be continuing in other areas for a little longer yet.

Browsing in a bookshop at Heathrow en route to Milan to see some relations of Penny's, I picked up a paperback copy of Jimmy Greaves's book, *The Heart of the Game*, a look at football today compared with the days when he left defenders floundering in his wake – and please don't tell me he wouldn't be able to do so in today's tighter defensive organisation. Glancing as one does – as you may have done now – at the index, with no expectation of finding Davies, B., among the likes of Dai, Ron, Wyn or even the Football Association's David, to my surprise I found a page which drew some interesting conclusions about my retirement from *Match of the Day* in September 2004.

Not just for that did his book lighten a journey he had himself once taken with Joe Baker to play for a season in Italian football in the defensive days of *catenaccio*. His spell there proved but a side road between his days at Chelsea and Tottenham but, by chance, qualified him to help start the television career of the man to whom he now bade farewell. I remember how he scribbled the odd note and pointed things out in off-mike whispers to help the new boy on his way.

His thoughts now were similarly provocative. His observation that I had become somewhat disillusioned with my successors in the football commentary box – as clearly he had – wasn't quite right, but wasn't a million miles from the truth. It was a question not of individuals but of the style and the way commentary was now treated which helped me to my decision. I thought it unlikely that in *Match of the Day*'s new format there'd be an opportunity to offer something different.

The programme is a comprehensive and enjoyable summary of the day's football, but surely gives little satisfaction to all but a few of the commentators. The highlights are now so condensed that the commentator is most of the time at a pitch of excitement and rarely to be heard reading the game. The throwaway line is now just that – thrown away.

I remember a conversation on a train with a chap who told me, with much glee, how often he spotted a tactical change before the commentator mentioned it. 'Ah,' I said, 'note next time when a point's made, for it's part of the art of commentating on edited highlights to make such comments following an incident which the commentator feels is likely to be included.' In that, of course, it was always a question of win some, lose some. But the best of the match editors would lift a line and drop it in at a suitable place. I am talking here of the days of twenty-minute edits. It was difficult enough then to get the pint into a glass less than a third that size. Now the task for the lesser matches is to put the pint into a thimble. The public see the goals and a dispute over the penalty not given: and the commentator who has given his all for the ninety minutes goes away – at times, I suggest – in search of a different pint to drown his sorrows. The only fair judgement of his or her worth is to listen to the live commentary. It's probably little consolation, but on a television channel in some far-flung country several weeks, months or even years later it may well be presented as though it is.

The role of the ex-player in live commentary, first really established in 1966, has changed much since Euro '96. The credits now say 'co-commentator' or, increasingly, just 'commentators'. The role used to be that of 'summariser', who offered a considered comment roughly every ten minutes. When football nearly came home, observations by the expert had increased but were still quite restrained. But since then the intervals have become shorter and shorter, to the point where a comment is required on every incident, and by becoming so involved with the minutiae of the game the original role has all but disappeared. As the commentator I've often wished for the chance to pull back from following the ball to see why, for example, a particular player has disappeared or why there's a problem. The man in what used to be the second seat has that chance.

As I use that phrase, I'm aware that some may feel that I'm trying to protect my position as commentator, and there have been times when I felt that that was the thought of my colleague for the ninety minutes. I once said to Don Howe, at half-time, that I had been fascinated by his observations but that I felt by offering so much he was in danger of losing the viewer. On the same point I once suggested to Trevor Brooking that if he said half as much he would inform twice as much. I feel guilty now, for the elegant Trevor was so comfortable to work with and one of the most restrained.

On another occasion I was on the receiving end. Arriving late from the hotel, I offered a few thoughts to Mick McCarthy just before the kick-off. At the end of the match, which seemed to me to have gone pretty well, particularly for him, he told me he'd felt very uncomfortable and unsure when it was all right for him to come in. It was by no means an argument – nor indeed were the other two conversations – but it left me concerned, for what is the point in having an expert if he isn't properly used? But, perhaps in part because experts can be working for radio one day and television the next, the style has become increasingly conversational, with the commentator too often feeling he has to react to the comment of the expert ('Yes, you're right, George') and some of Mark Lawrenson's quips deserve to stand alone to be appreciated.

In my view, commentators should be talking to the viewers and only occasionally to each other.

The result is few pauses in the flow of words, and little opportunity just to enjoy the atmosphere. I believe the viewer wants time for his or her own opinion. It's like finding a chatty companion sitting in the stand: after a while you want him to shut up so that you can enjoy the match with your own thoughts.

I believe that in most cases it's best if what the Americans call the 'play by play' commentator takes the first replay. He knows what he has seen and probably what he's looking for, so can confirm, or otherwise, his thoughts. The expert is therefore given two chances to look, and may spot something new or simply confirm in his mind what happened. As I said to Liam Brady, who worked with the BBC in Italia '90 and USA '94 (I'd been asked to give him some guidance), 'You've played this game at the highest level, so there should be things you can add.' I also suggested there was no rush: ninety minutes is a long time.

Obviously some combinations work better than others, but I've never felt completely lost, though one match came close. It was a recorded game at Southampton's old ground, the Dell, and I felt as some making their studio debut with him might have felt, for I could barely get a word in with Alan Hansen sitting alongside me. It was, I believe, but an over-enthusiastic one-off and I'm a great admirer of his punditry, as I was of his football. Fortunately, Bob Paisley eventually became used to him carrying the ball out to the halfway line and beyond. His absence from the Scottish squad for the 1986

World Cup was, I think, the worst selection decision in the superlative career of Sir Alex Ferguson. I've never asked but I suspect that Alan's main golf partner, Kenny Dalglish, who withdrew from the squad, might just agree with that observation.

The studio experts have plenty of time, of course, to discuss things during the match or event, though I've often thought it would be fun if they were given earphones and prevented from chatting to each other, leaving the presenter to discuss with editor and producer the points to be raised and the video replays to be included. I once tried to persuade Brian Barwick, then the BBC's editor of football, to separate Jimmy Hill and Terry Venables: an extreme argument, perhaps, but wouldn't it stimulate the conversation if one had really enjoyed the half and the other thought it rubbish and the first knowledge of the different opinions was on air. Interestingly, when those usually resident in the studio are found alongside the commentator they often comment on how a point raised during play is later introduced as though there'd been no previous mention of the subject. It's a fact which has often amused, and occasionally irritated, John Motson and me.

In January 2007 I found myself in the interesting position of being asked to interview Motty about the commentator's role for a programme for Radio Four's 'Archive Hour' called *Back to Square One*, marking the eightieth anniversary of the first football commentary. The programme told the story of commentary right from the first days when *Radio Times* printed a map of the pitch divided into eight squares and a second voice was used to call out the square where the action was taking place. Alas, we were unable to find a recording to prove the origin of the expression. The archive ranged from the 'over the line' FA Cup final in 1932 – when Newcastle's winning goal against Arsenal shouldn't have been allowed because the ball was out of play before it was crossed – to the Hungarians beating England at Wembley in 1953, and the more recent European Cup successes of Manchester United and Liverpool.

The commentary voices included the first, an Arsenal director and later manager, George Allison; Raymond Glendenning, the father of sports commentary; Brian Moore, Kenneth Wolstenholme, Peter Jones and two current representatives of radio and television, Alan Green and Motty, who both offered forthright but, at times, differing views. I had to accept the decision of the producer, Nicola Swords – a football fan as well as being the Manchester producer of *Women's Hour* – that my first commentary for the BBC be included; but it was a small price to pay for being asked to present the programme.

Towards the end of the recording, a thought made me quickly scribble a different closing link. The last lines of commentary were the most famous: Wolstenholme's 'They think it's all over . . . It is now' from the 1966 World Cup final. Alan used the word 'brevity' and led me to this: 'Brevity, a word which takes us back to square one: not a word to be heard describing football commentary these days. But while football is no longer the game of the man or woman in the street that it once was – these days enjoying the glamour and riches of superstardom – perhaps the style of football commentary still reflects the age in which it lives.'

Niall Sloane, the football editor for the last twelve years, always said he was happy to have the differing styles of his two main commentators, but once told me that I wasn't very good at conversation commentary and that that was the way to go. I concede that it can't have been easy for our experts to bounce between John and me, especially during tournaments, for his habit of ending sentences with the word 'Trevor' as a question mark, exclamation mark or full stop, invited an immediate response. Clearly it's best if you're pulling together as a team, and I've had a good deal of experience of doing that in many different sports; but I believe that the regular use of Christian names is unnecessary except if there's a need to distinguish expert from expert, as in the athletics box or, say, Dan and Chris in the Boat Race. Also, I've never seen the need to ask questions in commentary to which the viewers would expect me to know the answer, unless, as is more the case in interviewing, I am trying to illicit an opinion. Equally I've been quite happy to give an opinion my sidekick might embellish or even disagree with. There's no problem with the latter unless we become two dogs with a bone and dwell on the point too long.

During the four years in which Peter Salmon was the BBC's director of sport there was much comment about the increasing number of commentators appointed directly at the end of their sporting careers; the so-called 'cult of celebrity'. In Belfast, at a luncheon at the Reform Club, as a guest of Jim Neely, the BBC's boxing commentator (and incidentally a fine rugby commentator), I was expecting questions on the subject when, after our double act – he interviewing me – the subject of sports commentary was thrown open to the floor. I responded first by pointing out that employing commentators who had graced their sport was not exactly a new phenomenon, mentioning the likes of Denis Compton and Jim Laker from the past, and the long-serving Peter Alliss, Stuart Storey and, of course, Benaud who all began as 'ex-players'. The difference now, I suggested, was the assumption that a gold-medal-winner could overnight bring his on-field expertise to the role of professional broadcaster. There was, too, the frequent criticism made by journalists: that the ex-player was too close to his sport and therefore sometimes found it hard to pose the difficult question or offer the needed critical comment.

Among the points of discussion when the BBC offered an extension to my contract was the thought that I should conduct advisory classes on commentary. It was very tempting if a little surprising. I'd already been independently approached by a couple of new commentators on other sports, but I concluded that my advice might well have been non-beneficial to the careers of those who sought it; though I had private discussions with both. In football, in particular, having failed to persuade the decision-makers that my beliefs were right, it was a little ironic that I should be thought of as a guide to the future. But that the 'stars' should be given guidance and production there is no doubt: just as they were in their first careers.

The list of those who've had to put up with me in the

commentary box over the years would nearly fill the page – including, would you believe, an expert from the world of equestrianism when, back in Mexico '68, I found myself having to put words to dressage. In football, I could put out a star-studded team of quality, plus a full bench, though I'd have to be allowed to have all of them returned to the playing days of their prime.

In sports I haven't dwelt on in these pages, I should include from cycling the four-time world professional pursuit champion and Commonwealth Games gold medallist Hugh Porter, who rightly became the lead voice for the BBC on a sport he has graced as both performer and commentator. I did, though, stick around long enough to present the World Cycling Championship in Leicester in 1982. The most recent is now the boss of the Cardiff Devils, Brent Pope. New to the microphone, he brought his enthusiasm and added much to my knowledge of his sport in the Turin Olympics. It is a sport I've always liked and, as a student, wrote about for *Ice Hockey World*. It was later another sport I inherited from Alan Weeks, working with Red Imrie, of Streatham fame, in Britain and on my own in the Olympic final in Lillehammer. Four years later, when the National Hockey League players came to the Nagano games, I had the privilege of commentating on the great Wayne Gretzky.

When I started learning about sports broadcasting only one commentator was used. Then there was one microphone shared between two at the discretion of the man in the driving seat, the broadcaster, which meant that when David Coleman said, 'The men's Olympic one hundred metres final,' there was silence until the gun. Nothing which has been said in that gap since every commentator was given his own microphone has built the tension of the moment like that silence. Across the board of sports commentary on television – even allowing for the changing style of different generations – that is something worth remembering.

44

World Cup 2006

The World Cup in Germany 2006 was always going to be a strange experience for me. Not to be there after covering the previous ten finals was hard to take; though I make no complaint about it. I watched and listened to quite a lot, but tennis, first with preparation at the Stella Artois tournament at Queen's Club and then being fully involved at Wimbledon, meant that Sky Plus was well employed.

Much of it I enjoyed, although the demands of high-definition television led to too much of it, the earlier stages in particular, being covered too wide. I would have given a lot to be in the seat for the semi-final between Italy and Germany. The manner in which it was won was great to see, with the Italians putting on the style – unlike the agony too often in the past – and scoring two beautiful goals in extra time.

But I felt a bit sorry for the Germans, who under Jurgen Klinsmann were a breath of fresh air from the tournament's start. So what if their defence always looked vulnerable? Their attack always looked capable of scoring; and they were thoroughly entertaining to watch – in that respect their best side since 1990. Third place was way ahead of their public's expectation and Klinsmann, much criticised before the tournament – especially for living in California – got it right. The first task of a national coach is to instil belief and he did that in abundance when it mattered most.

Every winning side in a cup competition has a moment when luck keeps them on course. For the Italians it came in their second-round match, courtesy of Blackburn's, now West Ham's, Lucas Neill. Had he stayed on his feet when challenging Grosso in the penalty box, Australia would have taken the Azzurri to a very nervous extra time. By going down Neill invited Grosso to fall over him for the penalty which sent the 'Socceroos' back down under. And Grosso it was who scored Italy's winning goal in the penalty competition which meant that they and not France, for much of the final the better side, were world champions. In another way, perhaps justice was done because, but for Thierry Henry uncharacteristically feigning being injured by Puyol, France might have fallen in the quarter-final. The resulting free kick brought an equaliser against Spain and changed the match.

That was the worst part of Germany 2006: too many cheats – and how sad that in my view I have to include the brilliant Henry, for that one moment, among them – were allowed to prosper. FIFA should take the responsibility, for they have allowed it to become endemic in the game at the highest level – and consequently at every other level. As I said in 'Football Focus' at the start of the season following the World Cup in France '98, the evidence is there in the television coverage and, while the outcome of a match cannot be changed, future suspensions should be the punishment of the guilty. They took action against Italy's Mauro Tassotti for an assault back in 1994, so why have they – and UEFA – not adopted a policy of zero tolerance on blatant cheating to rid the game of this pestilence?

I further believe that the time has come for football to adopt the style of discipline first employed by hockey and later copied by rugby. In both games the temporary suspension of a player – the 'sin bin' if you like – has worked really well. In hockey it follows a second infringement after an earlier warning when a green card is shown. Football should stick with the yellows – there's no need to complicate the lives of future Graham Polls any further – but an offence which would at present bring a second yellow card and immediate dismissal should instead lead to a temporary suspension of, I suggest, ten minutes. A further infringement would automatically bring the red card. The referee, of course, would still retain the right to issue a straight red for offences as laid down in the laws of the game.

My one visit to the 2006 championship was to Gelsenkirchen on the middle Saturday of Wimbledon, courtesy of the managing director of Betfair, a certain Mark Davies. He found room for me among an interesting group invited to see the quarter-final – Alan Lee, racing correspondent of *The Times*; Keith Perry, sports editor of the *Daily Telegraph*; Mark Field MP; and Chris Heaton-Harris MEP.

Three weeks earlier I'd chaired a video debate for the company which compared form with available odds in a pretty comprehensive preview of the coming tournament. The panel was Derek McGovern, columnist of the *Daily Mirror*; Angus Loughran of the BBC, the *Daily Telegraph* and sundry other points of the compass at the same time; Tony Cascarino, of Republic of Ireland fame and *The Times*; and Bruce Millington, sports editor of the *Racing Post*. None of them gave England a prayer. I didn't expect that much from Eriksson's squad, either, but I couldn't believe they'd be so lacking in ideas and, to be frank, plain dull. Even the much-vaunted defence became a thing of parts: the goal from a long throw which gave Sweden a draw in the final group game is probably the worst goal I have ever seen conceded by an England team.

Of course, like Eriksson it's all history now, but I cannot resist putting on record the fact that shortly before the quarter-final with Portugal I asked Mark whether Betfair were offering odds on Wayne Rooney being sent off. It was, though, only possible to make a bet on a team losing a man and not on a specified individual. The youngster's injury had been so hyped by the media, and the role the manager asked him to play so frustrating for the player, that it was an accident waiting to happen. Nothing, it seemed, was learned from the qualifying match in Belfast when the manager should – huge talent though the young man unquestionably is – have taken Rooney off before he got himself sent off. His dismissal in Gelsenkirchen led to England's best spell of the tournament.

With only ten men they briefly looked a team. But in the end the only happy memory of England's football that summer was Joe Cole's volleyed goal against Sweden.

Why England failed so abysmally remains a mystery. They weren't as gifted as much of the media had us believe before the tournament; but neither were they as untalented as it became popular to suggest in the subsequent months, which saw a failure to qualify for Euro '08. It's true that Eriksson was again unlucky with injuries – especially poor Michael Owen – but my mind goes back to the first interview the Swede gave a few days before his debut as England's boss in the friendly match against Spain at Villa Park in February 2001. I asked him about the motto of the village where he was born, Torsby in Varmland. Roughly translated, it is, 'Never do today what you can put off until tomorrow.' We had a bit of a laugh about it. But did he ever decide what his best team was? Did he find a solution to integrating the similar attributes of Steven Gerrard and Frank Lampard? Did he solve the problem of the left side of midfield? Did he put off the decision to rest or replace David Beckham? And did he really decide how he wanted the team to play?

To be fair to Sven, on the last point I think we've become somewhat obsessed in this country with the England team formation. Danny Blanchflower once said that England started to play with four at the back simply because a slightly dodgy centre half needed support. At the time Ron Flowers was needed to support Peter Swan. Alf Ramsey found his winning combination only after trying all three of the wingers in his final squad – John Connelly, Terry Paine and Ian

Callaghan – in the group matches. But after the World Cup many First Division managers thought Ramsey had found a magic formula, and wingers withered on the vine. Alf just made the best of what he had available, and made decisions – including leaving his best goalscorer, Jimmy Greaves, out of the team. He won the World Cup, of course, at a time when there was no chance of getting it right second time by the use of substitutes. Subsequently he never really came to terms with their use. A basically simple game is surely all about balance, and round pegs in round holes, and for all the demands of the club game, which often leaves him short of key players, the national manager should be able to achieve that.

Perhaps Sven's farewell gift to England was his least understood selection, who was then ignored. Theo Walcott suffered for it at times in the 2006–07 season, but in the longer term what he learned from close quarters in Germany last year may prove invaluable when his real chance comes. Sven, meanwhile, seems to have taken his at Manchester City, adding to his reputation at club level.

Over the course of the tournament, I had a standard reply to those who sought my opinion of the commentary: 'I'm having my best World Cup ever; I haven't made a mistake yet.' I was, though, more than a little amused that both leading commentators on the main channels had their own newspaper columns to make points to their critics. I watched the opening match listening to a lot of different commentaries – none of them in English. Penny and I were staying with Gigi in her apartment in Lausanne, ten minutes from the headquarters of the IOC, and I took full advantage of the European channels available.

One German station had just one commentator and only Gunter Netzer as a half- and full-time expert. Another had many experts and a studio audience, as did an Italian channel. Generally there were two voices in the commentary box, the French most in conversation, but in all cases there were more moments with just the sound of the crowd than is now the case at home.

The next day we joined Mark and Miranda, who had travelled out that morning, at the Château de Divonne for the wedding of the daughter of long-standing friends. My only knowledge of England's afternoon struggle against Paraguay came from Mark's BlackBerry. With further hospitality the next day and a late flight home it was Monday before I saw for myself.

Almost the same scenario pertained for the final, but not quite; and the reasons were rather different. I'm always happy to be offered a finals commentary at Wimbledon and, as usual, the mixed doubles provided a good finale to the championships, with Andy Ram of Israel and Vera Zvonareva of Russia upsetting the top-seeded Americans, Bob Bryan and Venus Williams. But it meant that Sam Smith and I were the last of the commentary team to leave the All England Club. With apologies to Alan Green and Mike Ingham, who were covering their fifth World Cup final together, I ignored Five Live on the car radio and at home settled down with a supper tray to watch the final, delayed.

It was approaching half-time when Mark phoned wanting

to know what I thought of the match. I passed the message that I'd ring him back when the recording was finished, but from the reaction of Penny and Gigi it became clear that it wouldn't be over for some time. So I began to spin through, fully expecting extra time. Mark rang again: he had several meetings the next day and would soon be going to bed. Penalties, I thought, and I started to spin a bit faster, but then – what was that? I went back to watch in disbelief the Zinedine Zidane incident. How could he, in his last match? This wasn't a reaction: this was calculated. I quickly checked the outcome of the penalties and then rang back. 'He behaved like a hooligan,' I said. 'And he won the player of the tournament,' Mark responded. It shouldn't be, we agreed. I read the next day that the vote had been counted before the incident took place, but I believe that FIFA should have declared it null and void. Zidane was a truly great player but, whatever the provocation, what he did was disgraceful and FIFA's lack of a real reaction to it indefensible.

Fifteen months on, the vagaries of the local provider in Florida denied me the chance to listen to Five Live via my laptop when Croatia ended England's hopes of a place in the 2008 European Championships. It could be said that Scott Carson's goalkeeping howler cost Steve McClaren his job but the coach's position had been compromised from the very start by the overtures made to Portugal's Felipe Scolari and was further undermined by his own early errors of judgement. Sadly, the first attempt by the Football Association to appoint a successor from within the management team, once considered the best way to solve a regular problem, ended in failure.

Unlike Bobby Robson, who fell short on his first European qualifying test, there was little hope of a second chance. What support there was in Soho Square had long since faded away under media pressure.

Much of the comment which followed mirrored that of previous perceived debacles and only the coach carried the can while the board looked on. But this time there was greater blame apportioned to the players. To those to whom much is given, much is required, and there are some who have climbed too far from the world in which most of their supporters live.

The new incumbent, Fabio Capello, tends not to concern himself with egos so can be expected to bring the 'guilty' down to earth. The reaction to a second foreigner has been markedly different from the first; save for the FA, who, under pressure from the media for a quick appointment, seem again to have placed all the financial cards in the new coach's hands. Having more than once in this book taken issue with Italian coaches for stifling the natural ability of their gifted players it is hard to offer a fulsome welcome, but Capello's record at club level is excellent and, at sixty-one, he has a wealth of experience.

I suspect pragmatism with few frills will be his style, which will be in keeping with the goal he scored at Wembley to give his native country their first victory there thirty-five years ago – and with my low-key BBC commentary which accompanied it. 'Crikey,' was it really that long ago?

Postscript

•

'She's the One' and *The Big Train* are in the opinion of some my best claims to fame.

The first is easily explained. I was asked to voice the skating action on the Robbie Williams video of his hit song which won a BRIT award. We never met and he probably doesn't know, or indeed care, that I rewrote the script I was given, but it gave me a kick to be involved and wasn't bad for the image.

The World Staring Championships which ran in the first series of BBC 2's *Big Train* in 1998 was totally off the wall. I had no idea what to expect, and when I saw two cardboard characters eyeballing each other my first reaction was to tell the producer that I didn't think it was for me. But he persuaded me to say something about nothing and then phoned to tell

me that he wanted to team me with that very amusing imper-
sonator and comedian Phil Cornwell, of *Dead Ringers* fame. We
were first given a script and then asked to do an ad-libbed
version. What appeared in the programme was an amalgama-
tion of the two. It worked a treat and was a lot of laughs. Phil
and I have done a few commercial things together on the
strength of that partnership, and although I have yet to hear
it, he also does what he describes as an over-the-top impression of me.

Locally I found another claim to fame when, soon after I
gave up my regular Saturday commentaries, I was invited to
become the president of Windsor and Eton FC, the Royals,
filling a position which had been left vacant since the death
of David Hill-Wood, brother of the current Arsenal chairman.
As a result, most of the live football I've seen recently has
been in the Ryman and British Gas Southern Leagues. After
forty years I've learned again what it's like to watch a match
as a committed supporter.

It was two years before I saw a Premiership fixture – unfortunately a pretty tedious affair between Spurs and Fulham at
White Hart Lane – and although I've twice since watched
Arsenal in Europe I've yet directly to take up the invitation
offered by Arsene Wenger on my end-of-term day with *Match
of the Day*.

In spite of the failure to win anything for the last two seasons
I believe his team, when on form, are at club level the best
exponents of the beautiful game that I have seen. From distant
memories of the 'push and run' team of Arthur Rowe in the
early 1950s and the double team under Bill Nicholson a decade

later – the 1961 Cup final was the first I saw – I can certainly claim that as an objective view. I hope my fellow supporters of Spurs won't disown me for it. Not even Garth Crooks knew.

In my time in the commentary box there have been a number of home teams which at times deserved that most overused word in sport, 'great'. Manchester United have produced a few, with the Best, Charlton, Law side narrowly for me still the pick. So have Liverpool, with the 1977 team the best. Manchester City under Joe Mercer in the late '60s qualify, as do Don Revie's Leeds in the early '70s, Brian Clough's two championship sides, Howard Kendall's Everton of the mid-'80s and the modern Chelsea. But for purity of passing, positioning and invention my vote has to go to Wenger's Arsenal. Even their love of the ball, which seemed to have bred a reluctance to shoot for fear of losing it, has now found a sharper appreciation of priorities.

The wise heads of the *MotD* studio would at this point make clear to me that it is all about winning. But perhaps because I sadly lacked their playing ability I've always believed that winning with style should be the aim. Too much the idealist, too little the realist? Perhaps.

Index

Note: 'BD' stands for Barry Davies. Subheadings for individuals are in chronological order.

Now you can buy any of these other bestselling non-fiction titles from your bookshop or *direct from the publisher*.

FREE P&P AND UK DELIVERY
(Overseas and Ireland £3.50 per book)

Being Gazza   Paul Gascoigne   £6.99
Footballing hero Gazza, in the company of his therapist, confronts his demons and examines the reasons behind his depression and addictions.

There's Only One Neil Redfearn   Neil Redfearn   £7.99
The anatomy of a footballing career spanning more than a quarter of a century and over 1000 senior appearances as a professional.

Tom Finney Autobiography   Tom Finney   £7.99
The highs and lows of a remarkable career by England's greatest living footballer, who is idolised more than 40 years after his retirement from Preston North End.

1966 And All That   Geoff Hurst   £7.99
The updated autobiography of England's footballing legend, Sir Geoff Hurst, whose hat-trick won the World Cup in 1966.

Cloughie: Walking on Water   Brian Clough   £7.99
A special commemorative edition of the bestselling autobiography of arguably Britain's greatest ever football manager.

Chelsea FC: The Official Biography   Rick Glanvill   £6.99
The only official publication to celebrate 100 years of this fascinating, controversial and glamorous club, with a foreword by Roman Abramovich.

To order, simply call 01235 400 414
visit our website: www.headline.co.uk
or email orders@bookpoint.co.uk

Prices and availability are subject to change without notice.